Women, Children, and the Collective Face of Conflict in Europe, 1900-1950

Edited by
Nupur Chaudhuri
Texas Southern University
Sandra Trudgen Dawson
Berkshire Conference of Women Historians

Series in World History

Copyright © 2024 by the Authors.

All rights reserved. No part of this publication may be reproduced, stored in a retrieval system, or transmitted in any form or by any means, electronic, mechanical, photocopying, recording, or otherwise, without the prior permission of Vernon Art and Science Inc.

www.vernonpress.com

In the Americas:
Vernon Press
1000 N West Street, Suite 1200
Wilmington, Delaware, 19801
United States

In the rest of the world:
Vernon Press
C/Sancti Espiritu 17,
Malaga, 29006
Spain

Series in World History

Library of Congress Control Number: 2023942834

ISBN: 978-1-64889-875-4

Also available: 978-1-64889-747-4 [Hardback]; 978-1-64889-795-5 [PDF, E-Book]

Cover design by Vernon Press. Cover image: SCI, evacuation, Spanish Civil War, 1937. Authorization from Philipp Rodriguez, in charge of the SCI International Archives. https://commons.wikimedia.org/wiki/File:Es_sci_1937_spainish-civil-war_02_Evacuation.jpg

Product and company names mentioned in this work are the trademarks of their respective owners. While every care has been taken in preparing this work, neither the authors nor Vernon Art and Science Inc. may be held responsible for any loss or damage caused or alleged to be caused directly or indirectly by the information contained in it.

Every effort has been made to trace all copyright holders, but if any have been inadvertently overlooked the publisher will be pleased to include any necessary credits in any subsequent reprint or edition.

Table of Contents

List of Figures — vii

Preface — ix
Jean P. Smith

Introduction — xi
Nupur Chaudhuri
Texas Southern University

Sandra Trudgen Dawson
Berkshire Conference of Women Historians

Section One. War and Identity:
The Personal and the Collective — 1

Chapter 1 **'One of the Boys': Identity, Crisis and Vera Brittain's War** — 3
Mary Laurents
University of Maryland, Baltimore County

Chapter 2 **Saving Russia: Women's Contributions to Russia's First World War Effort** — 21
Laurie S. Stoff
Arizona State University

Chapter 3 **Who is a Soldier? Rethinking French Women's Military Identity during the Second World War** — 39
Andrew Orr
Kansas State University

Chapter 4 **Children and the Character of Italy: Consuming Juvenile Literature in Wartime and Conflict** — 57
Allison Scardino Belzer
Georgia Southern University

	Section Two. Humanitarian Aid and International Solidarity	77
Chapter 5	**The Armenian Genocide, Women Aid Workers, and World War I in the Middle East**	79
	Michelle Tusan *University of Nevada, Las Vegas*	
Chapter 6	**Guernica, Politics, and International Humanitarianism: Spanish Child Refugees in Britain and the Soviet Union**	99
	Sandra Trudgen Dawson *Berkshire Conference of Women Historians*	
	Patrick José Dawson *University of Maryland, Baltimore County*	
Chapter 7	**One with the Wounded: American Nurses in the Spanish Civil War**	117
	Gina Benavidez *University of New Mexico*	
Chapter 8	**Standing in Solidarity: British Women and the China Campaign Committee, 1937-1945**	135
	Mark J. Crowley *University of Utah*	
	Section Three. Consumption and Conflict	153
Chapter 9	**Indoctrinating Dinners: Feeding Ideology to the Hungry during the Franco Dictatorship in Spain, 1937-1948**	155
	Suzanne Dunai *Southwestern Oklahoma State University*	
Chapter 10	**Women, Children, and "Slow Starvation" in Occupied France**	173
	Kenneth Mouré *University of Alberta*	

| Chapter 11 | **Patriotism and Austerity: Finnish Children and Youth in World War Two** | 195 |

Marianne Junila and Tiina Kinnunen
University of Oulu

Contributors	213
Bibliography	217
Index	231

List of Figures

Figure 4.1:	Barbara Allason, *Italia nostra!* Palermo: Biondo, 1916.	61
Figure 4.2:	Amilda A. Pons, *Piccole storie della storia grande 1915-1916*. Milano: Società editrice Dante Alighieri, 1916.	65
Figure 4.3:	Haydée [Ida Finzi], *Bimbi di Trieste: Scene dal vero*. Firenze: Bemporad, 1916, page 18.	67
Figure 5.1:	Ann Mary Burgess, Studio portrait, c, 1910.	80
Figure 5.2:	Zabel Yessayan.	81
Figure 10.1:	"Tickets S.V.P.," Collection B. Le Marec, photo © Pierre Verrier.	188
Figure 10.2:	"Comme Maman - Pour jouer à la marchande," Collection B. Le Marec, photo © Pierre Verrier.	189
Figure 10.3:	"Jeu de rutabaga," Collection B. Le Marec, photo © Pierre Verrier.	190
Figure 10.4:	"Jeu des 7 familles," Collection B. Le Marec, photo © Pierre Verrier.	191

Preface

Jean P. Smith

Through its attention to the experience of women and children in European conflicts across the first half of the twentieth century, this wide-ranging collection both adds nuance to familiar historical narratives and a broader perspective on important themes of gender and social history in the period. These range from the professionalization of nursing and aid work to the vital role of women in navigating the shortages of food and other crucial resources during times of conflict. While each chapter provides a rich and specific portrait, the collection as a whole and, in particular, its transnational scope, also highlights points of continuity in the challenges faced by women and children and, crucially, how they navigated them. It draws attention to the important, and often overlooked, roles women played in conflicts during this era, in the international brigades during the Spanish Civil War, as aid workers responding to the Armenian genocide and the Japanese invasion of China, in the Russian army during the First World War and the French military, the French resistance and the Free French during the Second World War.

Another important focus, of many, of the book's chapters is an exploration of how women and children were both subject to state ideologies and policies and were able to influence and subvert them. This was true in relation both to the Basque child refugees sent to the United Kingdom and the Soviet Union during the Spanish Civil War, the working-class families who were the targets of food relief programs in Spain under Franco and French women and children who navigated food shortages during the Second World War. Taken together, the chapters highlight the contradictions between state ideologies that sought to reinforce traditional family structures and women's domestic roles and the exigencies of conflict that both forced women out of the home whether to queue for food or to eat in state-run canteens and provided some women a wider range of opportunities than they might otherwise have encountered. Held together by a wide-ranging introduction with a comprehensive and engaging account of relevant scholarship, the collection breaks new ground in its attention to the experience and agency of women and children across Europe in the first half of the twentieth century.

Introduction

Nupur Chaudhuri
Texas Southern University

Sandra Trudgen Dawson
Berkshire Conference of Women Historians

The opening years of the twentieth century in Europe were characterized by an optimism that, from a historical perspective, belies the widespread conflict and chaos that followed. The ostensible stability of this brief era, informed by the political projects of nineteenth-century liberalism and national unification, gave way to decades of increasingly complex crises. In the Great War (1914-1918), European Empires fought each other using new technologies and obsolete strategies that aggravated existing tensions within and between nations.[1] Despite efforts to reestablish peace, the crises continued: revolutions in Russia and civil war in Spain threatened parliamentary governments; the Armenian genocide began in 1915, foreshadowing the systematic destruction of European Jews in the 1930s and '40s[2]; and dictators seized power, establishing authoritarian regimes in Russia, Italy, Germany, Spain and Portugal that stymied democratic expression and censored the press.[3] The

---

[1] John Keegan, *The First World War* (Vintage, 2000).

[2] See, for example, Ronald Grigor Suny, "They Can Live in the Desert but Nowhere Else": A History of the Armenian Genocide (Princeton University Press, 2015); Saul Friedländer, *Nazi Germany and the Jews*, Volume I: *The Years of Persecution, 1933–1939* (New York: HarperCollins, 1997), and *The Years of Extermination: Nazi Germany and the Jews, 1939 – 1945* (New York: HarperCollins, 2007). Other groups were also targeted by Nazi Germany and other authoritarian regimes, including communists, Roma and Sinti people, homosexuals, and Jehovah's Witnesses. See, for example, Anton Weiss-Wendt, ed., *The Nazi Genocide of the Roma: Reassessment and Commemoration* (New York: Berghahn, 2015).

[3] Benito Mussolini seized power in Italy in 1921, António de Oliveira Salazar took power in Portugal in 1932, Adolph Hitler became Chancellor of Germany in 1933, and Francisco Franco became leader of Spain at the end of the civil war in 1939. There were also authoritarian regimes in Poland, Romania, Bulgaria, Greece, and elsewhere. See John Connelly, *From Peoples into Nations: A History of Eastern Europe* (Princeton: Princeton University Press, 2020).

League of Nations, formed after the Great War as an arbiter of world peace, failed to prevent the Italian invasion of Abyssinia (1935-36), the militarization of the Rhineland (begun in 1936), or the annexation of the Sudetenland (1938) by Nazi Germany.[4] Ultimately, when Germany invaded Poland on September 1, 1939, Europe descended into a second world war.

The scale and ubiquity of the suffering that marked the first half of the twentieth century often overshadows the rapid, progressive social and cultural changes that occurred during the same period. Broad shifts in public opinion expanded rights and freedoms for two interconnected demographics: specifically, women demanded and gained political enfranchisement, and childhood came to be widely seen as a discrete and significant period of the life cycle.[5] Just as the social and economic dislocations wrought by industrialization in the nineteenth century had led to philanthropy and the establishment of national charities for poor women and children, so the conflicts of the twentieth century saw the creation of international networks of care.[6] The establishment of the League of Nations created a space for

---

[4] For the establishment of the League of Nations, see Susan Pedersen, *The Guardians: The League of Nations and the Crisis of Empire* (New York: Oxford University Press, 2016). The remilitarization of the Rhineland was in direct contravention of the Treaty of Versailles, 1919. See Norman A. Graebner and Edward M. Bennett, *The Versailles Treaty and Its Legacy: The Failure of the Wilsonian Vision* (Cambridge: Cambridge University Press, 2014).

[5] Childhood has been described as an invention of the Romantic period. See Linda M. Austin, "Childhood: Nostalgia and the Romantic Legacy," *Studies in Romanticism* 42.1 (2003) 75-98. By the 1920s and 1930s, children's summer and holiday camps had emerged in France, Britain, and the Soviet Union. See Sandra Trudgen Dawson, *Holiday Camps in Twentieth-Century Britain: Packaging Pleasure* (Manchester: Manchester University Press, 2011) and Laura Lee Downs, *Childhood in the Promised Land: Working Class Movements and the Colonies de Vacances in France, 1880-1960* (Duke University Press, 2002). When Spanish refugee children were taken to the Soviet Union, many were housed in summer camps. See Karl D. Qualls, "From Hooligans to Disciplined Students: Displacement, Resettlement, and Role Modelling of Spanish Civil War Children in the Soviet Union, 1937-51," in *Displaced Children in Russia and Eastern Europe, 1915-1953: Ideologies, Identities, Experiences,"* ed. Nick Baron (Leiden-Boston: Brill, 2017).

[6] See, for example, Susan Ash, *Funding Philanthropy: Dr. Barnardo, Metaphor, Narrative and Spectacle* (Liverpool: Liverpool University Press, 2016); Christine Adams, Poverty, *Charity, and Motherhood: Maternal Societies in Nineteenth-Century France* (Champaign: University of Illinois Press, 2010), and Rachel G. Fuchs, *Abandoned Children: Foundlings and Child Welfare in Nineteenth-Century France* (Albany: SUNY Press, 1984).

Introduction xiii

international humanitarianism, which was largely taken up by white women and often focused on the plight of children.⁷

But women and children were not simply proponents of social progress, peacekeeping, or antiwar efforts. Often overlooked in early studies of European conflict, they experienced these tumultuous decades as political actors, civilians, workers, consumers, victims, exiles, humanitarian laborers, and combatants. Authoritarian governments often compelled women into subservient positions as wives and mothers, while children of all ages were corralled into political youth organizations that promoted the values and ideology of the state.⁸

---

⁷ Eglantyne Jebb established the Save the Children Fund in 1919 after the Great War. Jebb went on to draft the Declaration of the Rights of the Child, which was adopted by the League of Nations in 1924. See Linda Mahood, *Feminism and Voluntary Action: Eglantyne Jebb and Save the Children, 1876-1928* (London: Palgrave Macmillan, 2009). See also Tehila Sasson, "From Empire to Humanity: The Russian Famine and the Imperial Origins of International Humanitarianism," *Journal of British Studies* 55.3 (2016) 519–37, and Linda Mahood and Vic Satzewich, "The Save the Children Fund and the Russian Famine of 1921–23: Claims and Counter-Claims about Feeding 'Bolshevik' Children," *Journal of Historical Sociology* 22.1 (2009) 57–83. See also Bruno Cabanes, *The Great War and the Origins of Humanitarianism, 1918–1924* (Cambridge: Cambridge University Press, 2014); Caroline Shaw, *Britannia's Embrace: Modern Humanitarianism and the Imperial Origins of Refugee Relief* (Oxford: Oxford University Press, 2015); Emily Baughan, "The Imperial War Relief Fund and the All-British Appeal: Commonwealth, Conflict and Conservatism within the British Humanitarian Movement, 1920–25," *Journal of Imperial and Commonwealth History* 40.5 (2012) 845–61, and Gabriel Pretus, *Humanitarian Relief in the Spanish Civil War (1936–1939)* (Lewiston: Edwin Mellen, 2013).

⁸ See, for example, Michael H. Kater, *Hitler Youth* (Cambridge: Harvard University Press, 2006); Dagmar Reese, *Growing Up Female in Nazi Germany*, trans. William Templer (Ann Arbor: University of Michigan Press, 2006); R. J. B. Bosworth, *Mussolini's Italy: Life Under the Fascist Dictatorship, 1915-1945* (New York: Penguin, 2007); Gerhard Rempel, *Hitler's Children: The Hitler Youth and the SS* (Chapel Hill: University of North Carolina Press, 1990); Victoria de Grazia, *How Fascism Ruled Women: Italy 1922-1945* (Berkeley: University of California, 1993); Alan M. Ball, *And Now My Soul Is Hardened: Abandoned Children in Soviet Russia, 1918-1930* (Berkeley: University of California Press, 1994); Julie Gottlieb, *Feminist Fascism: Women in Britain's Fascist Movement, 1923-1945* (London: I. B. Tauris, 2003); Perry Willson, *Peasant Women and Politics in Fascist Italy: The Massaie Rurali* (London: Routledge, 2002) and *The Clockwork Factory: Women and Work in Fascist Italy* (Oxford: Oxford University Press, 1993); Alexander De Grand, "Women under Italian Fascism," *The Historical Journal* 19.4 (1976) 947-968; Wendy Goldman, *Women, The State and Revolution: Soviet Family Policy and Social Life, 1917-1936* (Cambridge: Cambridge University Press, 1993) and *Women at the Gates Gender and Industry in Stalin's Russia* (Cambridge: Cambridge University Press, 2002); Adrienne Edgar, "Bolshevism, Patriarchy, and the Nation: The Soviet 'Emancipation' of Muslim Women in Pan-Islamic Perspective," *Slavic Review* 65.2 (2006) 252-272; Gisela Bock, "Racism and

Women, Children, and the Collective Face of European Conflict, 1900-1950 focuses on the experiences and behaviors of women and children as they navigated the multiple crises, conflicts, and ideological extremes of the first half of the twentieth century. It complements and adds to the existing literature on the experiences of women and children in European conflicts by bridging the histories of women, children, and conflict. The volume considers revolution, world war, civil war, and exile as overlapping categories. Chronologically, the conflicts of the first five decades are discrete events and often responses to economic, political, or cultural fissures and shifts. Many scholars have maintained continuities, particularly between the first and second world wars.[9] While some chapters in this collection do observe continuities between conflicts, the volume as a whole does not explore this larger historical question. Rather, it examines individual and group responses to the everyday stresses of conflict as they impacted the lives of women and children.

Since the rising interest in social history in the 1970s, scholarship on conflict has expanded to include histories of women, gender, and sexuality.[10] More

---

Sexism in Nazi Germany", *When Biology Became Destiny: Women in Weimar and Nazi Germany*, ed. Bridenthal et al (New York: Monthly Review Press, 1984); Claudia Koonz, *Mothers in the Fatherland: Women, the Family, and Nazi Politics* (New York: St. Martin's Press, 1987); Gisela Bock, Antinatalism in National Socialist Racism," *Nazism and German Society, 1933- 1945*, ed. David Crew et al (New York: Routledge, 1994); Atina Grossmann, "Feminist Debates about Women and National Socialism," *Gender and History* 3.3 (1991) 350-58; Adelheid von Saldern, "Victims or Perpetrators? Controversies about the Role of Women in the Nazi State," *Nazism and German Society, 1933-1945*, ed. David F. Crew (New York: Routledge, 1994); Elizabeth D. Heineman, *What Difference Does a Husband Make? Women and Marital Status in Nazi and Postwar Germany* (Berkeley: University of California Press, 1999); Jill Stephenson, *Hitler's Home Front: Württemberg under the Nazis* (New York: Hambledon Continuum, 2006); Vandana Joshi, *Gender and Power in the Third Reich: Female Denouncers and the Gestapo, 1933-1945* (New York: Palgrave MacMillan, 2003); Cynthia Crane, *Divided Lives: The Untold Stories of Jewish-Christian Women in Nazi Germany* (New York: St. Martin's Press, 2000), and Tim Mason, "Women in Nazi Germany," *History Workshop Journal* 1 (1976) 74-113.

[9] See, for example, Michael Alpert, *A New International History of the Spanish Civil War* (London: Palgrave, 1998).

[10] Joshua Goldstein, *War and Gender: How Gender Shapes the War System and Vice Versa* (Cambridge: Cambridge University Press, 2003); Jutta Schwarzkopf, "Combatant or Non-Combatant? The Ambiguous Status of Women in British Anti-Aircraft Batteries during the Second World War," *War & Society* 28.2 (2009) 105–31; Gerard J. DeGroot and C. Peniston-Bird, *A Soldier and a Woman: Sexual Integration in the Military* (London: Longman, 2000); Tessa Stone, "Creating a (Gendered?) Military Identity: The Women's Auxiliary Air Force in Great Britain in the Second World War," *Women's History Review* 8.4 (1999) 605–624; Melissa Herbert, *Camouflage Isn't Only for Combat: Gender, Sexuality and Women in the Military* (New York: NYU Press, 1998), and Nancy Goldman, *Female Soldiers–Combatants or Non-*

Introduction   xv

recent research on the history of childhood has broadened the field to include the experiences of children.[11] The education of children was the focus of authoritarian regimes that desired to reshape the future by indoctrinating the young with their ideology. Children were participants, politicized by propagandist literature, subject to sectarian education, and sometimes silent observers. Their experiences were shaped by politicians and leaders and by the politics of their families and friends. Many served as resistance couriers and even as underaged combatants. Others were refugees, exiled from their homes and countries, used as political pawns or the focus of international humanitarianism.[12] Like adults, children confronted authoritarianism, violence,

---

Combatants?: Historical and Contemporary Perspectives (Westport: Greenwood Press, 1982). See also: Cynthia Enloe, *Maneuvers: The International Politics of Militarizing Women's Lives* (Berkeley: University of California Press, 2000); Linda Grant De Pauw, *Battle Cries and Lullabies: Women in War from Prehistory to the Present* (Norman: University of Oklahoma Press, 1998); Julie Wheelwright, *Amazons and Military Maids: Women Who Dressed as Men in the Pursuit of Life, Liberty and Happiness* (London: Pandora, 1994); Jeanne Holm, *Women in the Military: An Unfinished Revolution* (Novato: Presidio, 1982); Jean Bethke Elshtain, *Women and War* (Chicago: University of Chicago Press, 1987); Cynthia Enloe, *Does Khaki Become You? Militarisation in Women's Lives* (Boston: Pluto Press, 1983).

[11] See, for example, Mischa Honeck and James Marten, eds., *War and Childhood in the Era of the Two World Wars* (Cambridge: Cambridge University Press, 2019); Karl D. Qualls, *Stalin's Niños: Educating Spanish Civil War Refugee Children in the Soviet Union, 1937-1951* (Toronto: University of Toronto Press, 2020); Tara Zahra, *Kidnapped Souls: National Indifference and the Battle for Children in the Bohemian Lands, 1900–1948* (Ithaca: Cornell University Press, 2008), and Nick Baron, ed., *Displaced Children in Russia and Eastern Europe, 1915-1953: Ideologies, Identities, Experiences* (Leiden-Boston: Brill, 2016).

[12] See, for example, Vera K. Fast, *Children's Exodus: A History of the Kindertransport* (London: I. B. Tauris, 2011); Mark Jonathan Harris and Deborah Oppenheimer, *Into the Arms of Strangers: Stories of the Kindertransport* (London: Bloomsbury, 2017); John Welshman, *Churchill's Children: The Evacuee Experience in Wartime Britain* (Oxford: Oxford University Press, 2010); Muriel Emanuel and Vera Gissing, *Nicholas Winton and the Rescued Generation: Save One Life, Save the World* (London: Vallentine Mitchell, 2002); Bertha Leverton and Shmuel Lowensohn, *I Came Alone: The Stories of the Kindertransports* (Lewes: The Book Guild, 1996); Bob Moore, *Refugees from Nazi Germany in the Netherlands, 1933–1940* (Dordrecht: Nijhoff, 1986); Vicki Caron, *Uneasy Asylum: France and the Jewish Refugee Crisis, 1933–1942* (Stanford: Stanford University Press, 1999); Paul Weindling, "Medical Refugees in Britain and the Wider World, 1930–1960: Introduction," *Social History of Medicine* 22.3 (2009) 451–59; Louise London, *Whitehall and the Jews, 1933–1948: British Immigration Policy, Jewish Refugees and the Holocaust* (Cambridge: Cambridge University Press, 2001); Irving Abella and Harold Troper, *None Is Too Many: Canada and the Jews of Europe, 1933–1948* (Toronto: University of Toronto Press, 1982). For Australia, see Michael Blakeney, *Australia and the Jewish Refugees, 1933–1948* (Sydney: Croom Helm, 1985); Anil Bhatti and Johannes H. Voigt, eds., *Jewish Exile in India, 1933–1945* (New Delhi: Manohar, 1999).

hunger, famine, and starvation. This volume seeks to complicate the distinction between child and adult in order to present a more collective understanding of conflict in Europe in the first half of the twentieth century.

Women, Children and Conflict complements and adds to the existing literature by straddling the fields of women's history, women and war, histories of childhood and conflict, as well as war and consumption. Recent anniversaries commemorating the start of the Great War and the end of the Second World War have renewed scholarly and popular interest in both conflicts, expanding the hitherto narrow category of women's war work.[13] Early studies had explored the idea that war changed women's social and economic positions irrevocably.[14] Similarly, later research maintained that war, revolution, and conflict altered little for women and certainly did not bring about lasting change.[15] More recent studies explore the way women

---

[13] Perry Willson, *Peasant Women and Politics in Fascist Italy: The Massaie Rurali* (London: Routledge, 2002) and *The Clockwork Factory: Women and Work in Fascist Italy* (Oxford: Oxford University Press, 1993); Alexander De Grand, "Women under Italian Fascism," *The Historical Journal* 19.4 (1976) 947-968; Wendy Goldman, *Women, The State and Revolution: Soviet Family Policy and Social Life, 1917-1936* (Cambridge: Cambridge University Press, 1993) and *Women at the Gates: Gender and Industry in Stalin's Russia* (Cambridge: Cambridge University Press, 2002).

[14] See, for example, Harold L. Smith, "The Effect of the War on the Status of Women," *War and Social Change: British Society in the Second World War* (Manchester: Manchester University Press, 1986).

[15] See, for example, Penny Summerfield, *Women Workers in the Second World War: Production and Patriarchy in Conflict* (Manchester: Manchester University Press, 1984); Adrienne Edgar, "Bolshevism, Patriarchy, and the Nation: The Soviet 'Emancipation' of Muslim Women in Pan-Islamic Perspective," *Slavic Review* 65.2 (2006) 252-272; Gisela Bock, "Racism and Sexism in Nazi Germany," *When Biology Became Destiny: Women in Weimar and Nazi Germany*, ed. Bridenthal et al (New York: Monthly Review Press, 1984) and "Antinatalism in National Socialist Racism," *Nazism and German Society, 1933-1945*, ed. David Crew et al (New York: Routledge, 1994); Claudia Koonz, *Mothers in the Fatherland: Women, the Family and Nazi Politics* (New York: St. Martin's Press, 1987); Atina Grossmann, "Feminist Debates about Women and National Socialism," *Gender and History* 3.3 (1991) 350-58. Adelheid von Saldern, "Victims or Perpetrators? Controversies about the Role of Women in the Nazi State," *Nazism and German Society, 1933-1945*, ed. David F. Crew (New York: Routledge, 1994); Elizabeth D. Heineman, *What Difference Does a Husband Make? Women and Marital Status in Nazi and Postwar Germany* (Berkeley: University of California Press, 1999); Jill Stephenson, *Hitler's Home Front: Württemberg under the Nazis* (New York: Hambledon Continuum, 2006); Vandana Joshi, *Gender and Power in the Third Reich: Female Denouncers and the Gestapo, 1933-1945* (New York: Palgrave MacMillan, 2003); Cynthia Crane, *Divided Lives: The Untold Stories of Jewish-Christian Women in Nazi Germany* (New York: St. Martin's Press, 2000), and Tim Mason, "Women in Nazi Germany," *History Workshop Journal* 1 (1976) 74-113.

navigated conflict and used it as a platform for professionalization and political reform, often bringing to light the private conflicts they faced alone. For example, Christine Hallett argues that Allied nurses in the Great War faced hostile working conditions and misogynistic preconceptions as they nursed the wounded. Far from passive actors, they fought to gain professional recognition as nurses and political recognition as women.[16] Susan Grayzel and Tammy Proctor's recent volume, *Gender and the Great War*, offers insight into previously overlooked relationships between age and experience in World War One, using gender as a focus of analysis.[17] Since the fall of the USSR and the opening of the archives, scholarship on the Russian Revolution and women in the Soviet Union has expanded to account for formerly skewed historical conclusions. Wendy Goldman suggests that work and communist ideology did not mean that women were free of patriarchy, and that conflicts continued in the workplace and at home.[18] In this volume, women challenge patriarchy through their war work and through the ways in which they cope with conflict and the overarching reach of the state.

In the aftermath of revolution and war, nations responded in ways that created opportunities for women to engage in international humanitarianism, albeit in limited and limiting ways. Transnational organizations like the League of Nations comprised layers of male-dominated diplomacy and international committees, while post-conflict displacement and hunger gained the attention of women. Female-headed organizations like Save the Children were established in response to the famine that followed the Russian revolution and

---

[16] Christine Hallett, *Veiled Warriors: Allied Nurses of the First World War* (Oxford: Oxford University Press, 2021). See also Charissa J. Threat, *Nursing Civil Rights: Gender and Race in the Army Nurse Corps* (Urbana: University of Illinois Press, 2015). Threat looks at the intersections of race, war, and civil rights to argue that African American nurses in World War II and the Vietnam War used their positions to fight for civil rights.

[17] Susan Grayzel and Tammy Proctor, *Gender and the Great War* (Oxford: Oxford University Press, 2017).

[18] See Wendy Goldman, *Women, The State and Revolution: Soviet Family Policy and Social Life, 1917-1936* (Cambridge: Cambridge University Press, 1993) and *Women at the Gates: Gender and Industry in Stalin's Russia* (Cambridge: Cambridge University Press, 2002); Sheila Fitzpatrick, *Everyday Stalinism: Ordinary Life in Extraordinary Times: Soviet Russia in the 1930s* (Oxford: Oxford University Press, 2000). Tatjana Takseva and Arlene Sgoutas have curated an excellent collection of essays about motherhood during global conflicts in the second half of the twentieth century. See Tatjana Takseva and Arlene Sgoutas, eds., *Mothers Under Fire: Mothering in Conflict Areas* (Ontario: Demeter Press, 2015).

the continuing need for international aid during the subsequent civil war.[19] Quakers organized relief for those suffering after the breakup of the Austro-Hungarian Empire. Many of the volunteers were women.[20] Fundraising for child refugees from the civil war in Spain and Nazi Germany often fell to women and children, who went door to door or organized concerts, lectures, and fashion shows.[21] This volume adds to the literature on humanitarianism by exploring refugee work during and after the Armenian genocide and during the Spanish Civil War.

The first half of the twentieth century was dominated by severe shortages, famines, and starvation. Some of this was purposeful, as Lizzie Collingwood observes.[22] Other studies examine rationing policies and the black market, as well as nutrition and the politics of meals.[23] For example, Mark Roodhouse argues that despite a flourishing black market, notions of fairness underpinned rationing and austerity in Britain. Kenneth Moure takes a different approach, claiming that in France, the black market was essential to the occupied population, who subverted Vichy rationing and food policies during the Second World War as a basic survival mechanism.[24] This volume looks at food

---

[19] The Save the Children Fund was established by Eglantyne Jebb and Dorothy Buxton. See Tehila Sasson, "From Empire to Humanity: The Russian Famine and the Imperial Origins of International Humanitarianism," *Journal of British Studies* 55.3 (2016) 519–37; Linda Mahood and Vic Satzewich, "The Save the Children Fund and the Russian Famine of 1921–23: Claims and Counter-Claims about Feeding 'Bolshevik' Children," *Journal of Historical Sociology* 22.1 (2009) 57–83. See also: Bruno Cabanes, *The Great War and the Origins of Humanitarianism, 1918–1924* (Cambridge: Cambridge University Press, 2014), and Caroline Shaw, *Britannia's Embrace: Modern Humanitarianism and the Imperial Origins of Refugee Relief* (Oxford: Oxford University Press, 2015).

[20] See Norah Curtis and Cyril Gilbey, *Malnutrition: Quaker Work in Austria 1919–24 and Spain 1936–39* (London: Oxford University Press, 1944).

[21] Sandra Trudgen Dawson, "Refugee Children and the Emotional Cost of International Humanitarianism in Interwar Britain," *Journal of British Studies* 60 (2021) 115-139.

[22] Lizzie Collingwood, *Taste of War: World War Two and the Battle for Food* (London: Penguin, 2013).

[23] Nadja Durbach, "British Restaurants and the Gender Politics of the Wartime Midday Meal," *Home Fronts: Britain and the Empire at War, 1039-45*, eds. Mark J. Crowley and Sandra Trudgen Dawson (London: Boydell and Brewer, 2017); Sherene Seikaly, "A Nutritional Economy: The Calorie, Development and War in Mandate Palestine," in ibid; Ian Mosby, *Food Will Win the War: The Politics, Culture, and Science of Food on Canada's Home Front* (Seattle: University of Washington Press, 2015), and Graham Broad, *A Small Price to Pay: Consumer Culture on the Canadian Home Front, 1939-45* (Seattle: University of Washington Press, 2014).

[24] Kenneth Moure, *Marché Noir: The Economy of Survival in Second World War France* (Cambridge University Press, 2023).

shortages and hunger with a specific focus on Finland and France as ordinary citizens engaged in activities to endure hunger and want.

For many women and children, surviving the first half of the twentieth century meant living through sexual violence and slavery. Stories of Belgian women and girls raped by invading German troops in the Great War dominated the public discourse in Britain, particularly after the publication of the Bryce Report in 1914.[25] Similar stories of the rape of German women by Soviet troops saturated post-1945 Germany.[26] More hidden histories of sexual slavery and violence in China and Korea have recently been made public. Yoshimi Yoshiaki's study explores the official role of Japanese "comfort stations," established wherever Japanese troops were sent. Early in the war with China and Korea, single Japanese women were invited to "serve" the troops in comfort stations.[27] Once there, they found that the service included prostitution. Chinese and Korean women were forcibly enslaved. The shame of sexual slavery has meant that the voices of the women involved have remained silent. Peipei Qiu's pioneering work, *Chinese Comfort Women: Testimonies from Imperial Japan's Sex Slaves*, is one of the few studies using personal statements from coerced Chinese women to illuminate the sexual slavery that characterized the comfort stations of the Japanese Imperial Army.[28] This is an important and timely area of research that continues to grow.

In other research, historians have begun to examine the politics of race and personal intimacy during wartime. Yasmin Khan looks at the impact of thousands of British servicemen on the gendered wartime economy in India. Khan maintains that increased prostitution was closely linked to the militarization of the economy and the effects of the 1943 famine in Bengal.[29] Angela Wanhalla and Judith Bennett's research explores the impact of war on the economies and cultures of the South Pacific. Their essays examine the genealogies of the generation of children born of war and the resilience of the Indigenous women who shared intimacy with American servicemen during

---

[25] Report of the Committee on Alleged German Outrages Appointed by His Britannic Majesty's Government
and Presided Over by the Right Hon. Viscount Bryce, O. M., December 1914.
[26] Atina Grossman, "A Question of Silence: The Rape of German Women by Occupation Soldiers," *October* 72 (1995) 43–63.
[27] Yoshimi Yoshiaki, *Comfort Women: Sexual Slavery in the Japanese Military During World War II* (New York: Columbia University Press, 1995).
[28] Peipei Qiu, *Chinese Comfort Women: Testimonies from Imperial Japan's Sex Slaves* (Vancouver: University of British Columbia Press, 2013).
[29] Yasmin Khan, "Sex in an Imperial War Zone: Transnational Encounters in Second World War India," *History Workshop Journal* 73.1 (2012) 240–58.

the Second World War.³⁰ Karen Hughes explores the significance of the legal status of children of US servicemen and Aboriginal women in Australia during the Second World War. The status of the couples and their children was complicated by racial categories and army regulations, which greatly impacted their relationships after the war.³¹ Lucy Bland has also explored the legacy of children born to African American servicemen and British women during the Second World War. Many of Britain's "brown babies" were born to couples who, for reasons of racial prejudice or marital status, were placed in children's homes.³² The plight of children born of wartime encounters continues to be of interest to scholars of women, war, and sexuality. This volume adds to the literature by examining the experiences of displaced children sent to Britain, Sweden and the Soviet Union.

Histories of childhood have greatly enriched the focus of literatures on conflict, authoritarianism, consumption, and emotions. Mischa Honeck and James Marten's collection on war and childhood is an exceptional volume examining the experiences of children globally during the two world wars.³³ Nick Baron's recent collection examines children in wartime as well as during times of revolution, forced resettlement, and indoctrination. In *Stalin's Niños*, Karl Qualls focuses on the educational experiences of Spanish Civil War child refugees in the USSR, from the Soviet perspective. The children were carefully educated to engage with the Spanish language, culture, and traditions while learning the Russian language and traditions—particularly Soviet ideals of hard work, sacrifice for ideals, comradery, and internationalism.³⁴ Other volumes explore the experiences of the children in exile, using letters and interviews to illustrate the way children understood the political landscape

---

[30] Judith Bennet and Angela Wanhalla, eds., *Mothers' Darlings of the South Pacific: The Children of Indigenous Women and U.S. Servicemen, World War II* (Honolulu: University of Hawai'i, 2016). See also Angela Wanhalla, *Matters of the Heart: A History of Interracial Marriage in New Zealand* (Auckland: Auckland University Press, 2014), and Jacqueline Leckie, Angela McCarthy, and Angela Wanhalla, *Migrant Cross-Cultural Encounters in Asia and the Pacific* (London: Routledge, 2016).

[31] Karen Hughes, "Transnational Struggles for Racial Justice: Australian Indigenous Women's Marriages to American Servicemen during the Second World War," *Engendering Transnational Transgressions: From the Intimate to the Global*, eds. Eileen Boris, Sandra Trudgen Dawson, and Barbara Molony (London: Routledge, 2011).

[32] Lucy Bland, *Britain's "Brown Babies": The Stories of Children Born to Black GIs and British Women in the Second World War* (Manchester: Manchester University Press, 2019).

[33] Mischa Honeck and James Marten, eds., *War and Childhood in the Era of the Two World Wars* (Cambridge: Cambridge University Press, 2019).

[34] Karl D. Qualls, *Stalin's Niños: Educating Spanish Civil War Refugee Children in the Soviet Union, 1937-1951* (Toronto: University of Toronto Press, 2020).

and took sides in the civil war.[35] The chapters in this volume underscore the way that children were aware of the politics of their time and took sides in the conflict.

This volume is divided into three sections. The first section, "War and Identity: The Personal and the Collective," asks how women's participation in war complicated their own identities and challenged the collective binary relationships that characterized war as a masculine arena. In the first chapter of this section, Mary Laurents reexamines the journals, letters, and pre-war writings of Vera Brittain, arguing that her disillusion on experiencing the conflict had less to do with feminine solidarity with the "lost generation" than with Brittain's own pre-war desires that aligned more closely to accepted masculine norms. In the second chapter, Laurie Stoff reveals the extent of Russian women's activity in the First World War: that they worked and supported the war effort in all areas as nurses, in munitions factories, in agriculture and in industry. Unlike the western front, the eastern front was mobile, which made former distinctions—between home front and battlefront, civilian and combatant—fluid categories, enabling women to work in all areas. Andrew Orr's chapter interrogates a binary category—specifically combatant and noncombatant—that dominates military histories. This chapter uses trans theory to examine the experiences of French women during World War II as they served in military roles under German occupation. Finally, Allison Scardino Belzer explores Italian national identity in Fascist Italy using children's fictional accounts of the Great War. As Italy shifted politically during the War and in the 1920s, juvenile consumers were "taught" about the changes through books that personified Italy and revealed an ideal version of the Italian character. Belzer reminds us that children were imagined as a malleable group waiting to be politicized.

The second section, "Humanitarian Aid and International Solidarity," opens with Michelle Tusan's chapter on humanitarian aid workers during the Great War, one of whom was a victim of the Armenian genocide. Tusan decenters the image of the "white woman" as the face of modern international

---

[35] See, for example, Hywel Davies, *Fleeing Franco: How Wales Gave Shelter to Refugee Children from the Basque Country during the Spanish Civil War* (Cardiff: University of Wales Press, 2011); Colomina Limonero, *Dos patrias, tres mil destinos Vida y exilio de los niños de la guerra de España refugiados en la Unión Sovietica* (Madrid: Ediciones Cinca, 2010); Adrian Bell, *Only for Three Months: The Basque Refugee Children in Exile* (Earls Barton: Wrightsons, 2007); Natalia Benjamin, ed., *Recuerdos: Basque Children Refugees in Britain* (Oxford: Mousehold Press, 2007), and Dorothy Lagarreta, *The Guernica Generation: Basque Refugee Children of the Spanish Civil War* (Reno: University of Nevada Press, 1984).

humanitarianism by examining the work of two very different aid workers. Dawson and Dawson examine the experiences of Spanish refugee children as they arrived in Britain and the Soviet Union. Using letters and oral interviews of the children, Dawson and Dawson reveal a range of behavioral differences between them, arguing that the children were political actors even as their exile and humanitarian aid was sentimentalized by the governments who took them in. Gina Benavidez examines the motivation and ideologies of three American women who went to Spain on the first US medical mission, observing that the women used nursing as a platform to engage in international politics. While most histories of the international brigades focus entirely on male participation, Benavidez reminds us that women also participated as international actors in the conflict. In the final chapter of the section, Mark Crowley examines British women's consumer campaigns to boycott Japanese goods to assist China after the Japanese invasion of Nanking in 1937. Spearheaded by trade union women, the China Campaign Committee raised funds and offered Chinese citizens direct assistance to fight Japanese fascism.

In the final section, "Conflict, Consumption and Survival," the first chapter examines Franco's food policies during and immediately following the Spanish Civil War. Suzanne Dunai argues that wartime divisions persisted after the war and divided families. This impacted family traditions, particularly those around food. Franco's food policies aimed to replicate the family by providing recipes that required less food items, as so many were unavailable—even breast milk for babies. By using food as a lens, Dunai interrogates the myriad ways civil conflict transformed everyday life for Spanish families. Kenneth Moure's chapter explores the black market in Vichy, France. Rationing and shortages forced women and children to use ingenuity to gain access to much-needed black-market food. Moure argues that while the war separated families, it also encouraged families to work together to survive. The final chapter of the collection, by Marianne Junila and Tiina Kinnunen, examines the way Finnish youth and children dealt with rationing, shortages, and austerity during the three wars that make up Finland's experience of World War II. Without aid from Germany, four million Finns would have faced famine. Even with the grain from Germany, Finnish children and youth experienced malnutrition and other diseases—yet magazines aimed at youth encouraged children to grow food and consume less to illustrate patriotism. The chapter is a welcome addition to the literature on children and war and state expectations of the child citizen.

While the volume brings to attention conflicts in Europe, the editors acknowledge the global ramifications of revolutions, wars, and genocides, as well as the diversity of individual experience. By expanding our understanding of the personal *as* the political in European conflicts from 1900-1950, we believe our focus on women and children offers a representative and collective perspective on five tumultuous decades of European history.

Section One.
War and Identity: The Personal and the Collective

Chapter 1

'One of the Boys': Identity, Crisis and Vera Brittain's War

Mary Laurents
University of Maryland, Baltimore County

Abstract: The writings of British author and Pacifist Vera Brittain are often seen as a definitive description of the "Lost Generation" in their vivid portrayal of the First World War's destructive effects on a generation of young British men and women. Her writings are regarded as especially significant because they deal with a young woman's experience of war – a rarity in an overwhelmingly male category of historical literature. Her account provides evidence that young women, along with their male counterparts, suffered initial illusion about the war's purpose and nature and then deep disillusion with the experience of war. An examination of her pre-war writing and her early war journals and letters, however, offers a different perspective. Viewed through the lens of early 20th-century British collective identity, her experience does not typify a young woman's. Rather she describes a struggle to shape an identity and life aligned with contemporary masculine, not feminine, values and ambitions. Her war experience reinforced her desire to follow a traditionally masculine life path, while her early view of the war and journey into disillusion, anger, and alienation was not an indicator of a collective female experience but the adoption of a collective identity that was distinctly male and upper class. This chapter examines Brittain's alignment with the collective identity that defined young upper-class men of the war generation and formed the core component of the "Lost Generation" narrative. Tracing this identity alignment and following its effects on Brittain throughout the war illuminates the workings and significance of the process of collective identity development and transformation under traumatic conditions.

Keywords: Great War, Vera Brittain, Collective Identity, Pacifism, Lost Generation, feminism, masculinity, disillusion

***

Introduction

"The Great War of 1914-18 lies like a band of scorched earth dividing that time from ours. In wiping out so many lives which would have been operative on the years that followed, in destroying beliefs, changing ideas, and leaving incurable wounds of disillusion, it created a physical as well as a psychological gulf between two epochs."[1]

Barbara Tuchman's description of World War I as a band of scorched earth echoed the feelings and memories of many young men and women whose lives were devastated by that conflict. Among them was the future writer, pacifist, and feminist Vera Brittain, who wrote one of the most influential war memoirs, *Testament of Youth*.[2] Her story is seen as a definitive description of what came to be known as the "Lost Generation" in its vivid portrayal of the destructive effects of war on a generation of young British men and women. Brittain's wartime and post-war writings are especially significant because they deal with a young woman's experience of war——something of a rarity in a category of historical literature that is overwhelmingly male. Her account provides evidence that young women, along with their male counterparts, suffered from initial illusions about the war's purpose and nature, followed by deep disillusion with the experience of war.

However, an examination of Brittain's pre-war writing and her journals and letters from early in the war offers a different perspective. Brittain's experiences, viewed through the lens of early twentieth-century British collective identity, does not typify a young woman's experience. Rather Brittain describes a struggle to shape an identity and life aligned with contemporary masculine, not feminine, values and ambitions. Her war experience reinforced her earlier desires to follow a traditionally masculine life path. Brittain's early view of the war and her journey into disillusion, anger, and alienation is not an indicator of a collective female experience but an adoption of a collective identity that was distinctly male and upper class.

This chapter examines Brittain's alignment with the collective identity that defined young upper-class men of the war generation and formed the core component of the "Lost Generation" narrative. Tracing this identity alignment and following its effects on Brittain throughout the war illuminates the workings and significance of the process of collective identity development and transformation under traumatic conditions.

---

[1] Barbara Tuchman, *The Proud Tower: A Portrait of the World before the War, 1890-1914* (MacMillan, 1996), xv.
[2] Vera Brittain, *Testament of Youth* (Penguin, 1995).

British Upper-Class Collective Identity in the Early Twentieth Century

At the beginning of the twentieth century, British upper-class[3] male identity was defined by an awareness of the responsibilities of the ruling class in political, military, and social leadership.[4] Upper-class men were aware of their duty to serve the nation, and of the value of self-sacrifice for the nation. They also held deep admiration for those who had sacrificed their lives. War, especially for the younger generation, was seen as a desirable undertaking that provided individuals with opportunities to demonstrate the qualities that confirmed their upper-class status and the group's right to lead and to rule.[5]

While upper-class female identity shared certain characteristics—including the sense of being part of the ruling elite—there were also distinct differences. Upper-class female identity focused on providing the support structure that enabled upper-class men to fulfil their leadership roles in society. Women also validated values and behaviors that defined male upper-class identity. Upper-class women reacted to the deaths of husbands, brothers, and sons in World War I in a way that confirmed the desirability of the sacrifice of upper-class lives in the service of the state. For example, after losing her youngest son at Loos (1915), Mary, Countess of Wemyss, authored a memoir in which she wrote that her son, like many of his friends, had died "gallantly flinging to his country the gift of his life." In a stunning exposition of support for traditional upper-class male identity, she stated that her son and his friends had served and died because "they felt they owed this debt of honour […]. They did not hesitate, they rushed with all the exuberance of inspired youth." She asserted that families who had lost sons should not mourn them "for they had the glory and the glamour in their hearts."[6] Similar sentiments can be seen in an account written by Ettie, Countess of Desborough, in which she described the death of her son, Julian Grenfell. During the battle of Neuve Chapelle (1915),

---

[3] For the purposes of this paper, the terms "upper-class" and "upper classes" encompass both traditional upper-class and upper-middle class. Upper-class usually refers to traditional British aristocracy and gentry families and upper-middle class is usually taken to refer to families who have gained wealth and enhanced social status through some form of commercial activity. While young men dealt with in studies of WWI's Lost Generation belong to both upper-class and upper-middle class families they also, critically, belong to a common masculine collective identity that is clearly aligned with the traditional British upper class and transmitted through the public schools which served the sons of both the traditional upper class and the up and coming upper middle class.
[4] For an in-depth examination of British upper-class collective identity in the early twentieth century and its fracture under the pressure of World War I, see Mary Laurents, *British Identity in World War I: The Lost Boys* (Lexington, 2020).
[5] Laurents, *The Lost Boys.* 7-40.
[6] Angela Lambert, *Unquiet Souls* (Harper & Row, 1984), 191.

Grenfell sustained a serious head wound that became infected. He spent an agonizing three days dying from a combination of the wound and subsequent infection. His mother was at his bedside throughout those three days and witnessed the agony of his death. Yet, in her later account, she referred to "the blessedness" of Grenfell's death and even forbade the wearing of mourning at a memorial for him held at the family's country house.[7]

While they filled critical support roles, women were not expected to participate in ruling or defending the nation in any active or direct way. They were keepers of home and tradition whose job was to ensure that the next generation were prepared to fulfill their responsibilities. Young upper-class women were expected to marry men from "good" families with prospects for leadership roles in government, the military, or society. After marriage, women were expected to confine their activities to managing households, supporting husbands, and ensuring that children were properly prepared to follow appropriate life paths.

The pacifist and feminist activism that Vera Brittain demonstrated after World War I is usually perceived as driven by the motivations that also drove the prewar Women's Suffrage movement. Yet when viewed in terms of collective identity, and specifically the collective identity that defined the British upper classes[8] in the early twentieth century, the motivations for her actions before and throughout the conflict can be seen quite differently. Rather than a radical feminist identity, Brittain identified strongly with the men of her generation and adopted their values, goals, and behaviors. As a result of that alignment, Brittain suffered the same disillusion and alienation as many of the young men of her generation.

An Unconventional Young Woman

Vera Brittain was an unconventional young woman with a personality and ambitions that did not fit the mold of traditional, prewar, upper-class womanhood. Born into a conventional, financially successful family, she was expected to follow a well-defined path that included a limited education, a brief period as an eligible young woman "in society," and eventually, marriage to a man of similar social status with good financial prospects. However, as both her wartime diaries and later accounts show, her aspirations did not align in any way with those expectations. Brittain was acutely aware that she was not a typical young woman and took pride in that difference. An entry in her journal written at the beginning of 1913 summed this up. She noted that,

---

[7] Peter Parker, *The Old Lie* (Constable and Company Limited, 1987), 220.
[8] Again, "upper classes" denotes both traditional upper class and upper middle class.

for her, 1912 had been "a miserable year" in spite of the fact that "It was my year of being eighteen [...] a girl's traditional age for happiness." Her explanation for her unhappiness was that "it is like me to go contrary to this tradition as to so many others!"[9]

Brittain's tendency to "go contrary to" traditionally feminine expectations had been present since her early teens, rooted in dissatisfaction with the limitations that traditional feminine identity imposed on her intellectual and personal development and on the independent adult life she envisioned for herself. Brittain attended a preparatory school that provided a higher quality and more challenging education than was typically offered to girls of her class. This education encouraged Brittain to apply to attend one of the few women's colleges. At school, she was disappointed in her fellow students' lack of support for her ambitions and disapproved of their attitudes. "My classroom contemporaries," she wrote, "Regarded my ambitions [...] with no particular interest or sympathy." They were, Brittain explained, "fashionable young women to whom universities represented a quite unnecessary prolongation of uselessness and distasteful studies." She added, "they looked upon my efforts to reach the top of the form, and my naïve anxiety to remain there, as satisfactorily exonerating them from the troublesome endeavour to win that position for themselves."[10]

Brittain's descriptions of the attitudes of her peers reflected the features and characteristics of the dominant identity of young British women in the upper classes at that time. In sociological terms, this identity was a hegemonic (or legitimizing) feminine identity—one that defined women's traditional roles and the requirements that women would have to meet to be accepted as a member of the upper classes. From her writing it is evident that Brittain's ambitions signaled her development of an alternate and opposing identity. This is apparent in her descriptions of her days at school where she defines her interactions with fellow students in terms of what they were and what she was not. In diaries and later writing, she noted that none of her fellow students "coveted the reputation [...] unenthusiastically conceded to me for brains" but instead "regarded these assets as mere second-rate compensation for my obvious inferiority in the advantages that they valued most." For most of her fellow students and their parents, "the potential occurrence that loomed largest upon the horizon was marriage" and "almost every girl left school with only two ambitions—to return at the first possible moment to

---

[9] Vera Brittain, *Chronicle of Youth: The War Diary, 1913-1917* (Morrow, 1982), 25. Entry for January 1, 1913, 25.
[10] Brittain, *Testament of Youth*, 33.

impress her school-fellows with the glory of a grown-up *toilette*, and to get engaged before everybody else."[11]

From an early age, Brittain separated herself from the traditional feminine image to which she was expected to conform. Her ambitions—to go to a women's college, to become a novelist, and to support herself financially—were clearly outside of ambitions expected or even allowed. She recorded multiple instances in which she was reminded of this. For example, after the eighteen-year-old Brittain turned down a proposal from a young man who people in her parents' social circle regarded as a good prospective husband, she recorded a conversation in which her mother, while sympathetic, "said she wished she might have a more ordinary daughter."[12] A few months earlier, Brittain recorded a similar but much stronger reaction from her mother over her determination to attend one of Oxford's women's colleges. During a series of family arguments about Vera's ambitions, her mother wished that Brittain was a more conventional daughter—a desire that Brittain sarcastically characterized as her mother wishing that she limit herself to "living & sleeping & dying & leaving no impress behind." Her mother's friends treated Brittain's ambitions as childish and amusingly unrealistic. After spending an evening with her mother's friends, she recorded their negative response to her ambitions. "They all *would* talk of literature & my going to Oxford. They seemed amused when I said I wasn't going to get married .... Mrs. Green said people wouldn't let me embrace a literary & virginal career."[13]

Having her ambitions rejected and mocked was made even worse by comparison with the very different expectations levied on her brother Edward. Where Vera's desire to go to Oxford was viewed as strange and unacceptable, Edward was expected to go to Oxford after completing his studies at his public school. The fact that Edward had no desire to go on to university only made the situation worse for Vera. The situation in which her brother, who was not enthusiastic about going to Oxford, was being sent there despite his lack of enthusiasm while her own desire for a university education was resisted by her parents was shown by a wry comment in her journal: "Of course E. will go to Oxford in any case."[14]

Brittain's self-definition as "contrary," the differences between her ambitions and those of other young women of her class, and her resistance to traditional feminine collective identity were forms of deliberate self-exclusion from that identity. Once Brittain excluded herself, she had then to define the group to

---

[11] Brittain, *Testament of Youth*, 34.
[12] Brittain, *Chronicle of Youth*, 82. Entry for July 26, 1914.
[13] Brittain, *Chronicle of Youth*, 58. Entry for February 22, 1914.
[14] Brittain, *Chronicle of Youth*, 51. Entry for January 2, 1914.

which she did belong. Sociologists and theorists who deal with collective identity theory posit that an individual's rejection of a traditional, hegemonic or legitimizing collective identity leads that individual to adopt a resistance identity formed in opposition to the rejected identity. Adoption of a resistance identity provides the individual with membership in a new collective that defines itself and its members by an identity that not only differs from the rejected traditional identity, but that also excludes anyone who still defines themselves according to the rejected identity.[15]

While there were feminist groups in pre-WWI Britain that constituted resistive collectives to which Vera could have gravitated and which would have supported her rejection of traditional feminine identity, she chose not to align with them. The collective and the identity she chose to align with, however, presented significant difficulties. The group and identity with which she felt the most kinship, and the one that offered her the life path she most desired, was not one into which she could, realistically, be accepted. Brittain most closely identified with the group of young men to which her brother Edward and his close friends belonged. Her ambitions to attend university and pursue a career that would give her financial independence were ones that matched the expectations levied on young men like her brother and his friends.

Along with the ambitions and expectations that characterized upper-class male collective identity, she also adopted the values and behaviors indicative of that identity. Those were instilled in young upper-class men in the public schools which, during most of the nineteenth and into the twentieth century, were the major mechanism through which upper-class identity was inculcated into generations of young men. Brittain's relationship with her brother—and later with his close friends—was the avenue through which she absorbed the values and behaviors that defined upper-class male identity. Her desire to go to Oxford and to establish a career that would give her intellectual satisfaction and financial independence was one demonstration of the internalization of those defining values and behavior and of her commitment to a male, rather than female, collective identity.

---

[15] Collective identity is described in work by sociologists Alberto Melucci and Manuel Castells. The concepts of legitimizing, resistance, and project collective identities are described by Castells in *The Power of Identity*. Castells notes that resistance identities define groups within modern societies that form based on resistance or opposition to hegemonic social or religious norms, political systems, or ideologies. Examples can be seen in groups that include early Protestant "Dissenter" sects, nineteenth-century utopian communities, and mid-twentieth century socio-political activist groups. See Melucci *Nomads of the Present* (Temple University Press, 1989) and Castells, *The Power of Identity* (Wiley-Blackwell, 2010).

Brittain's commitment went beyond educational and career goals. In her journals and the memoir published after the war, she also demonstrated her adoption of the belief that young upper-class men had a military duty as defenders of the nation and a political duty as its natural rulers. Brittain described attending Uppingham Public School Speech Day in July 1914 when her brother graduated. She recorded the headmaster's address in which he urged students to seek to be of service to the nation and to be prepared to take up military service should the nation be threatened. Quoting the headmaster, Brittain wrote, "if a man could not be useful to his country he was better dead."[16] Finally, in her prewar journal, she demonstrated her belief in the highly romanticized idea of self-sacrifice in the interest of the nation. This belief, central to upper-class male identity and promoted in public schools, motivated many young men to volunteer to fight in the First World War. Indeed, when Brittain commented on the disastrous Scott Antarctic expedition, she unquestioningly accepted the popular narrative that depicted the failure of the expedition and deaths of its members as heroic sacrifice rather than the result of faulty planning and preparation. In early 1913, she described the news of the deaths of Scott and the expedition members as "terrible" but added, "how grand the way they died—especially Captain Oates who went out into the blizzard to die that his weakness might not delay his four companions, who refused to leave him. 'Greater love hath no man than this.'"[17]

Even the one area in which Vera appeared to conform to traditional feminine expectations was an indicator of her resistance to traditional feminine identity: her relationship with her brother's friend, Roland Leighton. Their relationship began as a friendship formed when Leighton spent several days at the Brittain's family home during the summer of 1914. The friendship continued through intense correspondence and eventually became a serious relationship with both anticipating eventual marriage. While anticipating marriage could indicate adherence to traditional feminine values, Vera's expectations regarding marriage were anything but traditional. In her journals, letters, and her post-war memoir she makes it very clear that the marriage she envisioned with Leighton was far from conventional. Writing to him late in the summer of 1914, Vera made her feelings about marriage clear: "I would be satisfied with nothing less than a mutually comprehensive loving relationship. I would not endure to be constantly propitiating any man…"[18] One of the things about Leighton that appealed to Brittain was that his mother (romance novelist Marie Connor Leighton) not only had a thriving

---

[16] Brittain, *Chronicle of Youth*, 78. Entry for July 11, 1914.
[17] Brittain, *Chronicle of Youth*, 51. Entry for February 12, 1913.
[18] Brittain, *Testament of Youth*, 102.

career but also provided a large part of the Leighton family income through her writing. Leighton was therefore used to the idea of a married woman with a career who was financially independent. In her descriptions of marriage to Leighton, Brittain envisioned a nontraditional partnership in which both she and Leighton would pursue individual careers while she would maintain her financial independence. Marriage with Leighton was, in fact, another demonstration of opposition to traditional feminine identity and traditional forms of marriage.

When Brittain was accepted at Oxford in 1914, she must have seen it as validation of her identification with masculine collective identity and perhaps even a sign of her acceptance into that collective. This was, however, completely upended by the beginning of WWI and the actions of her brother and his friends. Edward Brittain, Roland Leighton, and their other friends immediately applied for commissions in the British army and sought active duty in the war. For Vera, this must have been like having the rug pulled out from under her—just as she had attained some of the status that she sought vis-à-vis masculine identity, her brother and his friends were moving on to something that she absolutely could not join them in.

Brittain recorded a conversation with Leighton in September 1914 that had caused her pain and frustration as it confirmed her inability to be part of that young, upper-class, masculine collective with which she so strongly identified. Leighton informed her that he would not be going to Oxford but was, instead, seeking a commission in a regiment that would enable him to quickly be posted to the front. Leighton said, "I don't think in the circumstances I could easily bring myself to endure a secluded life of scholastic vegetation. It would seem a somewhat cowardly shirking of my obvious duty."[19] He added that he felt he was "meant to take an active part in the War" and described war as "a very fascinating thing—something, if often horrible, yet very ennobling and very beautiful, something whose elemental reality raises it above the reach of all cold theorizing."[20] Brittain's reaction was also telling. She found Leighton's reference to "scholastic vegetation" hurtful as "it seemed to definitely put me outside everything that now counted in life"—a significant comment that clearly expressed her feeling of exclusion. She further expressed identification with male, rather than female, collective identity when she wrote: "Women get all the dreariness of war, and none of its exhilaration." She expressed frustration because the place at Oxford that she had worked so hard to achieve was now "worth so little."[21] Oxford, in other

---

[19] Brittain, *Testament of Youth*, 103.
[20] Brittain, *Testament of Youth*, 103-4.
[21] Brittain, *Testament of Youth*, 104.

words, would no longer guarantee her membership in that young upper-class male collective. While the price of admission had been raised to a level that exceeded her ability to pay, Brittain had no intention of abandoning her efforts to join the club.

War, Loss, and Identity Fracture

Despite finally getting to Oxford, Brittain again felt left behind and excluded from the group with which she most closely identified. This exclusion, however, only sharpened her desire to take some form of action that would validate her striving for inclusion in the group typified by her brother and his friends. Throughout the autumn and winter of 1914, Brittain frequently expressed dissatisfaction with her inability to participate in the war on the same level as her male counterparts and complained about the marginal role that her gender forced her to play. In journal entries and letters, Brittain lamented that knitting socks and scarves for soldiers and attending first-aid classes needed to qualify as a volunteer nurse were "the only work it seems possible as yet for women to do."[22] In response to a letter from Leighton expressing his impatience with delays in sending his unit to the front, Brittain emphasized her unhappiness with "women's enforced inactivity in the military part of the war."[23]

In an apparent effort to reconcile her actions with those of her male counterparts, Brittain made an interesting comparison between the necessity to concentrate on her academic work and the foremost of soldierly virtues. In her journal, she wrote that she had "tried to work to-day, & with some success, realizing that if I could not feel interested in my work I must do it without feeling interested. Such is the only form of courage I can practice."[24] That her effort to see her academic work as equivalent to the military service undertaken by her brother and his friends was not successful can be seen in a later journal entry in which she states, "It is not the things that happen in Oxford that count now but those that happen in Flanders."[25] Brittain reinforced this when, after reading a newspaper account of some action that had taken place near the area occupied by Leighton's regiment, she wrote that she would "not fear the danger" faced by young men in the trenches "if I could share it."[26] She was even more straightforward when commenting on Leighton's description of the experience of having been under shell fire for

---

[22] Brittain, *Chronicle of Youth*, 89.
[23] Ibid.
[24] Ibid, 164.
[25] Ibid, 179.
[26] Ibid.

more than 2 hours. After quoting from his description in her journal, she added the wish that she "could be enduring [the danger] with him instead of waiting in suspense in soft surroundings."[27] The similarity between this particular remark and Leighton's statement rejecting "scholastic vegetation" in favor of doing what he saw as his duty is striking and again demonstrates Brittain's buy-in to male, rather than female identity.

Along with her desire for active participation in the war, Brittain's attitude about the loss of young men in the war paralleled the heroic view expressed by many young upper-class men at the beginning of the war. On hearing about the death of one of Leighton's friends, she wrote, expressing sentiments that reiterated the traditional heroic view of young men who die in battle. In that letter, Brittain urged Leighton to remember "these [words] which Francis Thompson said of the great Victorian dead—they passed, they passed, but cannot pass away, for England feels them in her blood like wine."[28] She sounded the same note when, in June 1915, she saw the obituary of Murray Drummond Fraser—a young man who had been part of her social circle. "He was only 21," she wrote in her journal, adding that she had "often played tennis or bridge with him, & always liked him very much."[29] She followed with a quote comparing the dead to Homeric heroes, talented, brave, and doomed to early death "they are all departing: fulfilling like the Achaeans of Homer's *Iliad*, a cruel fate—'the eloquent, the young, the beautiful & brave.'"[30]

The standards of behavior, values, and goals to which Brittain aspired were ones that defined men rather than women of her social class and generation. This identification motivated her to exercise the option that was the closest thing to military service that she could find—a nursing assignment in a military hospital.[31] In late spring 1915, she decided to take a leave of absence from Oxford and request a nursing assignment with the Voluntary Aid Detachment (VAD) in a field hospital as close to the front as possible. Her decision to leave Oxford and volunteer for nursing duty in military hospitals was supported by many of her tutors and fellow students—support that reinforced her alignment with young, upper-class, male identity. One of her tutors clearly equated nursing duty in military hospitals with men's military

---

[27] Ibid, 183.
[28] Ibid, 213.
[29] Ibid, 206.
[30] Ibid, 207.
[31] See Juliette Pattinson, *Women of War: Gender, Modernity and the First Aid Nursing Yeomanry* (Manchester: Manchester University Press, 2020); Christine E. Hallett, *Veiled Warriors: Allied Nurses of the First World War* Oxford: Oxford University Press, 2014), and Janet S. K. Watson, "War in the Wards: The Social Construction of Medical Work in First World War Britain," *Journal of British Studies* 41: 4 (2002) 484-510.

service at the front. Brittain wrote that one tutor had "put it quite on the level of a man's deed by agreeing with me that I ought not to put the speedy start of my career forward as an excuse, any more than a man should against enlisting."[32]

Brittain began her war service in hospitals in London, tending to civilian patients and to an increasingly large number of military casualties. Her experiences with war casualties and the increasingly bleak picture of the war communicated to her by her brother, Leighton, and two of her brother's friends serving on the western front, brought home the realities of war and the danger faced by those young men. During the late summer and autumn of 1915, Brittain realized that there was a strong likelihood that Leighton would be killed at the front and formulated a plan for that eventuality. The plan, which Brittain detailed in her journal, was a significant indicator of her attitude toward the war. Given the pacifist beliefs and activities she publicly espoused and promoted in the interwar years, and for which she subsequently became famous, one might reasonably expect any contingency plan after the death of her fiancé would include some negative reaction to the war. The plan, however, was one that supported the war effort and reinforced the values and attitudes that defined the masculine identity with which she identified and that had motivated her generation's participation in the war. Her intention was to ask for duty in a hospital close to the front lines—one in which the work that she would do would be "hard" and "dirty," emulating, as closely as possible, the actions of her male counterparts.

Brittain's plan has some striking similarities to the reactions of many young officers to the deaths of close friends. One of the best-known examples is Siegfried Sassoon's reaction to the death of David Thomas, a fellow officer in the Royal Welch Fusiliers and a man who was close to both Sassoon and Robert Graves. Graves described the terrible anger that Sassoon experienced over Thomas' death and wrote that even though Sassoon was, at the time, acting as Transport Officer (and not obligated to perform patrol duty or to participate in routine trench raids), his desire for revenge was so great that "every evening […] when he came up with the rations, [he] went out on patrol looking for Germans to kill."[33] Brittain's intention to be as near to the front lines as possible was similar to the disregard for personal safety illustrated by Sassoon's unnecessary forays in response to loss. Brittain's planned reaction to Leighton's death, like Sassoon's reaction to Thomas' death, validated the war by responding to loss through an escalated participation in that war.

---

[32] Brittain, *Chronicle of Youth*, 195.
[33] Peter Parker, *The Old Lie*, 178.

Many young officers like Sassoon, Graves, and Leighton held on to their heroic view of the war and their place in it during the first year of the war but could not maintain that under the increasing pressure of the war's reality and of the horrendous death rate suffered by junior officers. By the autumn of 1915, many of the young upper-class men who comprised the large majority of the junior officer corps were firmly rejecting traditional beliefs about war. Sassoon and Graves became iconic members of the group of war poets who memorialized the squalidness of trench warfare and the feeling of many young officers that they had been betrayed by the older members of their own class and duped into fighting a pointless war. Traditional upper-class collective identity was fracturing along generational lines to form a new, resistance identity that defined itself by its opposition to that traditional identity.[34]

Hospital duty and the deaths of young men whom she had known exerted the same type of pressure on Brittain and her alignment with traditional male upper-class identity. Her initial response validated the war but, like many of her male contemporaries, her sentiments were changing, and she was questioning the war's conduct and purpose. Brittain's definitive break with traditional identity occurred in December 1915. In mid-December, she received a letter from Leighton saying that he had left and expected to be in England on Christmas Day. Brittain spent the days before Christmas on hospital duty and, on Christmas Day, traveled to join her parents in a hotel in Brighton. She waited all Christmas Day for word from Leighton. The following morning Brittain was summoned to the hotel telephone to take what she assumed would be a call from Leighton. The call was not from Leighton but from his younger sister, Clare. Leighton had not arrived safely in England. Instead, a telegram from Leighton's commanding officer had arrived at the Leighton home: "Regret to inform you that Lieut. R. A. Leighton 7th Worchesters died of wounds December 23rd."[35]

The shock of Leighton's death brought into focus all the negative things that Brittain had begun to feel about the war. A journal entry written on New Year's Eve 1915 made clear the devastating loss that she felt. In it, she wrote, "This time last year ... I had just begun to realise I loved Him. Today He is lying in the military cemetery at Louvencourt—because a week ago He was wounded in action, and had just 24 hours of consciousness more and then went 'to sleep in France.' ... All has been given me, and all taken away—in one year." [36] True to the plan that she had intended to put into action in the event of

---

[34] Laurents, *British Identity in World War I*, chapter 2.
[35] Brittain, *Chronicle of Youth*, 196. Entry for December 27, 1915.
[36] Brittain, *Chronicle of Youth*, 196-197. Entry for December 31, 1915.

Leighton's death, she immediately applied for overseas duty and was assigned to a military hospital in Malta.

Vera Brittain spent the remainder of the war working in military hospitals in Malta, northern France, and, at the end of the war, in England. From the moment that she found out about Leighton's death to the time she left hospital service at the end of 1918, Brittain's war was a story of continual loss and increasing disillusion and bitterness with the government, society, and the social structure that she viewed as responsible for duping her generation and then sacrificing the members of that generation in a war that, for her, served no good purpose. In April 1917, approximately a year and a half after Leighton's death, another of Edward Brittain's close friends (Victor Richardson) sustained a head wound that left him blind. Having lost Leighton and being a close friend of Richardson's, Brittain made the decision to marry Richardson and use her nursing experience to help care for him. In writing about this decision, she stated that she had nothing left in life but her brother Edward and "the wreckage of Victor" and concluded that as Victor had "stood by me so often in my blackest hours" she felt that it was now her duty to "stand by him in his."[37] Sadly, Brittain's intention to marry Richardson and spend her life caring for him proved futile. After two months in which his health improved, though his sight did not return, he suffered what was probably a stroke caused by the aftereffects of his head wound and died.

In this she echoed feelings expressed by young men like Sassoon and Graves who, as their disillusion with the war and the older upper-class men (senior military leaders and government officials) that they saw as responsible for beginning, pursuing, and prolonging it increased, turned their loyalty and their sense of duty to their friends and fellow soldiers—other members of their own generation (and, with regard to their close friends, of their own class) that they saw as also being victimized by the older men. Brittain delivered a very clear statement of these sentiments when she wrote to her brother, "No one could realise better than I our responsibility towards him [Victor]—not only because of our love for him, but because of his love for us, and the love felt for him by the one we loved and lost [Leighton]." She followed this by writing that, while the dead were "beyond any aid of ours," she and Edward had an obligation to them that could only be repaid through service to "those young men who still remained."[38] In a letter to Brittain written after she had arrived in England intending to marry Richardson, Edward echoed these sentiments about war. Edward wrote, "we have lost

---

[37] Brittain, *Testament of Youth*, 347.
[38] Ibid.

almost all there was to love and what have we gained? Truly as you say has patriotism worn very threadbare [...]."[39]

Brittain's sentiments, as repeated here by her brother, reiterated the feeling expressed by many young upper-class men. We see a striking similarity between this statement, and one made by Alec Waugh in his autobiographical novel *The Loom of Youth* (1917), which is set at an elite public school. In a key scene, a former student returns from the front on leave and, while visiting his friends at his former school, tells them, "All our generation has been sacrificed," and that while they had been "deceived by the tinsel of war" they were "done with fairy tales. There is nothing glorious in war."[40] The loss of Leighton followed by the loss of Richardson, had shattered Vera's belief in the upper-class view of self-sacrifice in the interest of the nation as a defining virtue. She no longer held with the statement made by Uppingham's Headmaster that any young man who would not be of use to his nation was better off dead. For her, the loss of young men who died while trying to be of "use" to their country—and who might have been of significant use to the nation had they lived normal lifespans—was simply "cruel waste."[41]

After the death of Richardson and another of Edward Brittain's closest friends (also in 1917), Vera wrote bitterly that while "it is better to have had such splendid friends [...] than not to have had any particular friends at all [...] now that all are gone, it seems that whatever was of value in life has all tumbled down like a house of cards."[42] Here again, her sentiments echo those of many young men who, by 1917, felt that the war had cost them too much. In late 1917, Duff Cooper (future Conservative party politician, author, and diplomat) noted in his journal a conversation that he had had with one of his few surviving friends, Patrick Shaw Stewart. In that conversation, they discussed the friends they had lost, concluding that "we can make no new friends worthy of the old ones." Within a month of that conversation, Shaw Stewart was killed, leaving Cooper to remark that he believed the war had cost his generation "more than our fair share" and that, for his generation "the dance is already over and it is time to go."[43]

The final blow for Brittain came with the death of her brother, Edward, on the Italian front in June 1918. Her brother's death crystallized her rejection of all the features of traditional upper-class identity that she had formerly embraced so fervently and that had led her into war service. Her final

---

[39] Brittain, *Testament of Youth*, 360.
[40] Alec Waugh, *The Loom of Youth* (Cassell & Company, Ltd., 1917), 307.
[41] Brittain, *Testament of Youth*, 358.
[42] Ibid, 360.
[43] Duff Cooper, *Old Men Forget* (Faber and Faber, 2011), 201.

rejection is shown in an incident recorded in her journal. When invited to dine with an elderly cleric who was acting as the administrator for a military hospital in which she was serving, Brittain declined because "I did not propose to submit to pious dissertations on my duty to God, King and Country. That voracious trio had already deprived me of all that I valued most in life." Like so many young men who had survived the war but lost the values and beliefs that had defined them as well as any hope for the kind of futures that they had looked forward to, Vera wrote that her "only hope now was to become the complete automaton, working mechanically and no longer even pretending to be animated by ideals."[44]

Building a New Identity

I have, in *British Identity in World War I*, provided an in-depth discussion of the social, political, cultural mechanism that defined upper-class male collective identity and that enabled the transmission of that collective identity to young upper-class men. That work also demonstrates that the experiences of young upper-class men in the First World War resulted in a fracture, along generational lines, of traditional upper-class identity. That fracture resulted in the formation of a different type of collective identity, a resistance identity, among many young upper-class men. The major characteristic was its opposition to the traditional (legitimizing) identity, its rejection of the values, beliefs, and behaviors on which that traditional identity was based, and its embrace of young upper-class men who had rejected the values and behaviors that defined traditional upper-class identity.

By the end of the war, Brittain was expressing the same type of resistance identity demonstrated by young men like Waugh, Graves, and Sassoon. She, however, differed from them in one significant way. Those men and other war survivors adopted a resistance identity that was essentially "retreatist." Their postwar lives exhibited an aimlessness or disengagement from the careers and futures expected of young men of their class. While Brittain's response to the war was similarly grounded in an awareness of what she saw as cynical lies and the betrayal of her generation by the nation's leadership, resistance was not the final step in her journey. Brittain had no intention of retreating permanently from taking an active role in shaping a postwar world. Even some of her most dramatic expressions of resistance demonstrated a desire to be productive. Writing about the peace negotiations that led to the Treaty of Versailles, Brittain noted the negotiations "did not seem to me to represent at all the kind of victory that the young men whom I had loved would have

---

[44] Brittain, *Testament of Youth*, 450.

regarded as sufficient justifications for their lost lives." She added that while her brother and her fiancé would have welcomed a League of Nations, she did not believe either would have given their lives "in order that Clemenceau should outwit Lloyd George, and both of them bamboozle President Wilson, and all three combine to make the beaten, blockaded enemy pay the cost of War."[45] Brittain's statement clearly shows her opposition to the results of the peace negotiations, which she saw as evidence of her generation's betrayal. There is also, however, in that statement and its reference to the League of Nations, the hope that a world might be established to prevent anything like the war from happening again.

On her return to Oxford, Brittain changed her area of study from English to History and described the motivation as a desire to understand how the war—and the associated disaster that her generation had suffered—had come about. It was also clear, however, that understanding was not her only motivation. This is where we see the difference between Brittain and her male counterparts. For Brittain, the change in her studies was part of an emerging plan for a future and a career in which she felt a responsibility to find the causes of the war and "try to prevent it from happening to other people in the days to come."[46] Where many young men were, and would continue to be, detached from career expectations and resisted any efforts to play a part in shaping the future of the nation, Brittain struck out on her own, very different path. Brittain used the trauma of the war to shape not only her own future, but to shape a better future for fellow survivors and future generations.

---

[45] Brittain, *Testament of Youth*, 470.
[46] Ibid. 472.

Chapter 2

Saving Russia: Women's Contributions to Russia's First World War Effort

Laurie S. Stoff
Arizona State University

Abstract: Russia's involvement in World War I was harrowing, as in many other countries that fought in this conflict, but until very recently, scholarly studies have largely overlooked its experiences. Not only is Russia generally neglected in Western historiography of this war (which, perhaps unsurprisingly, is dominated by Western experiences), it was similarly largely disregarded in Soviet scholarship. Immediately preceding and in a number of important ways, predicting, the Russian Revolution of 1917, it was overshadowed by histories of that event. Moreover, the new Soviet regime was loath to commemorate what was perceived as a "bourgeois imperialist war." Yet, Russia's war experience during this conflict is historically significant for a number of reasons. Although it withdrew its forces from the fighting earlier than other belligerents, Russia put approximately 15 million men into battle and lost nearly half to wounding, illness, death, and desertion. To allow for the operation of its military machine in this total war, the country depended heavily on the mobilization and participation of women in virtually every aspect of service. Female workers performed nearly half of all wartime labor in agricultural, commercial, and industrial sectors. More than thirty thousand women worked in wartime medical capacities, treating the wounded and ill among both the soldiering and civilian populations. Perhaps most saliently, thousands of Russian women actually participated directly in Russia's military efforts on the battlefields. Moreover, Russia's war was fundamentally different from the static trench warfare that dominated the Western front. Instead, military operations were highly mobile on the Eastern Front, which meant that it was often impossible to separate women from frontline activity. As a result, the actions and experiences of Russian women in the Great War indicate the extent to which war often has been mischaracterized as a masculine endeavor, and call into question the notion of ossified divisions between "front" and "rear," "combatant" and "non-combatant," even "masculine and feminine."

Keywords: Russia, Eastern Front, Sisters of Mercy, Great War, combatant, Western Front, Soviet Regime

***

Introduction

The participation of millions of women was fundamental to waging war in the First World War. The "total" nature of the war meant that military activities were highly dependent on the mobilization of broad swaths of the civilian population and their active involvement in the war effort. Conventionally, male and female participants in warfare have been understood to belong to significantly different categories: military personnel versus civilians, front versus rear, with correspondingly gendered associations of masculine versus feminine. Such a view presents an ossified division of activity that fails to consider the multiple ways that women affected and were affected by the conflict. Furthermore, the traditional scholarly narrative of the Great War was shaped largely by experiences on the Western Front as a static, trench-bound war of attrition centered on male combatants. Women in this narrative are featured in secondary positions, as workers on the "home front," as nurses in medical facilities and in other forms of auxiliary labor far behind the frontlines, and as temporary replacements for conscripted men on the "home front."[1] This dichotomous understanding of warfare and the military is challenged by scholarship that reveals how vital the roles women played in the war efforts were for their respective nations.[2] But here, too, the historiography is focused primarily on the Western experience and neglects Eastern Europe and Russia, despite the fact that much of the conflict actually took place in those lands.[3]

---

[1] See, for example: B. H. Liddell Hart, *The Real War 1914-1918* (London: Faber & Faber, 1930), later republished as *History of the First World War*; John Keegan, *The First World War* (London: Hutchinson, 1998); Hew Strachan, *The First World War* (New York: Oxford University Press, 2003); David Stevenson, *1914-1918: The History of the First World War* (New York: Penguin, 2004).

[2] See, for example, Susan Grayzel and Tammy Proctor, *Gender and the Great War* (New York: Oxford University Press, 2017) and Billie Melman, ed., *Borderlines: Genders and Identities in War and Peace, 1870-1930* (New York: Routledge, 1998).

[3] See Allison Scardino Belzer, *Women and the Great War: Femininity under Fire in Italy* (New York: Palgrave Macmillan, 2010); Kimberly Jensen, *Mobilizing Minerva: American Women in the First World War* (Champaign: University of Illinois Press, 2008); Margaret Darrow, *French Women and the First World War: War Stories of the Home Front* (New York:

The Eastern Front featured a different dynamic, one of much greater mobility. Although the Russian armies did use trenches along the frontlines, those lines shifted rapidly and required troops to relocate as enemy armies pushed them back or as they advanced. Areas designated as military zones changed often and civilian spaces transformed quickly into battlefields and then back again. The zones of conflict came to encompass not only the millions of soldiers engaged directly in combat, but also millions of others: medical personnel and support services who moved with the troops; railway workers who transferred troops, auxiliaries, and the goods necessary for their work; prisoners of war who existed in a liminal zone between active warfare and civilian life; and millions more laborers who engaged in the agricultural and industrial production that fed, clothed, and provided arms, munitions, and supplies necessary to carry out this gargantuan undertaking.[4] The result of this was greater fluidity and porosity of categories and spheres of activity, wherein many women operated directly in war zones. The separations of front/rear, military/civilian, and their gendered associations of masculine/feminine, were difficult to maintain. Several recent scholarly works have examined Russia's experiences in the Great War in-depth and restored them to the overall picture of the conflict.[5] Yet women and gender have figured only peripherally in most of the scholarship.[6]

Berg, 2000); Susan Grayzel, *Women and the First World War* (Essex: Pearson Education, 2002); Gail Braybon, *Women Workers in the First World War* (London: Routledge, 1989); Margaret Higonnet et al., eds., *Behind the Lines: Gender and the Two World Wars* (New Haven and London: Yale University Press, 1987); Lettie Gavin, *American Women in World War I: They Also Served* (Boulder: University of Colorado Press, 1999).

[4] See Laurie S. Stoff et al, eds., *Military Affairs in Russia's Great War and Revolution, 1914–22, Book 1: Military Experiences* (Bloomington: Slavica Publishers Indiana University, 2019) and Joshua Sanborn, *Imperial Apocalypse: The Great War and the Destruction of the Russian Empire* (New York: Oxford University Press, 2014).

[5] See for example, the multivolume series entitled *Russia's Great War and Revolution*, published by Slavica Press of Indiana University (first volumes appeared in 2014, and they continue to be published each year since, with multiple books scheduled to come out in the next several years), as well as Peter Gatrell, *Russia's First World War: A Social and Economic History* (Harlow: Pearson: 2005).

[6] There is, to date, no comprehensive study of Russia's war through the lens of gender or that examines the totality of women's wartime experience in Russia. Some works focus on women's wartime activities. These include my own works, from which much of the present article is drawn: *Russia's Sisters of Mercy and the Great War: More than Binding Men's Wounds* (Lawrence: University Press of Kansas, 2015) and *They Fought for the Motherland: Russia's Women Soldiers in World War I and the Revolution* (Lawrence: University Press of Kansas, 2006); Peter Gatrell, "The Epic and the Domestic: Women and War in Russia, 1914-1917," in Gail Braybon, ed., *Evidence, History, and the Great War: Historians and the Impact*

This chapter examines Russian women and the gendered aspects of their participation in the Great War effort in order to re-establish their place in the scholarly narrative. Rather than depicting the war and the mass participation of women in it merely as an unintended result of the exigencies and specific features of total, mechanized warfare, I argue that the mobilization and employment of women in multiple facets of the conflict, including directly in zones of conflict, was deliberate and desirable. Women were seen by many in Russia as a source not only of necessary labor, but one of salvation for a troubled nation in an increasingly troubled war effort As laborers, women nourished the nation, producing the goods and providing the services needed. As nurses, women were believed to possess unique abilities, stemming from essentialist notions of "natural" propensities for caring and nurturing, for literally curing men of wounds and illness, physically and, perhaps more importantly, both mentally and spiritually. This positioned women as especially important in the process of restoring damaged men so that they could return to their masculinized duties as soldiers. And as soldiers, they were intended to "heal" the army by restoring its fighting spirit, and "save" Russia from collapse as a result of an external existential threat. Indeed, female soldiers were recruited and employed not only because of the desperate need for fresh troops toward the end of the war, but specifically to serve as examples for war-weary men who were faltering, and to remind them (some even conceptualized this in terms of shaming) to reciprocate their duty specifically as men, as defenders of the nation, to continue fighting.

The role of women in staving off national collapse was instrumental (even if unsuccessful). Although in Russia, warfare was traditionally understood as a male preserve, the notion of women as strong, both physically and morally, in Russian tradition is well-documented. Vera Dunham reveals that, in Russian literary sources, "'Russian womanhood' is remarkable in that it is a perceptible motif" which "extols that coherence and strength of the woman in a historical sequence and in divergent class settings," and is portrayed by multiple Russian authors as "a vital source of national salvation."[7] Barbara Heldt demonstrates that strong female figures are replete in modern Russian literature, and "the inadequacies and weaknesses of some male protagonists find their complementary awesome strengths in the young heroines of

---

of 1914-1918 (New York: Berghan Books, 2003), 198-215; and Alfred Meyer, "The Impact of World War I on Russian Women's Lives," in Barbara Clements, Barbara Engel, and Christine Worobec, eds., *Russia's Women: Accommodation, Resistance, Transformation* (Berkeley: University of California Press, 1991), 208-224.

[7] Vera S. Dunham, "The Strong Woman Motif," in Cyril Black, ed., *The Transformation of Russian Society* (Cambridge: Harvard University Press, 1960), 462, 468.

Russia."⁸ As Heldt contends, "the Russian heroine is generally taken as a marvelous given of nature, a being in whom not only her own and her family's future, but the future hope of Russia resides."⁹ These ideas were accompanied by the view that a woman's greatest attributes were embodied by motherhood and the creation and preservation of life, and uniquely feminine.¹⁰ Russian peasant women in particular were associated with fertility, purity, and importantly, nurturance. Their image was, as Cathy Frierson describes, "merge[d] with the image of the Russian land, the earth, the soil from which the most basic necessities for cultural survival must spring."¹¹

The perception of the gender-specific strength of women influenced ideas about women's wartime roles. Although much of this centered on supportive roles, it nonetheless indicated ways in which women's participation was significant to the success and very survival of the nation. As one author commented in 1914, "The war has delegated a very large role for women in the arena of social activity. It has given woman the opportunity to show her spiritual strength decisively to all."¹² Journalist Valentina Kostyleva asserted that "the strength of woman is in what she brings into the world, *that* which man is *unable* to bring... And so the role of woman in war predisposed her to the very fate that she must fulfill, that which men are unable to do." Feminine influence had healing, restorative power, with applications in the context of the destructiveness of war and more broadly. "Aside from healing wounds received in battle, a woman can heal many sores received in life," Kostyleva argued, and "woman can play an especially important role there, where she is a guardian angel, where her authority has especially spiritual strength."¹³ While this may seem more obvious in relation to female nurses, even women's soldiering was conceptualized in ways consistent with the image of strong female healers and saviors of the *narod* (people) and the *rodina* (motherland). From the very start of the war, women entering combat were seen as passionately driven by the desire to save the country from the impending

---

[8] Barbara Heldt, *Terrible Perfection: Women and Russian Literature* (Bloomington: Indiana University Press, 1987), 12.
[9] Heldt, *Terrible Perfection*, 12.
[10] See nineteenth-century works on women, such as Vitalii Shul'gin, *O sostoianii zhenshchin v Rossii do Petra Velikago: Istoricheskoe issledovanie* [*On the conditions of women in Russia to Peter the Great: Historical research*] (Kiev, 1850)
[11] Cathy Frierson, *Peasant Icons: Representations of Rural People in Late Nineteenth Century Russia* (New York: Oxford University Press, 1993), 162.
[12] *Zhenskaia zhizn': Zhurnal dlia khoziek* [*Women's Life: Journal for Housewives*] 2 (October 7, 1914): 8.
[13] Valentina Kostyleva, "Nashi Amazonki" ["Our Amazons"], *Zhenskaia zhizn': Zhurnal dlia khoziek* [*Women's Life: Journal for Housewives*] 1 (October 1, 1914): 24.

doom of conquest by the enemy. Such notions were greatly amplified by the conditions of 1917. As the Russian army continued to falter and the collapse of tsarist authority because of the February Revolution, many argued that the troops were "ailing" and in need of "healing" influences to restore their morale and battle readiness.

Women's Wartime Labor

The Russian armed forces conscripted 15 million men, 36 percent of the population, to fight.[14] The vast majority were peasants engaged in agricultural work. Agrarian production was necessary to feed the civilian and military populations. Millions of women took up the labor previously done by men. While women had been intensively involved in agricultural production, the war needs increased numbers dramatically. Exemptions were supposed to prevent the conscription of men who were the sole able-bodied male laborers in peasant households, but corruption and uneven application of policy meant they often failed. This was compounded by the shift in production from agricultural machinery to military equipment that significantly reduced the number of peasants available for cultivation and harvesting.

As a result, women filled the gaps.[15] On peasant farms, women constituted 72 percent of laborers, and on landowner estates they made up 58 percent of workers.[16] The transition to a predominately female labor force was eased by the fact that Russian women had always worked in agriculture, often in the most physically exertive tasks. Although there was strictly gendered division of labor in rural households—domestic activities conducted within the home were the domain of women—field work was undertaken by both male and female peasants. Therefore, women did not need to learn new skills to carry out wartime labor.

This shift was not entirely unproblematic. Some men viewed the "feminization" of agricultural labor as threatening to male prerogative and authority in highly patriarchal peasant communities.[17] Nonetheless, the country desperately needed women to undertake the bulk of food production. In this, they performed the vital role of literally nourishing the nation and, even more importantly for the war effort, keeping millions of troops fed. But

---

[14] N. N. Golovin, *The Russian Army in the World War* (New Haven: Yale University Press, 1931), 49.
[15] Gatrell, *Russia's First World War*, 154-157; Lewis H. Siegelbaum, *The Politics of Industrial Mobilization in Russia, 1914-17* (London: Macmillan Co., 1983), 152.
[16] Alfred Meyer, "The Impact of World War I on Russian Women's Lives," in Clements, Engel, and Worobec, eds., *Russia's Women*, 208-224.
[17] Meyer, "The Impact of World War I on Russian Women's Lives," 214-216.

as with the traditional agricultural work that peasant women had long done, there was little reward, despite the acknowledgment of their indispensability.

Russia's industrial labor force similarly experienced great expansion of women's participation, as the war increased demand for production and decreased the availability of male workers. Although the numbers were smaller because some skilled men were given exemptions from conscription to carry out vitally needed production, they were still significant. Women undertook training for the skilled labor work traditionally done by men. Prior to the war, the number of women in industrial employment had been rising, but numbers increased dramatically (around 39 percent) in the first years of the war. By 1917, women constituted nearly 50 percent of the industrial workforce. In some areas, such as metal work, women came to dominate.[18] More resistance came from men who believed skilled labor was a male domain. The presence of women was seen as competition and threatened their conscription exemption status. Yet, as in agriculture, industrial production was necessary for the Russian war effort in an increasingly mechanized war and could not have been completed without women workers. Nevertheless, despite their contributions, women workers remained underpaid even in highly skilled jobs, often earning as little as 35 percent of male wages.[19]

Women's work in the service sector also increased dramatically, especially in transportation and utilities. They worked as mechanics, chimney sweeps, mail carriers, janitors, truck drivers, police, and other roles previously designated "men's work." Although educated Russian men were more likely to receive draft exemptions (often through bribery), their numbers in white-collar office work also diminished, necessitating the greater use of women in these jobs. This was especially true in lower-level clerical work. In Moscow alone, the number of female office employees increased by 80 percent during the period of the war.[20]

Civilian Women's "War Work"

Women from all segments of society responded to the outbreak of war by mobilizing their labor and resources in a variety of ways. Those from the economic and social elite, often already involved in well-developed charitable efforts, retooled their activities to meet the needs of a nation embroiled in total war. Though philanthropy and charitable volunteer work operated

---

[18] Richard Stites, *The Women's Liberation Movement in Russia: Feminism, Nihilism, and Bolshevism, 1860-1930* (Princeton: Princeton University Press, 1991), 287.
[19] Meyer, "The Impact of World War I on Russian Women's Lives," 214.
[20] Stites, *The Women's Liberation Movement in Russia*, 281.

largely in the public (i.e., masculine) domain, it had come to be considered appropriate for women during the nineteenth century. This work was framed in terms of women's special role as caring nurturers. While men labored in "hard" fields like industry and politics, women contributed in "softer" ways that provided necessary support to a suffering population.

In the top-heavy environment of autocratic rule, civil society was somewhat curtailed and looked upon with great suspicion by a government that sought to limit the involvement of potentially subversive subjects. As Joshua Sanborn explains, "mobilization as a regular feature of political and social life was the last thing that the besieged autocracy wanted."[21] The scope of the war, however, soon made clear that the tsarist administration could not rely solely on official entities it controlled directly. Shortages of nearly every good, significant obstacles in distribution, and inadequate means of transportation plagued the Empire. As a result, the Russian government turned to civilian sources of production, labor, and service provision. While the autocracy attempted to maintain oversight of such activities by creating centralized organizations, often headed by trusted members of the royal family, this proved insufficient to meet wartime needs. Additional efforts were required to fill the gaps, and many of these were staffed and even led by women. Women from Russia's elite social circles undertook efforts to sew linens and undergarments, prepare care packages, and collect material resources for the troops.

Role of the Russian Women's Movement

For feminists seeking to expand rights and opportunities for women, the war presented a chance to demonstrate their value to the nation. Many progressives believed women would be rewarded with the rights of full citizenship in return for war work. Organizations such as the Mutual Philanthropic Society and the League for Women's Equality were quick to express their support for the conflict and called for "women's mobilization."[22] Dr. Poliksena Shishkina-Iavein, leader of the League for Women's Equality, exhorted the "daughters of Russia" to join the war effort: "We women have to unite and forgetting personal misfortune and suffering, each of us must come out of the narrow constraints of the family and dedicate all of our energy, intelligence, and knowledge to our country. This is our responsibility to the fatherland, and it

---

[21] Joshua Sanborn, *Drafting the Russian Nation: Military Conscription, Total War, and Mass Politics, 1905-1925* (DeKalb: Northern Illinois University Press, 2003), 96.
[22] Edmonson, *Feminism in Russia, 1900-1917*, 158.

will give us the right to participate as equals with men in the new life of a victorious Russia."[23]

When the war began, most Russian feminists, like many of their Western counterparts, abandoned their pacifism and aligned themselves with their country's interests (again, as a strategy undertaken in the hopes of political payoff). Leaders such as Maria Pokrovskaia, formerly a sharp critic of what was understood as a masculine drive toward violence and war, joined the patriotic chorus in support of the war effort from its outbreak in 1914. A journalist writing for Pokrovskaia's *Zhenskii Vestnik* [*Women's Herald*] asserted the necessity of women's participation in military action: "The homeland and freedom are threatened with deadly danger from without. Women cannot remain indifferent and passive," she wrote. "They must take part in the defense of the homeland, whenever they can, either in the rear or at the front. Women are strongly for the side of peace and against war, but when the motherland and freedom are threatened with danger, they will take up arms and sacrifice their lives."[24] Others argued that women's participation was vital to saving the nation in its time of crisis and that women were particularly well-suited to such activity as a result of their long history of self-sacrifice for the good of their families and communities.[25]

Even as Russian feminists engaged in war work, they did not entirely abandon the notion that feminine influence was necessary to temper male aggression and restore a war-torn nation. Anna Shabanova, head of the Mutual Philanthropic Society, lamented that the conflict had caused a rift in international sisterhood centered on peace and unity. Shishkina-Iavein vindicated women and laid the blame for causing the violence squarely on the shoulders of male-dominated state action. For her, women had a special role as mothers to ensure that the next generation was brought up steeped in an understanding of universal love.[26] Pokrovskaia lamented, "If women had possessed a 'decisive voice' in the affairs of the nation, this dreadful war would never have been waged." Now, she argued, it was up to women: "having precipitated Europe into the conflict, men have proved incapable of bringing it to a successful conclusion. It is left to women to take on the

---

[23] *Zhenskoe delo* (August 15, 1915), 1-2.
[24] "Zhenskii batal'ony smerty," *Zhenskii Vestnik* (July-August, 1917): 4.
[25] Rochelle Goldberg Ruthchild, *Equality and Revolution: Women's Rights in the Russian Empire, 1905-1917* (Pittsburgh: University of Pittsburgh Press, 2010), 213-215.
[26] Poliksena Shishkina-Iavein, "Zhenshshina i Voina [Women and War]," in M. I. Tugan-Baranovksii et al, eds., *Chego zhdet Rossiia ot voiny? Sborkin statei* [*What awaits Russia from the War?: Collection of articles*] (Petrograd: Kn-vo "Prometei" N. N. Mikhailova, 1915), 214-220.

responsibility."[27] In so doing, women would save Russia from another devasting military conflict.

Wartime Nursing

In addition to extensive work on the "home front," women also undertook a variety of labor as auxiliaries to the Russian military machine. They worked in clerical positions, dug ditches, and worked on railways along the front. The most popular auxiliary wartime service for women was nursing. Indeed, wartime nursing was transformed into the patriotic equivalent of soldiering and seen as national service for women. Nurses performed vitally important medical services for Russia's armed forces and carried out much of this work, outnumbering doctors three to one. And they often did so in zones of conflict, close to and sometimes even during combat, unlike most nurses who served for other belligerents.

The combination of ideas concerning women's natural proclivities and the historical tradition of Russian women in healthcare made women's medical service, even in the hyper-masculinized context of a war zone, not just palatable but highly sought-after. The image of women as healer had roots not only in universal associations of women with caring and nurturing, but also, more specifically, in a long history of women as healers in the Russian context. In peasant communities through the early twentieth century, women made up the majority of village folk healers (*znakharki*), who were preferred by rural inhabitants as sources of medical treatment over scientifically trained doctors. Women midwives steeped in traditional practices (*povitukhi*) also predominated over scientifically trained *akusherki*.[28] Because healthcare was viewed as an appropriate occupation for women, Russia was one of the first countries to allow women into medical schools and to practice as physicians.[29]

The "healing" and "saving" of Russia by women was understood quite literally as nurses worked to restore the nation's defenders to health, both physically and mentally, and return them to fighting capacity. This paired well not only with prevalent ideas of women as caring and nurturing, but also prescriptions that they be selfless and devoted to others, in keeping with both

---

[27] As quoted in Linda Edmondson, "Mariia Pokravskaia and *Zhenskii Vestnik*: Feminist Separatism in Theory and Practice," in Barbara Norton and Jehanne Gheith, eds., *An Improper Profession: Women, Gender, and Journalism in Late Imperial Russia* (Durham: Duke University Press, 2001), 211.
[28] Rose Glickman, "The Peasant Woman as Healer," in Clements, Engel, and Worobec, eds., *Russia's Women*, 148-162.
[29] Jeanette E. Tuve, *The First Russian Women Physicians* (Newtonville, MA: Oriental Research Partners, 1984), 46.

secular and religious ideals of femininity. The image of wartime nurse as savior was a particularly well-developed trope with strongly religious connotations. Although Russian wartime nursing was secularized, it had long-standing connections to the Russian Orthodox Church. Women's nursing in Russia developed as an extension of religious communities and, until the Soviet period, retained its quasi-religious nature. This is reflected not only in the organization of nursing, but also in the name assigned to Russian nurses in the Imperial period, "sisters of mercy," as well as the requirements for sexual modesty in dress and behavior. In fact, the uniform of Russia's pre-revolutionary nurses closely resembled that of nuns and nurses were often mistaken for monastics.[30] Imagery of wartime nurses often reflected religious tropes, with sisters in poses that mimicked iconography, particularly that of the Virgin Mary. Other representations featured nurses as "angels of mercy" providing comfort and care for soldiers, particularly when they had little chance for survival. The nurse offered solace and spiritual succor for men in their last earthly moments. A popular history of women's nursing activities during the Great War was titled *Angely Khraniteli* [*Guardian Angels*].[31] Some even suggested that sisters of mercy served as conduits between this life and the next.[32] Thus, they were presented as literal saviors of souls.

Many saw female nurses' greatest contributions as emotional and even spiritual, something only women could do. Thus, the nature of their work was often understood as less scientific and practical, despite the fact that they performed medical procedures and assisted in nearly every aspect of treatment and care of wounded and ill patients. The Russian press often described nurses as providing wounded and dying men with "cheer" and "easing their souls." High mortality rates as a result of extremely destructive modern weaponry, lack of sufficient medical supplies, the rapid influx of the wounded, and the spread of deadly and contagious epidemic diseases often meant that Russian medical personnel could do little to save the lives of their patients. The extreme shortage of and high demand for trained medical personnel resulted in wartime nurses often receiving very cursory training (some as short as six weeks) before being sent to work in medical facilities. For many, it was enough that nurses provided comfort and solace for the dying and emotional support for troops. When approached by a sister of mercy who asked how to proceed with the treatment of seemingly hopeless cases, one

---

[30] Although wartime nurses were paid for their services during the First World War, nursing in Russia was not professionalized until the 1920s.
[31] Iurii Khechikov, *Angely Khraniteli* (Moscow: Agenstvo vmeste, 1993).
[32] See, for example, images such as "Voina" ["War"], *Novyi Satirykon* [*The New Satiricon*], March 1915, 3, and "Poslednee videnie v Podzhestvenskuiu noch'" ["Last Vision on Christmas Eve"], *Letopis' Voiny* [*Chronicle of the War*] December 26, 1914, 1137.

doctor responded, "How do I know how to make a man live? I'm not God. You should know better than I, you should feel it with your heart."[33]

Despite such gendered associations, women who served as nurses during the Great War often did so in conditions that were distinctly outside feminized conventions. The highly mobile nature of the fighting meant that sisters of mercy had to move quickly with the troops, serving in "flying columns" and other movable medical units, often very close to, and at times even in the midst of the fighting. They were subject to living conditions similar to those of soldiers, in extreme cold and heat, amid filth and vermin, with poor quality and limited quantities of food. They were even exposed to the same dangers: artillery and rifle fire, aerial bombing, gassing, and contagion from deadly diseases. Operating in these similar situations, female nurses were also awarded medals of bravery for carrying out their duties "under heavy enemy fire," "in deadly danger," "in the midst of battle," and "in conditions of clear threat to their own lives,"[34] reflecting the same kinds of heroic deeds as those associated with male combatants. Women nurses also experienced the same psychological and emotional traumas as soldiers because of their participation in modern, mechanized warfare.[35]

Thus, even highly feminized notions of the female nurse as healer and savior were complicated by the conditions of warfare. As a result of the hardships and depravations of wartime service, they were often encouraged to abandon more conventionally understood aspects of femininity. The uniform of the wartime nurse, long skirts and women's shoes, proved impractical on dirt roads and in muddy fields and dugouts, and were often traded for men's leather jackets, boots, and even trousers. Cosmetics and personal hygiene items were seen as unnecessary impediments to the light travel required to service moving troops. Even female emotionality, the element so highly prized

---

[33] Sophie Botcharsky [sic] and Florida Pier, *The Kinsmen Knew How to Die* (New York: William Morrow & Co., Inc., 1931), 46-47.

[34] See reports to the Main Directorate of the Russian Society of the Red Cross from various command personnel of the armies of the Northern Front, Russian State Military-Historical Archive (RGVIA), fond (f.) 12675, opis (op.) 2, delo (d.) 2, as well as reports in *Vestnik Krasnago Kresta* [*Chronicle of the Red Cross*], 1915-1916, and in *Vserossiskii Zemskii Soiuz pomoshchi bol'nym i ranenym voinam: Izvestiia Glavnogo Komiteta* [*The All-Russian Zemskii Union for aid to ill and wounded soldiers: News of the Main Committee*], 1914-1916.

[35] A. S. Preobrazhenskii, *Materialy k voprosu o dushevnykh zabolevaniiakh voinov i lits, prichastnykh k voennym deistviiam v sovremenoi voine* [*Materials on the problem of psychological illness of soldiers and personnel participating in military activity in the present war*] (Petrograd, 1917), 79-80. Preobrezhenskii included medical workers, male and female, in his study.

in nurses, was sometimes considered a hindrance to efficient care of scores of ill and wounded soldiers who flooded medical facilities. In a number of instances, wartime nurses were told to "harden their hearts" and not become attached to patients, lest they spend precious time on cases whose prognoses for survival were dim. When told that a young nurse cried profusely after the death of a soldier in her care, the head doctor in her unit retorted, "If all the nurses are going to weep like this over every death-case, we shall be drowned. Once they have come to the War they must learn to control their emotions. Otherwise they can't work."[36]

Sisters of mercy were seen as active and heroic rather than passive, hand-holding supporters of male soldiers. They were understood as working to save Russian soldiers and Russia itself. Textual and visual images depicted nurses in dangerous battles where they rescued wounded men under the hail of artillery fire or treated soldiers' wounds despite bombs exploding around them.[37] The participation of nurses in violent activity was even celebrated when undertaken to assist the war effort.[38] In a wartime film by famed director Evgenii Bauer, "Glory to Us—Death to the Enemy," the heroine becomes a sister of mercy to avenge her husband's death. As Denise Youngblood contends, "the idea of a nurse as a murderous avenging angel might strike those familiar with the conventions of Western, especially American, cinema of this period as strange, but the strong, independent, even murderous heroine was a recurring motif in prerevolutionary Russian film melodramas."[39]

Women's Soldiering

From the start of Russia's entry into the hostilities, women participated in soldiering. For the first three years of the war, hundreds of women disguised as men entered the conflict. Others were granted exceptions to Imperial law

---

[36] Mary Britnieva, *One Woman's Story* (London: Arthur Barker, 1936), 19.

[37] See, for example, "M. F. Kokh," *Letopis' Voiny [Chronicle of the War]* 15 (November 29, 1914): 248; P. Petrov, "Podvig Sestry E. P. Korkinoi" [The Feat of Sister E. P. Korkina" (Moscow: Litografiia T-va. I. D. Sytina, 1915), Hoover Institution Poster Collection, RU/SU 322; A. Lavrov, Untitled, (Moscow: Nikol'skaia Obshchina R. O. Krasnago Kresta, n.d.), Helsinki University Slavonic Library

[38] Iu. N. Khristinin, "Ne radi nagrad, no radi tokmo rodnogo narodu" ["Not for the sake of awards, but for the sake of the motherland's people"], *Voenno-Istoricheskii Zhurnal [Military-Historical Journal]* 1 (1994): 92-93.

[39] Denise Youngblood, "Fade to Black: The Russian 'Bourgeois' Film Industry during War and Revolution," in Murray Frame, Boris Kolonitskii, Steven G. Marks, and Melissa K. Stockdale, eds., *Russian Culture in War and Revolution, 1914-22, Book 1: Popular Culture, the Arts, and Institutions* (Bloomington: Slavica Publishers of Indiana University, 2014), 85.

prohibiting women from combat service and served as known women. They had a variety of motives for joining the fighting. Some had a personal desire for adventure and freedom from the constraints of patriarchal life, others joined because of patriotic impulses. The latter often expressed the desire to ensure Russia was "saved" from enemy occupation and domination. In the spring of 1917, the Provisional Government (which replaced the tsarist autocracy following the February Revolution) undertook the unprecedented act of organizing all-female military units. Over 5,000 women were recruited and trained. Additionally, grassroots organizations created private women's combat units that were unsanctioned and uncontrolled by Russian military authorities.[40]

Advocates for and casual observers of these all-female units amplified the rhetoric of "saving" in describing them. One journalist commented, "Once again that saintly mission falls to the lot of woman: to save the homeland and the people!"[41] Women soldiers were also expected to play a "healing" role, despite the fact that their actions were decidedly destructive in nature. This epithet was applied to women's units because their creation was motivated by the dire situation the Russian army found itself in prior to the launch of the last offensive in the summer of 1917. Military and civilian commentators understood hesitant male troops as "sick," suffering from the "ailments" of war-weariness, low morale, and more dangerously, desertion, fraternization, and insubordination. As Allan Wildman asserted, these caused tremendous "public anxiety over the health of the army."[42] It was thought that it needed to be "healed" to restore its fighting spirit and successfully undertake one last, decisive assault against enemy forces. The Women's National Military Union of Volunteers, among other groups, saw women as essential to raising national consciousness among soldiers: "by directly participating in military activity, we women citizens must raise the spirit of the army and carry out educational-agitational work in its ranks, so as to convey a logical understanding of the duty of free citizens to the homeland."[43] The goal of the women's units was to demonstrate by example "the necessity of attack in

---

[40] For a fuller examination of the individuals, see Stoff, *They Fought for the Motherland*, chapter 2; for the women's military units formed in 1917, see chapter 3.
[41] "Muzhchiny k ochagam! Zhenshchiny k oruzhiiu!" ["Men to the hearths! Women to arms!"], *Birzhevye vedomosti [Commercial News]*, August 1, 1917, 2.
[42] Allen Wildman, *The End of the Russian Imperial Army, Volume 1: The Old Army and the Soldiers' Revolt, March-April 1917* (Princeton: Princeton University Press, 1980), 362-63.
[43] This appeal appeared in several newspapers: *Russkoe slovo [Russian Word]*, June 2, 1917, 3; *Russkii invalid [Russian Invalid]*, June 4, 1917, 4; and *Iskry [The Spark]* 23 (June 18, 1917): 183. Similar calls were published in other prominent periodicals of the day.

order to save the honor and freedom of Russia"[44] The women's units were thus understood by many to possess "healing" power through their moral influence and would be instrumental in "saving" the army and Russia.

The extensive press coverage Russia's women soldiers received both domestically and abroad suggests an attempt to include women in the narrative and mythmaking of war (despite their neglect in subsequent historiography). Fascinated by these female warriors, news outlets ran story after story featuring them. At first glance, it may be easy to conclude that the media found them compelling as sensational examples of defiance of conventional gendered behavior. However, much of this comported to traditional gender ideology, particularly in framing women soldiers as saviors of the motherland. While journalistic representations of male soldiers often focused on the active, killing aspects of their warrior activities, most narratives concerning women soldiers centered on their defensive roles. Much of the reporting indicated ways that female soldiers endured hardships associated with life at the front. Women provided aid to their male comrades-in-arms, even as far as shifting from active combatants that took life to those who worked to save it, pulling their wounded compatriots to safety after being wounded in battle. They volunteered to undertake dangerous reconnaissance missions to help their units. Women were often portrayed as compelled by positive patriotic impulses and love of the homeland to make the ultimate sacrifice of their own lives—to die in battle for the cause. Rarely, if ever, did the press write about women as participating in killing (despite the fact that they certainly did). This seems to have been a conscious effort on the part of journalists. The image of the woman soldier was contained within conventional understandings of women's role as nurturers and part of the effort to "save" Russia through self-sacrifice. Writers often used terms such as "martyrs" and "saints" when describing women soldiers. As one journalist remarked after watching a procession of the First Russian Women's Battalion of Death in Petrograd shortly before it was dispatched to the front, "there is a feeling that a great turning point is to be achieved, that now begins the saving of Russia from great misfortune, from great disgrace [...] And there is the desire to fall before the Russian women's battalion and to cry relieving tears of joy."[45] Another commented, "The Russian woman on the field of battle, in the ranks

---

[44] "Zhenskie marshevye otriadi" ["Women's Military Units"], Main Administration of the General Staff, Department of Organization and Service of Troops, RGVIA, f. 2000, op. 2, d. 1557, l, 4.
[45] "Provody pervogo zhenskago batal'ona" ["Procession of the First Women's Battalion"], *Novoe vremia* [*New Times*], June 22, 1917, 4.

of heroes, has made a memorable impression of her selfless, devoted love for the motherland, sacrificing her life."[46]

Conclusion

The First World War disrupted sexual divisions of labor and traditional conceptions of gendered behaviors. Women's participation in the war effort in Russia illuminates this well. Women simultaneously confirmed and transgressed conventional notions of femininity and obscured the gendered conceptions of war. This was acceptable, even desirable for many as a result of the specific exigencies created by a total war. Ultimately, the gender-nebulous activity of women at the front demonstrated that such divisions were difficult to maintain in total war, and more broadly, in a modernizing society requiring mass mobilization.

It is important to note that the presence of women in the male warzone was met with some ambiguity and criticism. When their activity was thought to be undertaken for personal benefit, it fell outside the confines of acceptable behavior as self-sacrificing healers and saviors. Having been given access to the bodies of strange men and with opportunities to pursue personal relationships and even engage in sex, some female nurses faced accusations of sexual impropriety. Eventually, even the positive "sister of comfort" took on pejorative, sexually charged connotations. Women thought to have entered medical service because it was "fashionable," or to enhance their own personal prestige, were labeled self-aggrandizing. Female soldiers, despite admiration for their patriotic impulses, were also viewed negatively for engaging in what was considered antithetical to femininity: killing and destruction. There was considerably more equivocation and even rebuke leveled against them by those who believed women could serve the nation in ways that did not involve repudiation of the life-giving and nurturing forces they were thought to naturally possess. Women's war work could be lauded only if conceptualized in keeping with feminized ideals centered on self-sacrifice and devotion to a higher cause.

Moreover, beyond the context of war, women's work in such distinctly masculine spheres was seen by many as problematic. War was considered anathema to "normal" life, and few wished to reproduce the same conditions created in a moment of crisis in peacetime society. Returning to peacetime "normality" meant removing women from military roles for the most part, despite that following the implementation of Bolshevik rule, women's public labor was deemed essential to the success of socialist society and heavily

---

[46] "O Russkoi zhenshchine" ["On Russian Women"], *Vremia* [*Time*], July 13, 1917, 1.

encouraged.⁴⁷ Thus while women transformed the temporary space of war in dynamic and important ways, the lasting effects of these experiences on Russian (soon to be Soviet) society are less pervasive. Despite the evidentiary experience of military conflict that indicated multiple ways gendered demarcations were not always possible nor efficacious, war continued to be understood by many as a male sphere. Female mobilization was only acceptable in times of exigency. This precedent established in the First World War endured as the cultural norm, even as the Bolsheviks attempted a cultural shift toward gender equality. Thus although strict demarcations were impossible to maintain during the upheavals of violent conflict, the gendered lines of separation in the division of labor were breached only out of necessity and understood as only temporarily desirable. This created a paradox in which the ideology of gender, which insisted on rigid dichotomies, was undermined and counteracted by the realities of war. The modern state was forced to rely on the active participation of millions of civilians in order to conduct war. The inability of gendered ideology to match the realities of war and women's wartime action remained unresolved.

Despite anxieties and reservations, the wartime participation of women during Russia's Great War was not only necessary, but welcomed and encouraged by many in multiple ways. The celebration and promotion of women's actions on the home front and in forward positions was consistent with the traditional "strong woman motif" and notions of women as saviors and healers in Russian culture. These ideas, however, were developed in conventional contexts, wherein women acted for the good of the family, and largely within domestic settings. What is unique about the war experience is that many women operated in a non-traditional and masculinized warzone. Removing her from the domestic context did not damage her image significantly, despite some criticism from those who saw such actions as inappropriate for women. For the most part, if her efforts were undertaken in the service of others, she was extolled. Within the context of the patriarchal nature of Russian society that portrayed the nation as an extended family and the tsar as the father of subject children,⁴⁸ nurses were mothers and sisters coming to the aid of their sons and brothers (if they adhered to standards of

---

⁴⁷ Women in Soviet society were fully integrated into the labor force and continued to serve in auxiliary capacities in the Red Army, but were only used in direct combat roles in significant numbers during World War II. Nearly one million women participated in this conflict. After the War, there was no integration of women in the Soviet armed forces, and women were encouraged to return to more traditional roles.
⁴⁸ See Sanborn, *Drafting the Nation*, and Karen Petrone, "Family, Masculinity, and Heroism in Russian War Posters of the First World War," in Billie Melman, ed., *Borderlines: Genders and Identities in War and Peace, 1870-1930* (New York: Routledge, 1998).

sexual purity). And although there was more ambiguity surrounding them, female soldiers were similarly conceptualized as sororal patriots fighting to preserve the motherland. Both were understood as working heroically in the face of great danger, subsuming their own needs and sacrificing their own lives for the sake of others. Their actions were seen as acceptable by many, even in this sphere, because they worked for the good of the family of the nation, and within the specific context of the national emergency of the war. Without their contributions, the nation would have been unable to sustain the total war effort.

Chapter 3

Who is a Soldier? Rethinking French Women's Military Identity during the Second World War

Andrew Orr
Kansas State University

Abstract: During World War II, French women's participation in national defense showed the diverse roles open to people during total war. Often women's wartime experiences defied the seemingly clear distinctions that laws and regulations used to define military identity and participation. This reflected total war's erasure of barriers meant to contain warfare and the inherent incapacity of dichotomous definitions of military identity to accurately describe modern warfare. This chapter leverages trans theory to rethink French women's wartime experiences and challenge the gendered civilian-military and combatant-noncombatant binaries that underlay Western military identity.

The first section draws on archival records to trace the experiences of women who worked inside the French Army during the 1940 campaign. The second section focuses on the military career of Susan Travers, an immigrant Frenchwoman who volunteered for the Free French Army, to expose the disjuncture between her legal status and her real military roles. The final section draws on the memoirs of several resistors, especially Marie-Madeleine Méric, to explore the varied options available to women working against the Germans in occupied France.

Keywords: World War II, French women, Military, Free French Army, Susan Travers, Marie-Madeleine Méric, Occupied France

***

In May 1940, Andrée Leonard was thirty-one years old and had worked for the French Army since 1931. Perhaps inspired by her anti-gas training while working for the Army General Staff in Paris, Leonard volunteered for specialist training as an "*infirmière* Z," a nurse specializing in treating gas patients. By late May, the General Staff was preparing to evacuate Paris and warned Leonard to be ready to leave. Fearing she would lose her chance to serve as a nurse near the frontlines, Leonard asked for permission to remain behind because the private organization she had volunteered for could call her up at any moment. Because she worked for the General Staff, Leonard probably already knew the battle was hopeless, but she pleaded for the chance to risk her life by joining the army's last stand.[1]

Leonard's immediate superiors approved her request, but on 1 June 1940, the Central Administration of the Ministry of War ruled that she could not serve as a volunteer nurse. Ministry regulations forbade Leonard from joining any organization that could interfere with her duties as a civilian employee of the army, which the army defined as a vital national defense function. Ironically, the Ministry fired her later that day. It had begun shutting down its operations in Paris, so officials ordered officers to fire civilians whose jobs would not continue during the retreat. Military officials interpreted the directive broadly, firing thousands of people, including a large proportion of women.[2]

There were many reasons for the purge, including cost, transportation shortages, and a desire to protect civilian employees. Many officers feared that the Germans could treat civilian employees, even women, as military auxiliaries by holding them as prisoners of war; they hoped severing civilians' connections to the army would protect them. This reflected the ambiguities of military membership. Civilian employees were legally not soldiers, but were vital to the army's functioning. In the interwar era, officers extended a form of military identity to women employees, partly because their long-term service made them resemble the army's professional officers and NCO corps, whose conscription service had shrunk, by the early 1930s, from three years to one. During the defeat of 1940, some feared the Germans, too, would see a similarity between women employees and soldiers, despite women's legal status as civilians and noncombatants.

Yet French women's wartime experiences often defied the seemingly clear distinctions that laws and regulations used to define military identity and participation. The diverse roles open to them during World War II—including working in armament factories, medical services, and war relief roles, but also direct military service and resistance roles—reflects total war's erasure of barriers meant to contain warfare, as well as the inherent incapacity of

---

[1] Service Historique de la Défense (Vincennes), Département Terre (DT) 5 YG 238 Leonard.
[2] Ibid.

dichotomous definitions of military identity to accurately describe modern warfare.

Scholars and political leaders have struggled conceptually to integrate women's resistance into the larger history of the Resistance because of their tacit acceptance of the combatant-noncombatant dichotomy. Initially, feminist scholars focused on women's contributions to total war economies, especially in war production.[3] Later, they explored a wider array of women's roles. In the process, they showed that France could not have fought either World War without women's active participation.[4] Historically, however, the majority of politicians, officers, and war scholars have devalued and obscured women's military engagement by defining them out of military service using legalistic definitions of military participation. This marked, and continues to mark, women as inferior contributors—even within militaries—by attaching them to auxiliary corps and labeling them non-combat soldiers.[5] (Because adherents to the Gaullist vision imposed this strict combatant-noncombatant dichotomy on resistors, only six out of 1038 winners of the Croix de la Libération were women.[6]) At first, scholars of women and the French resistance accepted the Gaullist vision. Later, they used social history to highlight women's roles and expand the pale of Resistance membership. Unfortunately, they also reproduced the civilian-military and combatant-noncombatant dichotomies by accepting a clear differentiation between

---

[3] Although her work was on German and American women's experiences, Liela Rupp's work laid the foundation for much of the subsequent historiography on French women and the world wars. See Leila Rupp, *Mobilizing Women for War: German and American Propaganda, 1939-1945* (Princeton, NJ: Princeton University Press, 1978).

[4] Chantal Antier, *Les Femmes dans la Grande Guerre* (Paris: Soteca, 2011); Jean-François Dominé, *Les Femmes au Combat: L'armé feminine de la France pendant la Seconde Guerre mondiale* (Paris: Service historique de la Défense, 2008); Margaret Higgonet, Jane Jenson, Sonya Michel, and Margaret Weitz, eds. *Behind the Line: Gender and the Two World Wars* (New Haven: Yale UP, 1987); Andrew Orr, *Women and the French Army during the World Wars, 1914-1940* (Bloomington, IN: Indiana University Press, 2017); Luc Capdevila, "La mobilisation des femmes dans la France combattante, 1940-1945," *Clio: Femmes, Genre, Histoire* 12 (2000) https://clio.revues.org/187.

[5] E. Anthony Rotundo, *American Manhood: Transformations in Masculinity from the Revolution to the Modern Era* (New York: Basic Books, 1993), 222-46; Karen Jenson, *Mobilizing Minerva: American Women in the First World War* (Urbana IL: University of Illinois Press, 2008), 14-20.

[6] Valerie Deacon, "Fitting into the French Resistance: Georges Loustaunau-Lacau and Marie-Madeleine Fourcade at the Intersection of Politics and Gender," *Journal of Contemporary History* 50 (April 2015): 268.

women who launched attacks and those who were couriers, hid fugitives, or helped the families of other resistors.[7]

This chapter rethinks French women's wartime experiences to challenge the gendered military-civilian and combatant-noncombatant binaries that underlie western military identity. It exposes the failure of historical (and contemporary) binary-based juridical categories of resistance and non-resistance. By bringing transgender theory's critique of dichotomous gender norms to bear on the combatant-noncombatant binary, it argues that military identity is best understood as a spectrum on which individuals have different roles and relationships to war both over time and simultaneously. The first section draws on firsthand accounts of women who worked inside the French Army during the 1940 campaign. The second section focuses on the military career of Susan Travers, an immigrant Frenchwoman who volunteered for the Free French Army, to expose the disjuncture between her legal status and her real military roles. The final section draws on the memoirs of several resistors, especially Marie-Madeleine Méric, to explore the varied options available to women working against the Germans in occupied France.

Beyond Binaries

The French military had clear rules and rituals it used to differentiate members from nonmembers. Then, as now, they included enlistment papers, oath-taking, uniforms, and the special system of military law. Two of the main axes of military identity were defined by difference: members of the military must be distinct from civilians (those who are not part of the military) and combatants must be separate from noncombatants. Both dichotomies are highly gendered in ways that seemingly normalized the distinctions while making them available to reinforce patriarchal social and political authority. The two dyads interlock to create a privileged identity for combat-eligible soldiers, a group which historically was almost always male. The theoretical basis for this hierarchical understanding of military identity was expounded in Margaret and Patrice Higonnet's introduction to *Behind the Lines: Gender and the Two World Wars*. The Higonnets used the metaphor of DNA's complementary double helix to argue that women's "wartime gains" were ephemeral because they never changed women's relative position compared to men. They understood gender as a hierarchical binary relationship tying and subordinating femininity to masculinity and built their conception of

---

[7] Paula Schwartz, "Partisanes and Gender Politics in Vichy France," *French Historical Studies* 16.1 (Spring 1989) 126-151; Margaret Collins Weitz, *Sisters in the Resistance: How Women Fought to Free France, 1940–1945* (New York: Wiley, 1995).

warfare and identity on dyads, implicitly accepting the military-civilian division as a binary distinction.[8]

The military-civilian and combatant-noncombatant dyads are foundational to modern military identity, but imperfectly reflect warfare. Binary military identity focuses cultural recognition on the national defense roles performed by legally recognized soldiers over the contributions of civilians, and by combatants (including combat-eligible soldiers who never enter combat) over juridical noncombatants. An alternate approach would recognize an array of identities that reflect the diverse ways people relate to armed conflict. The professional and public construction of military identity through binary instead of polychotomous constructions has been a barrier to women's citizenship rights and equal recognition of their roles in national defense because male officers and political leaders have often enforced these binaries to mark men as their societies' protectors, relegating women to the status of protected dependents. Though scholars of women's history and security have explored women whose actions defy the gendered assumption that women do not make war, their work has heavily focused on how women's violence challenges gender roles and the gendered construction of political violence.[9] This research focuses on women serving as regular soldiers and women's roles within partisan and terrorist organizations, and does not account for the majority of women whose roles most complicate the military-civilian and combatant-noncombatant dyads.

Although scholars of warfare have been reluctant to embrace it, transgender theory challenges the dominance of binary categories in identity studies. For example, Riki Lane and Laura Sjoberg have observed that transgender theory exposes the artificiality of dichotomous thinking, championing "diversity against dichotomy."[10] Susan Stryker argues that by exposing, disputing, and denaturalizing "the normative linkages" between "the sexually differentiated human body, the social roles, and the statuses that a particular form of body is supposed to occupy [...] and the cultural mechanisms that work to sustain or thwart specific configurations of gendered personhood," transgender theory

---

[8] Margaret and Patrice Higonnet, "The Double Helix," in *Behind the Line: Gender and the Two World Wars*, eds. Margaret Higonnet, Jene Jackson, Sonya Muchel, and Margaret Weitz (New Haven, CT: Yale University Press, 1987), 34.

[9] Linda Grant DePauw, *Battle Cries and Lullabies: Women in War from Prehistory to the Present* (Norman, OK: University of Oklahoma Press, 2000); Caron E. Gentry and Laura Sjoberg, *Beyond Mothers, Monsters, Whores: Thinking about Women's Violence in Global Politics* (London: Zed, 2015).

[10] Riki Lane, "Trans as Bodily Becoming: Rethinking the Biological as Diversity, Not Dichotomy," *Hypatia* 24.3 (2009) 136-7; Laura Sjoberg, "Towards Trans-gendering International Relations?" *International Political Sociology* 6.4 (December 2012): 341.

helps scholars break down persistent gendered hierarchies and assumptions about identity.[11] Gender scholars have called for a broadening of how historians understand women's wartime experiences. Valerie Deacon urges scholars to reassess the meaning of women's wartime experience by paying more attention to women whose experiences were uncommon.[12] Drawing on Judith Butler's work on performativity, Bernice Hausman argues "that gender identity is a juridical construction, as well as the effect of reiterated performances of one's sex that makes up the illusion of an identity inside that produces such expressions."[13] Like Deacon, Hausman goes on to call for "documenting" the "distinctive features" of identities that defy binary classifications in order to break down the dichotomous construction of gender. When applied to military identity, such a practice destabilizes normative classifications of people's relationships to warfare, opening space for a broader and more realistic definition of military identity and participation.[14]

Until the Very End: Civilian Women and the French Army in 1940

When France entered the Second World War in September 1939, French women remained legally disenfranchised and blocked from military service. However, since the First World War, the French military had employed civilian women in noncombat positions. From September 1939 to June 1940, tens of thousands of civilian women worked for the French Army. Most did clerical work; others were telephone operators, couriers, cooks, cleaners, drivers, and even ammunition handlers. Although they performed the same role as many uniformed male soldiers, women employees were legally civilians. Their labor allowed the army to feed, pay, provision, and command itself. They were clearly identified as noncombatants because they were defined as civilians and because regulations forbade exposing them to battle. They were neither issued weapons nor trained to kill, but they were trained in anti-gas measures in case they came under attack. Without them, the French Army could not have waged war, making them part of a combat system despite being noncombatants.[15] Outwardly, they conformed to gender and military

---

[11] Susan Stryker, "(De)Subjugated Knowledges: An Introduction to Transgender Studies," in *The Transgender Studies Reader*, ed. by Susan Stryker and Stephen Whittle (Los Angeles: CRC Press, 2006), 3.
[12] Deacon, "Fitting into the French Resistance," 271.
[13] Bernice L. Hausman, "Recent Transgender Theory" *Feminist Studies* 27.2 (Summer 2001): 476.
[14] Ibid, 480.
[15] SHD DT 9 NN 24, Dossier 1, Ministère de la Guerre, "Direction de Services du personnel et du matériel de l'administration central," No. 2.O/2-2; SHD DT 9 NN 24, Dossier 1 "Instructions 'Z' en 1936," May 18, 1936.

membership types, but they were firmly integrated into the army as an organization. At times sympathetic officers even recognized their place within a military community that was broader than the legal limits of military membership.[16]

Andrée Parreux's campaign resembled that of many French soldiers. In May 1940, she was forty years old and had worked for the army in Paris since March 1917. On 28 May, General Maxime Weygand, the supreme commander of French forces, assigned Parreux to General Julien Dufieux's personal staff. Weygand had entrusted a "delicate packet" of secret information to Dufieux, and he selected Parreux to protect and copy it amidst the coming battle. When French defenses collapsed, Dufieux's staff began a long and dangerous retreat.[17]

Although she was a civilian, Parreux stayed at her post when Dufieux's headquarters abandoned Paris. Keeping one step ahead of the Germans, her unit stopped in Vichy and continued to the La Courtine military camp before ending up in Montauban. When Dufieux reestablished contact with the chain of command and reported that Parreux had completed her task, he discovered that the army had fired her weeks earlier, on 1 June. Dufieux immediately protested that it was absurd to fire her while she was serving with a unit in the field. In a letter to the Ministry of National Defense, he described Parreux as if she were a soldier, praising her loyalty, stoicism, and hard work. He emphasized that she had volunteered to risk her life by staying with his headquarters in the field and, despite the hardships, she "never complained" during the month-long "disagreeable" retreat. Through it all, he explained, she had behaved with "courage and good humor," which was a high military compliment. He drew a contrast between her and the soldiers who deserted, saying she "remained at her post until the very end" and executed every command he gave her while rendering him the "most valuable services during the forty days she spent with my headquarters."[18] Dufieux had Parreux's firing redefined as a leave of absence and she returned to work at the Army General Staff in August 1940. Military officials recorded her service in her personnel file by including a copy of Dufieux's letter as if it was a military commendation.[19] The letter sits in a file that indicates she was on leave the entire time she spent in the field, creating a legal fiction that she was not part of the retreat even as the letter chronicles her experience in it. That contradiction

---

[16] Andrew Orr, *Women and the French Army During the World Wars* (Bloomington, IN: Indiana University Press, 2017).
[17] SHD DT 6 YG 266, Parreaux
[18] Ibid.
[19] Ibid.

suggests that the juridical limits created by the civilian-military and combatant-noncombatant dyads actively distorted reality.

Parreux's experience illustrates the difficulty of creating clear categories of military service in wartime France, as well as the failure of dichotomous definitions to accurately describe people's roles and experiences. Parreux was a civilian, whose gender marked her as unable to be a soldier, and she never took up arms. However, she risked her life to keep working for the army, and by extension, to defend France. By describing her in militarized language, Dufieux showed that he viewed her as like him in some relevant ways. In their day-to-day service, women like Parreux and Leonard performed roles that were theoretically inaccessible to them, crossing the boundaries defined by the military-civilian dyad. Officers' reactions to women employees showed that, at least sometimes, they recognized that there were other ways to conceive of military identity. Parreux and Leonard's experiences resembled those of French men who were labeled combatants and soldiers because their gender and legal military status aligned despite never experiencing combat. These soldiers were accepted as warriors, while civilian women's equivalent experience was written out of national defense history because their gender and legal status clashed with the reality of their roles, theoretically queering their service.

Susan Travers: Soldier, Combatant, and French Woman

In September 1939, French law banned women from serving in the military, but on 21 April 1940, President Albert Lebrun signed a decree opening the French Army to women. [20] After the defeat, the Vichy Regime repudiated the decree, but Charles de Gaulle's Free French accepted women as soldiers. In September 1940, de Gaulle created the first of several organizations to contain women's presence within his army, the Corps des Volontaires Française. Members had to be between eighteen and forty years old and French citizens by birth or marriage.[21] In practice, these rules were inconsistently applied.

Free French regulations recognized women as soldiers but defined them as noncombatants, forbidding them from entering combat. Many male soldiers were also given tasks that kept them out of combat, but they were not designated as noncombatant soldiers, creating a subjective juridical distinction among soldiers. The improvised nature of Free French forces sometimes helped women to get around bureaucratic restrictions through persistence, guile, and a

---

[20] Luc Capdevila, "La mobilisation des femmes," 4.
[21] Dominé, *Les Femmes au Combat*, 31-2.

willingness to perform roles without regard to juridical barriers. Susan Travers was one such woman.

Travers, a British citizen living in France, registered as a civilian ambulance driver for the French Red Cross because she viewed it as a more militarized role than nursing. She then volunteered to serve in Finland during the Winter War against the Soviet Union, Nazi Germany's de facto ally. Finland's surrender left her unit trapped in Sweden during the fall of France. There she "listened on a crackling wireless to the emotional and powerful broadcast by General de Gaulle." She "felt affronted" at the idea that "Nazi troops were marching in the Champs-Elysées" and inspired by de Gaulle's plea that "the flame of French resistance must not go out." After returning to Britain, she volunteered for the Free French because "it had been eighteen years since I'd lived in England; more than half of my life had been spent in France. I suppose I felt more French than anything..."[22]

The Free French military's improvised organization created opportunities for women, and men, to redefine themselves within an otherwise hierarchical organization. Despite her not being a French citizen, De Gaulle's army accepted Travers's enlistment. After being sent to French Congo as an ambulance driver, she was reassigned to be a nurse. When other women in her group shifted to clerical work, she instead traveled to the staging post for French forces about to leave for Ethiopia and convinced the chief medical officer to make her his driver.[23] Although officially a noncombatant, she repeatedly came under Italian artillery fire during the liberation of Ethiopia and Eretria because she accompanied the Foreign Legion's 13th Demi-Brigade for much of the campaign. She stayed with the unit when it moved to the Middle East for the Syrian and North African campaigns, ultimately becoming Brigadier General Marie-Pierre Kœnig's driver.[24]

Regulations limited women to non-combat roles, but the remoteness of Travers' postings from Free French leaders and her Travers'close relationships with senior officers allowed her to sidestep those rules. While stationed at Bir Hakeim with the First Free French Brigade in early 1942, Travers joined legion raiding columns that probed behind German and Italian lines. These raids sought out and engaged Italian and German forces, putting her on the front lines.[25] Even back in the fortified camp, she carried a rifle and ammunition.[26]

---

[22] Susan Travers and Wendy Holden, *Tomorrow to be Brave: A Memoir of the Only Woman Ever to Serve in the French Foreign Legion* (New York: The Free Press, 2000), 36-37, 44-45.
[23] Ibid, 58, 67-76.
[24] Ibid, 67-76, 93-98.
[25] Ibid, 148-50.

After an artillery barrage bracketed her dugout, she yelled "I am not a wretched military target," unintentionally highlighting the gap between her legal status and practical position.[27] Travers' experience emphasizes the inability of binary designations like combatant-noncombatant to accurately describe veterans' service.

Although evacuated when German and Italian forces began attacking Bir Hakeim on 26 May 1942, she refused to be separated from her unit and slipped back into the position with the last supply convoy.[28] By 9 June, the French were running out of ammunition and water. Faced with destruction if they remained, Kœnig ordered a breakout through enemy lines into the open desert. With Kœnig in her staff car, Travers took her position in the headquarters convoy and, after midnight on 10 June 1942, set out toward enemy lines. The convoy strayed off course and was soon "trapped under heavy fire in the well-lit corridor" by German and Italian troops.[29]

While infantrymen charged the enemy to buy time for the convoy to regroup, Travers picked up a second officer whose vehicle had been hit and drove through a minefield to reach the front of the stalled convoy. She then headed directly into German fire. She recalled, "I was exhilarated. It was an amazing feeling, going as fast as I could in the dark towards what looked like a mass display of beautifully colored fireworks dancing towards me, bringing what seemed like almost certain death."[30] While she did this, she was legally a noncombatant.

Seeing the general's car racing toward enemy lines spurred the stalled convoy into motion and other vehicles followed Travers. Despite the car being hit repeatedly by machinegun fire she drove her charges through three German defense lines while "behind us, vehicles and men were burning." Many of the survivors credited her with leading them through the main Axis gun line.[31] That summer, Travers received the Croix de Guerre and the Ordre du Corps d'Armée. Fourteen years later, retired legionnaire Travers, by then a Frenchwoman, received the Médaille Militaire for her actions, along with a select group of other former legionnaires, even though she was not a legionnaire during the battle of Bir Hakeim and was strictly forbidden from entering combat.[32]

---

[26] Ibid, 3.
[27] Ibid, 163.
[28] Ibid, 154-59.
[29] Ibid, 177.
[30] Ibid, 180.
[31] Ibid., 189.
[32] Ibid., 191-2, 269-71.

Later in the war, Travers drove staff cars and ambulances in Tunisia and Italy, and landed in southern France during Operation Anvil. After being assigned to drive a supply truck, a legion officer offered her a place in his anti-tank unit. While still officially a noncombatant and not a member of the legion, she was regularly in combat, pulling guns into position to engage the Germans. In 1939, she was a British expatriate living in France, but by 1945, she was a French soldier who was "proud to be back and about to contribute to my adopted country's liberation from the Mediterranean to the Vosges."[33] At the end of the War, she was satisfied she had "done my duty for the country I loved" and used her wartime connections to enlist in the Foreign Legion, despite it not officially accepting women. At the end of her legion service, she received French citizenship, having become French first conceptually and then legally through military service.[34]

Travers defined her own military identity by performing roles she was legally barred from for long enough to win qualified acceptance from superior officers. She was an outlier, but her experience challenged several of the binaries that define military identity. Travers was not French, and yet served in the Free French Army when it banned foreigners and as a legionnaire before it allowed women to join. She enlisted as an ambulance driver, the same function she had as a civilian before the defeat, which emphasizes the limitations of relying on formal enlistment to categorize military roles. She was legally a noncombatant who acted as a raider and was decorated for her combat exploits.

Journalistic and commercial retellings of Travers' story undermined her extraordinary achievements by sexualizing her. Her *Daily Telegraph* obituary recorded her military service and medals but also noted that she "enjoyed several romantic liaisons, notably with a tall White Russian prince, Colonel Dimitri Amilakvari [the officer she rescued during the Bir Hakeim breakout], but none of these proved lasting," and became General Kœnig's mistress.[35] Three years earlier, in an interview pertaining to the publication of her memoir, *Tomorrow to Be Brave*, the *Guardian's* Jon Henley emphasized her sexuality over her service by identifying her as "the mistress of a French general" before mentioning her military record.[36] Travers fueled some of these comments herself because she and her coauthor, Wendy Holden, featured her

---

[33] Ibid., 235.
[34] Ibid., 250.
[35] "Susan Travers," *Daily Telegraph*, December 23, 2003 https://www.telegraph.co.uk/news/obituaries/1450081/Susan-Travers.html.
[36] "'I think actually they thought I was a man,'" *The Guardian*, December 7, 2000 https://www.theguardian.com/Columnists/Column/0,,407808,00.html.

love affairs prominently in her memoir. Holden, a journalist, novelist, and frequent ghostwriter, likely influenced how the book represented and integrated Travers' romantic as well as military experiences. The memoir cast Travers' life as an adventure story, using her romances as proof that the heroine was feminine and heterosexual despite her martial exploits.

Hedgehogs and Partisans: Women of the Resistance

The French Resistance challenged the binary construction of military identification and combatant status. Its members were a mix of soldiers and civilians, women and men, and foreigners and French nationals. Most resistors never fired a weapon against a German. Because they were living under occupation, resistors regularly moved between categories. Even armed guerillas and saboteurs lived as civilian noncombatants when not conducting attacks, and propagandists, spies, and couriers tried to retain the illusion that they were uninvolved in the conflict even as they violated the legal norms of behavior for civilian noncombatants. The nature of resistance groups meant that they lacked the juridical barriers to entry that often excluded women from formal military organizations and officially limited their roles within them.

Some women resistors came close to fitting the stereotype of women as civilian noncombatants, participating in warfare by providing aid and comfort to men. Sabine Hoise helped Allied soldiers evade capture and try to reach safety to carry on the War. In July 1940, she sheltered and fed two British soldiers who were hiding from the Germans and got them false identity papers. The Germans arrested her in November 1940 and tried her before a court martial. After serving her prison sentence in Germany, Hoise was released in December 1941. She was arrested for espionage in December 1942 and spent the rest of the war in prison.[37]

Hoise was legally a civilian who never experienced combat, but she risked her life to help defeat the Germans and used her civilian and noncombatant status as a cloak, temporarily allowing her to pass as uninvolved in the conflict. Although far less violent than Travers' experience of direct combat, Hoise's actions were illicit under the laws of war. The Germans punished her for performing roles outside of the limits of her legal status by convicting her of criminal acts instead of holding her as a prisoner of war.

Hoise was unusual in resisting so early in the war. Support for resistance groups was meager until 1942, in part because there seemed little hope of

---

[37] Sabine Hoise, *Chambre 535 ou Mes cinq prisons pendant l'occupation, souvenirs des heures tragiques vécues* (Limoges: Société des Journaux et Publications du Centre), 7-18, 53-4, 99-100.

success. In 1942, support grew because of unpopular collaborationist policies, particularly the labor service law that sent French citizens to work inside Germany. Allied victories in late 1942 and 1943 encouraged more people to resist. Some French women fought as guerillas, but they made up a smaller proportion of armed fighters than did women in many other countries, especially Yugoslavia. Resistance groups concentrated women into a relatively limited set of tasks that they came to think of as being well-suited for women. These included being couriers and helping the families of arrested or killed resisters.[38]

In many ways, Simone Sequine's experience as a resister was typical, yet it also suggests that women could break out of stereotyped roles within resistance groups. In 1944, Sequine, then eighteen years old, assumed the name Nicole Minet and joined the local Francs-tireurs et partisans (FTP), the Communist Party's combat organization, to avoid being pressed into serving at a local German garrison. Her experience was typical in that she only joined the Resistance in 1944, when the Liberation was clearly approaching and only a small portion of her work involved violence and active combat.[39]

Her missions and roles changed over the course of that year. First, she served as a courier, a role frequently given to women because the Germans were less likely to aggressively search them. After being trained to use firearms, Sequine helped blow up bridges and derail a train. On 14 July 1944, she participated in an ambush that killed two Germans soldiers. She later told a *Life* reporter that nothing pleased her "so much as the killing of Germans," though she admitted that it was impossible to tell which of them killed the Germans.[40] She joined the FTP's uprising in Chartes in August 1944, helping to capture twenty-five German soldiers, and then accompanied a force of twenty FTP members to support the revolt in Paris.[41]

Sequine's experience demonstrates the challenge of defining who was part of the military. She only joined the FTP in the spring of 1944 and spent most of her time as a courier, a role that required keeping a low profile. She participated in acts of sabotage, ambushed an isolated patrol, and only openly took up arms during the FTP's local rising, which was carefully timed to anticipate the arrival of American troops. That act was enough for her to be

---

[38] Julian Jackson, *France: The Dark Years, 1940-1944* (New York: Oxford University Press, 2001), 492-96.
[39] Frantz Malassis, "Photographie de la jeune résistante armée de Chartres" Fondation de la Résistance http://www.fondationresistance.org/pages/rech_doc/jeune-resistante-arme e-chartres_photo1.htm.
[40] Jack Belden, "The Girl Partisan of Chartes" *Life*, September 4, 1944, 20, 23.
[41] Malassis, "Photographie de la jeune résistante."

transitioned into the French Army when resistance groups were brought into de Gaulle's forces. She then became a legally sanctioned soldier, but one who lacked the education and specialist military skills that usually defined military identity.[42]

Marie-Madeleine Méric had an unusual pathway to becoming a soldier and spy master. In 1937, she took a job with a publishing company founded by retired Commandant (Major) Georges Loustaunau-Lacau. Loustaunau-Lacau, a former officer on Marshal Philippe Pétain's staff, who had been forcibly retired from the army after the police discovered he was running the Corvignolles network, a secret anti-communist intelligence network inside the army. He hired Méric to help him edit anti-communist and anti-German magazines.[43] After the fall of Paris, Loustaunau-Lacau, who had returned to the army and then escaped German captivity, and Méric reorganized their sources into a spy ring. That network, initially called the Crusade, was heavily rooted in rightwing, sometimes far-rightwing, military circles, and Loustaunau-Lacau and Méric passed as Vichy supporters. While he organized a Vichy-sanctioned veterans league to use as a front organization, Loustaunau-Lacau tasked Méric with organizing the clandestine side of the operation. When she objected on the grounds that "I am a woman," he replied, "Even more reason." Over the next year, the two recruited hundreds of agents. Later called the Navarre Network (after Loustaunau-Lacau's codename), its members eschewed armed resistance. Instead, they infiltrated the government and security services and passed their information to the British.[44] Throughout the War, the network focused on operational military intelligence that would help Britain's war effort. Méric never fired a shot, but her life was increasingly in danger every day she remained in France. In July 1941, she became the network's leader when Vichy's police arrested Loustaunau-Lacau for spying.[45]

Loustaunau-Lacau's arrest left Méric in a complicated position. She was fulfilling a militarized role that was conceptually closed to her based on her gender and military status. The social construction of warfare defined civilian women as noncombatants, but she led a self-consciously military unit that aimed to affect the result of combat operations. Internally, she relied on the personal relationships she had built with agents and the respect she had earned through success to maintain her authority, but she chose to pass as a

---

[42] Ibid.
[43] Marie-Madeleine Fourcade, *L'Arche Noé* (Fayard: Paris, 1968), 16. Marie-Madeleine Méric (née Bridou) remarried after the war and published her memoir as Marie-Madeleine Fourcade.
[44] Ibid, 33.
[45] Ibid, 52-8, 61-2, 72-5.

male officer and thus a combatant to avoid being cut off by her British military patrons.

Méric radioed London, "N 1 [Loustaunau-Lacau] arrested this morning – STOP – Network intact – STOP – Work Continues." When asked who was taking command, she responded immediately, "Me as planned," and assured them she was surrounded by "faithful lieutenants" and that their operations would continue.[46] Her message was signed with her codename, POZ 55. The British, who knew her only through coded radio messages, assumed she was a male French officer.[47]

Méric's network survived by avoiding open conflict with the Germans, but she was in constant danger. She spent the rest of the War trying to evade German and Vichy security services, often losing her closest associates as she went. When the police raided her group's main base in late 1941, her chief of staff and her mother were arrested. Without most of her staff or a working radio transmitter, she needed to reestablish contact with the British and her sub-networks, so her surviving agents smuggled Méric into Spain inside a mail bag.[48] Her British contacts only discovered that POZ 55 was a woman and not a "mustached officer," as they had assumed, when she appeared in Madrid. Méric explained to a British officer, "I hid from you that I am a woman because of those who work and risk their lives every minute. I did not want them to be abandoned and deprived of support if you did not believe in me. I had to prove myself before revealing myself."[49] Until then, the British thought they were dealing with a career military professional, and POZ 55 performed the part to keep British support coming.

After infiltrating back into France, Méric shifted her operation to Marseilles and rebuilt her network, soon known as the Hedgehog network, after her internal codename. She strengthened connections with the British and, with their help, professionalized the organization by paying its members based on military pay grades.[50] The network was an illicit espionage operation focused on operational military intelligence: the location, numbers, and movements of troops, weapons, and warships. Its members, and Méric herself, were thus trying to shape coming battles, making them part of a combatant system even if they were denied recognition as combatants.

---

[46] Ibid, 112.
[47] Ibid, 113.
[48] Ibid, 136-40.
[49] Ibid, 142-3.
[50] Ibid, 250-7, 682-85.

As a woman and a civilian rather than a male officer, Méric had an ambiguous position in her own network, whose members thought of it as a military organization. She was universally acknowledged as its "chief" by her senior male subordinates, who were prewar officers and thought of themselves as on active duty, but she was not an officer. In October 1942, Méric held a court martial for a treacherous British agent who had betrayed her group. Despite leading the organization, she did not join the court, which was composed of what her chief subordinate, Commandant Léon Faye, described as "five French army officers who refused to surrender." She was present and read out the indictment, but she "sat to one side," marking herself as present but not fully a part of the military unit she commanded.[51] In this position of literal and figurative adjacency to perceived military identity, Méric defied the military-civilian binary by being seen as both a civilian and the commander of a military organization.

During 1943, the British intelligence officers in London dubbed the network Alliance, and General Giraud recognized it as a unit in the French Army. Legal militarization further highlighted Méric's paradoxical position. She remained the network's recognized chief, but the order identified Commandant Faye as the officer responsible for the Alliance Network, even though he was Méric's subordinate.[52] Implicitly, her officers recognized her as a military leader by taking orders from her and calling her "chief," a term used to refer to a commander inside the French Army. Her status defied the military-civilian dyad, which defined soldiers in opposition to civilians, but the fact that neither the officers in her network nor senior Free French leaders objected to her authority shows that they at least partially accepted that she could transgress the most critical and identity-defining boundary for soldiers. In 1949, French military and political leaders tried to retroactively normalize Méric's liminal position by appointing her a lieutenant colonel in the army retroactive to 1941, thus redefining her as having been Faye's superior the entire time. She thus passed from being a civilian to a retired officer without any period in which she really held her rank while on active service.[53] As with Andrée Parreux, military authorities used legal fictions to distort reality and sustain their juridical construction of military identity.

Méric's opponents sexualized her to explain her line crossing. Vichy investigators claimed she was Loustaunau-Lacau's mistress and some wrongly reported that she was pregnant by him. Valerie Deacon argues that these reports served to feminize her through their "constant emphasis on her sexual

---

[51] Ibid, 271-2.
[52] Ibid, 400-1, 495.
[53] SHD DT 16 P 67268.

and reproductive roles."⁵⁴ They also helped hostile male officers make sense of Méric's unusual position by pushing her into the mold of a camp follower, which Linda Grant DePauw has shown is a traditional way for men to belittle women's military roles.⁵⁵ Deacon convincingly argues that Méric herself, perhaps like Travers, edited her public testimony to assert her femininity and make her transgression of gender barriers more palatable, in this case by feigning reluctance to accept leadership roles and by claiming she was motivated by being a mother.⁵⁶

Conclusion

The civilian-military and combatant-noncombatant dyads do not explain French women's wartime experiences during the Second World War. Women in the Resistance often held multiple roles within their groups while trying to hide their overall affiliation, making it difficult to categorize them according to simplistic binary designations. Calling Marie-Madeleine Méric a civilian noncombatant obscures more than it clarifies about her role in the war. Nobody would deny that Susan Travers was in the French Army in 1942, but her experience still defied the legal limits of her military identity. She was legally classified as a soldier and noncombatant, and in addition to driving cars, trucks, and ambulances, she spent time working in hospitals beside British women who were classed as civilians and noncombatants. Yet the term "noncombatant" cannot accurately describe a soldier who conducted raids behind enemy lines, drove a general through enemy defenses under fire, and pulled anti-tank guns into position on the front lines. The limitations of binary constructions of military identity are even evident in the better-organized version of the French Army that fought the 1940 campaign. Women civilian employees were vital parts of that army, and officers often treated them as members of their institution despite their status as juridical civilians.

French women's experiences in the struggle against Nazi Germany and the Vichy Regime highlight the imaginary nature of the military-civilian boundary. The reliance on ideologically laden binaries to categorize military identity resembles the problem transgender theory emerged to solve: attempts to make people's identity conform to an allegedly organic, but artificial and arbitrary, male-female dyad that does not accurately reflect many people's lived experience. Journalists, as well as military and political

---

⁵⁴ Deacon, "Fitting into the French Resistance," 267.
⁵⁵ DePauw, *Battle Cries and Lullabies*, 20.
⁵⁶ Valerie Deacon, "From 'femme d'officier, mère de famille' to 'grand dame de la Résistance': Marie-Madeleine Fourcade during the Second World War," *Contemporary French Civilization* 42.2 (July 2017) 181-82.

leaders, resorted to expedients to obscure the insufficiency of gendered and juridical conventions governing personal status in warfare. These administrative actions, which altered women's legal status ex post facto, and the layering of sexualization narratives and feminine tropes on top of women's experiences highlight the instability and insufficiency of existing categories to accurately describe many people's relationship to modern warfare.

Just as scholars of sexuality and identity have expanded concepts of gender and challenged the existence of the male-female dyad, scholars of women and warfare are well-positioned to challenge the binaries at the heart of military history and organization. Strong legal, social, and political pressures have sought to enforce the military-civilian and combatant-noncombatant dyads. Scholars, activists, and military professionals' passive acceptance and active assertion of these dyads have serious and fatal consequences because they distort the understanding and practice of modern war and undermine attempts to regulate it. The ideological and legal structures that support these distorting dyads have created a hierarchy of relative prestige based on a system that denies and degrades women's experience and rights, making it all the more urgent that these structures are relegated to history.

Chapter 4

Children and the Character of Italy: Consuming Juvenile Literature in Wartime and Conflict

Allison Scardino Belzer
Georgia Southern University

Abstract: This chapter examines the Italian women who published individually bound books aimed at children during and immediately after the Great War to gauge contemporary attitudes about how girls were supposed to respond to war. Almost all Italian children's books (both fiction and non-fiction) about the war adopted a patriotic, pro-war stance that valorized soldiers and encouraged sacrifice. Almost none featured female characters. Despite sharing similar views about the war and how to present it, the Italian women writing about the Great War for children formed a diverse group. They came from different generations and were disproportionately Jewish. Some became avid Fascists, others committed anti-Fascists. This chapter discusses the central themes of the works published by women and investigates where their wartime patriotism took them during the Fascist regime.

Keywords: Italy, Italian, Great War, Fascist, fascism, children's fiction, children's non-fiction, patriotism, women authors

***

Complex geopolitical diplomacy and the ever-present reality of violence and death make it difficult to explain war to children. The problem is compounded when adults address the issue during the crisis. Because war might be more normal than peace, scholars need to attend to how societies communicate wartime messages across chronological and national borders. Although it is impossible to know how readers reacted to what they found on the page, contemporary publications offer a glimpse into wartime expectations.

The Great War (1914-1918) was markedly different from previous conflicts. Late to acknowledge how new technologies should breed new strategies, belligerent nations recruited millions of men to fight on multiple fronts. Meanwhile, the demands of total war created home fronts that focused on providing munitions and demanding sacrifice. Governments and social service groups called on entire populations to contribute, creating levels of civilian engagement unseen in prior conflicts and entrusting even women and children with responsibilities for achieving victory. Elsewhere my work explores how these new calls affected women individually and collectively by looking closely at the Italian front.[1] For this study, I hoped to examine what Italian children's books said about girls and their wartime responsibilities.[2] Alas, investigations revealed that most Italian juvenile literature was written by men for boys. Even the handful of women who published children's books addressed the same audience and emphasized the same themes of sacrifice and loyalty. A common belief was that girls would read boy-centered books but not vice versa.[3] Almost no books written during or just after the war diverged from the propagandistic belief that the war was vitally necessary for Italy's future, and only a few featured central female characters.

Despite sharing similar views about the war and how to present it, Italian women writing about the war for children were a diverse group. They came from different generations, born from the 1860s through 1890s, and were disproportionally Jewish. Some became avid Fascists, others committed anti-Fascists. Italy's postwar history was complex. Fascist ideals, ascendant in the 1920s, distorted the memory of war and, by the late 1930s, the state had taken control of the publishing industry, a process that artificially skewed which books would become the "classics" read by later generations. This chapter, which focuses on individually bound book publications that emerged during or within a decade and a half of the war, discusses the central themes of some canonical works produced by women and investigates where their wartime patriotism took them during the Fascist regime.

Italy in the Great War and Fascism

Italy entered the Great War over a year late, abandoning the Central Powers to join the Allies. While sharing the same war aims as its allies, Italy had a different

---

[1] Allison Scardino Belzer, *Women and the Great War: Femininity Under Fire* (New York: Palgrave, 2010) and "Women's Experiences with War" in *Italy in the Era of the Great War*, ed. Vanda Wilcox (Netherlands: Brill, 2018), 253-271.

[2] Note that these findings are limited in scope because the Covid-19 pandemic shut down many libraries and made travel impossible.

[3] Fred Erisman, *From Birdwomen to Skygirls: American Girls' Aviation Stories* (Fort Worth, TX: Texas Christian University Press, 2009), 3-6.

wartime experience. Italians fought on their own soil and in some of the harshest conditions. And Italy had a more conservative culture than France and Britain with a more pronounced religious identity and lower rates of education. Whereas Britain enjoyed a literacy rate approaching 100% in the early 1900s, Italy's hovered around 60%.[4] For the most part, Italy's middle class was both literate and patriotic, having been the chief beneficiary of unification in the 1860s. Although over half the Italian troops were peasant farmers (many of whom felt tied to their own region rather than the newly formed nation), civic discourse followed the middle-class sensibility and focused on rallying all citizens to the war effort.[5] Women, who had previously been marginalized in national conversations, and children became a vital audience that needed to be persuaded to join the war effort. The war ended with a victory that, for many Italians, felt tainted by the Allies' failure to follow through on territorial promises. Benito Mussolini channeled this national anger into the rise of Fascism as his early supporters derided the postwar world for straying too far from martial values—obedience, loyalty, hierarchy, order—and not properly esteeming veterans and their sacrifices. When Mussolini became prime minister in 1922 at the request of the king, the question of how to process the war years remained open. His consolidation of power, however, forced a re-examination of books and authors dealing with Italy's war experience and increasingly forced war memories to align with Fascist principles.

The Fascist government's growing power especially affected Jewish citizens. Although Mussolini was at first uninterested in anti-Semitic persecution, the alliance he sought with Hitler in the 1930s encouraged him to restrict the legal rights of Jews. Although only one out of every thousand residents in Italy had at least one Jewish or formerly Jewish parent, Jews were actively involved in education and publishing, giving them a disproportionate public visibility.[6] The Racial Laws of 1938 banished writers of Jewish heritage, regardless of their outlook or patriotic history, from the literary scene. Over the next two years, officials campaigned to pull books written by those named on a list of 900 authors "not welcome in Italy" from schools, libraries, and bookstores. By 1943, officials had banned all books with themes that ran counter to Fascist

---

[4] Charles Ferrall and Anna Jackson, *Juvenile Literature and British Society, 1850-1950* (New York: Routledge, 2009), 6 and Katharine Mitchell, *Italian Women Writers: Gender and Everyday Life in Fiction and Journalism, 1870-1910* (Toronto: University of Toronto Press, 2014), 9.

[5] Martin Clark, *Modern Italy 1871-1995* (New York: Longman, 1996), 186.

[6] Figures are from 1938 census of foreign and Italian Jews. Michele Sarfatti, "The Persecution of the Jews in Fascist Italy, 1936-1943" in *The Jews of Italy: Memory and Identity*, eds. Bernard D. Cooperman and Barbara Garvin (Bethesda, MD: University Press of Maryland, 2000), 413, 418-419.

ideals, and Jewish writers who had actively supported Italy in the Great War found themselves cast as outsiders in their own country.[7]

Nonfiction: Textbooks, Prescriptive Literature, and Valorizing Italy's Heroes

Every belligerent nation produced, in varying degrees, wartime literature aimed at rallying children to the home country, pitching the Great War as an existential crisis that required immediate attention. In his study of international publications, Stéphane Audoin-Rouzeau has demonstrated how these works transmitted cultural and patriotic attitudes from older to younger generations. He found that wartime publications valorized the wounds, suffering, and even deaths of children.[8] Quinto Antonelli has explained how, as the war progressed in Italy, it became accepted, normalized, and "minitiarized" for children. Postcards, toys, and texts aimed at the youngest citizens tried to explain the war and help them understand it.[9]

With lower literacy and higher poverty rates, Italy's juvenile literature market was not oriented towards the mass-produced, formulaic serials that were popular in the United States, Great Britain, and Germany.[10] British and American series tracked the varying fields of battle and glorified the leadership abilities of adolescent male characters who hailed from the upper classes.[11] American readers could imagine themselves in the center of the action in series such as the *Boy Allies*, *Uncle Sam's Boys*, the *Red Cross Girls*, and the *Camp Fire Girls*. Nothing similar existed in Italy. Major Italian publishers, especially Bemporad in Florence, offered mostly stand along juvenile books about the war and did not separate non-fiction from fiction.[12]

---

[7] Other policies required racial consciousness education be introduced from the first grade. Piero Boero and Carmine De Luca, *La letteratura per l'infanzia*, 2nd ed. (Roma: Laterza, 2009), 172-175.

[8] Stéphane Audoin-Rouzeau, *La guerre des enfants, 1914-1918: Essai d'histoire culturelle* (Paris: Colin, 1993), 186.

[9] Quinto Antonelli, "Piccoli eroi: Bambini, ragazzi e guerra nei libri italiani per l'infanzia." *Annali* 4 (1995), 67.

[10] In general, Italy had lower production of children's books and scholars have showered less attention on creating archives of juvenile literature. Alberto Cavaglion, "Judaism and Children's Literature: Emanuele Levi's *Giornale* (1822-1823)" in *The Jews of Italy*, eds. Cooperman and Garvin, 358.

[11] Michael Paris, *Over the Top: The Great War and Juvenile Literature in Britain* (Westport, CT: Praeger, 2004) and Erisman, *From Birdwomen to Skygirls*.

[12] On the wartime goals of Bemporad and other publishers see Antonio Gibelli, *Il popolo bambino: Infanzia e nazione dalla Grande Guerra a Salò* (Torino: Einaudi, 2005), 38.

Children and the Character of Italy

While Italy's fledgling children's book market was smaller than that of many other nations, Italians still needed textbooks for classroom use. The *Italia nostra!* (Our Italy!) line particularly engaged with the war and deserves more study. Different versions existed for each grade level, all offering patriotic celebrations of Italy's war effort, charting activity on land and sea, in the mountains and the plains. These books provide no room for questioning the war, as the laudatory dedication to the prime minister makes clear. The subtitle strikes an inclusive note, advertising that the intended audience was both "little Italian boys and little Italian girls." Nevertheless, as Image 1 shows, the cover suggests separate ways each gender should contribute to the war effort: males in uniform heading into outdoor adventures, females sitting in a sewing circle, facing each other.[13]

Figure 4.1: Barbara Allason, *Italia nostra!* Palermo: Biondo, 1916.

---

[13] The digital collection of the Biblioteca nazionale centrale in Florence includes multiple editions of *Italia nostra!* Barbara Allason, *Italia nostra!: forte sulle tue Alpi, libera nei tuoi mari: Il libro della nostra guerra per I piccoli italiani e le piccole italiane delle scuole medie* (Palermo: Biondo, 1916).

Under the masculine pen name Luigi di San Giusto, Luisa Gervasio Macina (1865-1936) published several volumes of *Italia nostra!* She was an educator, supporter of teachers' unions, and author of dozens of works, including didactic books for children and translations of international classics.[14] Her 1916 edition of *Italia nostra!* for second-grade students described the war through vignettes about a child, Tonino, and his soldier father. The fifty-page book delivers edifying explanations of the war effort, highlighting the sanctity of the "unredeemed" territory along the front, the sacrifices made by civilians, and the plight of refugees in the context of Tonino's daily life.[15] Her volume for fifth- and sixth-grade students offers a similar structure and tone but is over twice as long with more sophisticated discussions of history and current events.[16]

Barbara Allason (1877-1968) authored a middle-grades edition of *Italia nostra!* Across 200 pages, she covered various topics, including Red Cross nurses, soldier priests, and prisoners of war. The book engages with some of the difficulties caused by the war, for example, with an illustration of orderlies moving a wounded soldier off the battlefield. The book's tone, however, remains upbeat and patriotic, stressing Italian superiority by noting that Austrians sometimes fired on medics or took them prisoner.[17]

For twenty-first-century readers, this unquestioning support for the war prevalent in these books sounds suspiciously like something later mandated by Fascists. The call for obedience and loyalty and the lionizing of individual sacrifice for the greater good resonate with Mussolini's values. But it is important to look at these authors' biographies in order to chart the ways they responded to the rise of Mussolini's regime. Allason was a patriot in the liberal tradition. She rejected the conservative nationalism embedded in Mussolini's ideology and joined an important group of antifascists in Turin.[18] In contrast, Macina's relationship with the regime was more complicated. She wrote a lengthy handbook explicitly celebrating Fascist values but also a novel

---

[14] The Italian SBN lists over 200 editions of her works. She also wrote a separate book for children, *Armi e fedi d'Italia: Conversazioni coi giovani* (Torino: Lattes, 1916).

[15] Luigi di San Giusto, *Italia nostra! Forte sulle tue Alpi; Libera nei tuoi mari - Libriccino della nostra guerra per i piccoli italiani e le piccole italiane della seconda classe elementare: riccamente illustrato con fotografie e acquerelli* (Palermo: Biondo, 1916).

[16] Luigi di San Giusto, *Italia nostra! Il libro della nostra guerra per i piccoli italiani e le piccole italiane della quinta e sesta classe elementare: riccamente illustrato con fotografie, acquarelli e schizzi geografici* (Palermo: Biondo, 1916).

[17] Allason, *Italia nostra!: scuole medie*, 68-73, 133.

[18] Note the title of her memoir: Barbara Allason, *Memorie di un'antifascista, 1919-1940* (Roma: Edizioni U, [1940]).

examining the difficulties a Jewish family faced during the Great War.[19] That it remains difficult for historians to pin down an author's political ideology demonstrates there was a range of opinions about how far readers should take patriotism and wartime duty. Being pro-Italy during the Great War did not necessarily prime someone to accept Fascism later.

In the early twentieth century, literature for children was expected to convey social mores and values. Non-fiction works eased this transmission process. Freed from having to sneak lessons into adventure stories, publications that prescribed behavior or offered role models could convey directly what wartime society expected from children. Among the most forthright were two handbooks by Rachele Ferrari (dates unknown) aimed at children.[20] Ferrari would become, along with her husband and father, among Mussolini's first adherents, and she remained loyal even after his fall.[21] She worked as one of the highest-ranking women in the Fascist party, parlaying her enthusiasm into a paid role as the overseer of "culture, propaganda, and the press."[22] Her handbooks address the young male reader, affirming his (presumed) frustration that he could not join his relatives who were away fighting. She advised those unable to display honor on the battlefield to engage with opportunities at home and reminded readers that victory did not depend only on having courageous soldiers. To win, she explained, Italy needed to have the fullest warehouses, the most money and raw materials, and the largest crops. Her lack of interest in female readers, who could easily have followed her prescriptions, is surprising.[23] One can imagine that Ferrari's exhortations were not page-turners for either sex of young readers.

A focus on glorifying Italy's past and exalting present-day heroes might have been more entertaining. Historian Eric Johnson has explored some of the approaches that different types of publications can take to sell wartime messages to children, citing ABC-primers, picture books, and presentations of

---

[19] Luigi di San Giusto, *Il piccolo decamerone fascista: libro di fede e di storia per le scuole e per il popolo* (Torino: Petrini, 1929) and *Schemagn Israel! Storia d'una famiglia ebrea durante il primo anno della guerra mondiale* (Torino: Petrini, 1927).

[20] Rachele Ferrari, *A voi, fanciulli...(per il fronte interno)* (Milano: Abbiati, 1917) and Rachele Ferrari, *Avanti, ragazzi miei: per il fronte interno* (Milano: Abbiati, 1918).

[21] Perry Willson, "Group Portrait: The *Ispettrici Nazionali* of the Italian Fascist Party, 1937-1943," *The Historical Journal* 61.2 (June 2018): 444, 449.

[22] Her married name, used in her work as a national inspector, was Rachele Ferrari del Latte. Giuseppe Conti Calabrese, ed., *La cassina del duca: Proprietari, architettura e territorio di una grandiosa corte colonica a Milano* (Milano: Sistema Biblioteca Milano, 2015), 127-28. Willson, "Group Portrait," 438.

[23] She addressed adult women in a different publication: Rachele Ferrari, *A noi, donne...: per il fronte interno* (Milano: Captan Fracassa, 1917).

exemplary figures.²⁴ Italy produced few picture books but plenty of works about heroes.²⁵ In part, because Italy was only recently unified, many cultural commentators saw the war as a continuation of the Risorgimento, another opportunity to gain "unredeemed" Austrian territory. From the earliest days of Italy's war effort, women authors churned out ostensibly true stories about wartime heroes to model appropriate values.

A prototypical example is *Piccole storie della storia grande 1915-1916* (Little Stories of Big History) published by Amilda A. Pons (1876-1966), addressed to "the children of Rome while their Father and Brothers fought for the honor of Italy." The collection contains eight vignettes, each featuring a model of self-sacrifice for the greater good.²⁶ Unlike Ferrari, Pons did not channel her support for the war into Fascism. After Mussolini's fall, she became the first woman minister of public education, indicating her lack of collaboration with the regime.

Corinna Teresa Ubertis Gray (1877-1964) published a similar book under her pen name Térésah: *Piccoli eroi della grande guerra* (Little Heroes of the Great War). The 1916 volume was part of the Bemporad Illustrated Little Library series for "youth, soldiers, and general readers." Image 2 shows how the book's cover emphasizes the war's cost: a grieving young woman holds hands with a desolate child who hugs a toy soldier.

The book highlights how different people contributed to the war across Europe with stories culled from newspaper articles. The book's ending foreshadows Fascism with a call for national and racial unity to transcend class identity: "There is everything in racial pride."²⁷ The volume is an example of a publication that profiled courageous and brave acts to inform and inspire readers. Ubertis Gray followed this effort with similar books.²⁸ Her intense patriotism translated into support for Fascism; in 1928, she published

---

[24] Eric Johnson, "Under Ideological Fire: Illustrated Wartime Propaganda for Children" in *Under Fire: Childhood in the Shadow of War*, eds. Elizabeth Goodenough and Andrea Immel (Detroit: Wayne State University Press, 2008), 60.

[25] One fascinating exception, much discussed by scholars, is Golia, *Abcdario di guerra* (Torino: Lattes, [1920]).

[26] Amilda A. Pons, *Piccole storie della storia grande 1915-1916* (Milano: Società editrice Dante Alighieri, 1916). For more on Pons, see Antonelli, "Piccoli eroi," 71; Allison Scardino Belzer, "Identifying Patriots: Women in Uniform in Italy," in *Cutting a New Pattern: Women in Uniform in the Great War*, eds. Barton J. Hacker and Margaret Vining (Washington, DC: Smithsonian Institution Press, 2020), 189.

[27] Térésah, *Piccoli eroi della grande guerra*, 35-36. Full view available https://teca.bncf.firenze.sbn.it/ImageViewer/servlet/ImageViewer?idr=BNCF00004198764

[28] Térésah, *La ghirlandetta: Storie di soldati* (Firenze: Bemporad, 1915); *Essi e noi: commemorando Editta Cavell* (Firenze: Bemporad, 1916); *Soldati e marinai* (Firenze: Bemporad, 1918) For more on Térésah, see Louise Restieaux Hawkes, *Before and After Pinocchio: A Study of Italian Children's Books* (Paris: The Puppet Press, 1933), 132-134.

a moralistic, heavy-handed book featuring a Fascist father character exhorting his son to buy a black shirt.[29] Her husband Ezio Maria Gray became a prominent supporter of the racial laws and maintained his anti-Semitism even after the Second World War.[30]

Figure 4.2: Amilda A. Pons, *Piccole storie della storia grande 1915-1916*. Milano: Società editrice Dante Alighieri, 1916.

Another book that aimed to help children understand the war from a patriotic viewpoint was *A voi soldati futuri, dico…* (To you, future soldiers, I say…) by well-known author Anna Franchi (1867-1954).[31] Over almost 250 pages, Franchi described major figures from Italian history, emphasizing

---

[29] Ubertis Gray, *Balillino del suo papà una ne pensa una ne fa* (Firenze: Bemporad, 1928). Discussed in Boero and De Luca, *La letteratura*, 165.
[30] Walter Fochesato, "Nani, pinocchi e piccoli alpini: Il racconto della guerra" in *La grande guerra raccontata ai ragazzi*, ed. Marnie Campagnaro. (Roma: Donzelli, 2015): Part I, Ch III.
[31] Anna Franchi, *A voi, soldati futuri, dico (La nostra guerra)* (Milano: A. Vallardi, 1916).

Risorgimento heroes, popes, and political leaders. The book details the early stages of the Great War, covering everything from diplomatic negotiations to damage from bombings. It showcases numerous photographs and paintings alongside reprinted sources. It is hard to imagine a young reader finding the attention to delve so deeply into Franchi's long history, but the layout invites dipping into the book in parts, lingering over particular sections rather than absorbing the whole. No matter where one begins, the book celebrates patriotism and justifies wartime suffering as the price of victory. Few women could be included among Franchi's role models, but she did find one to discuss, Maria Abriani, who gained fame for escorting Italian troops to victory during the invasion of her small hometown in 1915.[32] Franchi was a prolific author, but she published only a few books during the war because she busied herself with war efforts. Her only son, Gino, was killed at the front in September 1917 and Franchi responded by organizing an aid group for mothers of the fallen and writing prescriptive prowar pamphlets. After the Armistice, she returned to writing, publishing both novels and non-fiction books with particular (but not exclusive) attention to young readers and women. Mussolini admired her work, but she never embraced the Fascist party line.[33]

Like Franchi, Ida Finzi (1867-1946) wrote in a variety of genres (journalism, poetry, novels, and memoirs) aimed at both young and adult readers. Published under her pseudonym, Haydée, her wartime books blended truth and fiction to exhibit ideal behavior during the real war. In *Bimbi di Trieste: Scene dal vero* (Children of Trieste: Scenes from Real Life) Finzi looked at the war specifically through children's eyes.[34] In addition to featuring children as main characters, Finzi also used slang and dialect to capture authentic young voices.[35] Finzi intended to be didactic, and her books instructed through storytelling. Image 3 illustrates a typical vignette – a well-off mother explains to her confused children that the Austrians have forbidden the Italian national anthem.

---

[32] For more on Abriani as a war hero, see Belzer, "Nurses, Spies, and Sacrifice: Female Citizenship and Patriotism in Italy" in *Italy and the Cultural Politics of World War I*, ed. Graziella Parati (Madison: Farleigh Dickinson University Press, 2016), 55-68.
[33] Elisabetta De Trojia, *Anna Franchi: l'indocile scrittura: passione civile e critica d'arte* (Firenze: Firenze University Press, 2016), 106-109.
[34] Haydée, *Bimbi di Trieste: Scene dal vero* (Firenze: Bemporad, 1916), published as part of the series *Biblioteca Bemporad per i ragazzi*.
[35] Laura Gaudino, *"Oh, Fatina, Fantina! How did they bring my poor puppet to such a state?": A Study of Emerging Political Instrumentalization and its Interrogation in Subversive Texts in Italian Children's Literature Published between the Beginning of the First World War and the Advent of the Fascist Regime (1914-1921)* (MA Thesis, University of Roehampton, 2019), 50.

Figure 4.3: Haydée [Ida Finzi], *Bimbi di Trieste: Scene dal vero*. Firenze: Bemporad, 1916, page 18.

In another book, *La passione di Trieste* (The Passion of Trieste), published with Bruno Astori, she described daily life in her hometown, a city hotly contested during the war. The city was technically part of the Austrian Empire, but Finzi and many others felt culturally more connected with Italy.[36] In fact, Finzi had fled to Milan when the war began, so the book offered a sampling of what was happening to others rather than her lived experience. The American literary critic Louise Restieaux Hawkes (writing in the 1930s) praised it as a "historical document..suffused with a deeply patriotic glow."[37] Indeed, Finzi's attention to detail and her ability to cast the daily sufferings caused by the war in a holy light (note the religiosity of the title) demonstrate her ability to transcend genres. Hawkes labeled Finzi's books as "among the masterpieces of Italian war literature" in large part because of how well they conveyed the importance of Italy's "unredeemed" territory and captured the language of

---

[36] Haydée and Bruno Astori, *La Passione di Trieste* (Firenze: Bemporad, 1920).
[37] Hawkes, *Before and After Pinocchio*, 139-141.

patriotic devotion.[38] As a native of Trieste, Finzi wrote from her life but concealed that she came from a Jewish family with roots in the Veneto region. She continued to publish novels and short stories after the war, picking up on Fascist themes, including nationalism and the valorization of motherhood. But the introduction of the Racial Laws forced her out of work. She barely escaped the Second World War with her life, hiding out in Portoguardo to avoid deportation after the German occupation.[39]

The Errera sisters found themselves in a similar situation. Rosa (1864-1946) and Anna (1870-1940) hailed from a wealthy Venetian Jewish family; both worked as educators and published popular children's books. Rosa also translated children's works.[40] In keeping with other notable texts of the era, their publications emphasized the importance of moral characteristics, such as moderation, honesty, and sincerity.[41] Rosa distinguished herself by winning first prize from the Treves publishing house for her patriotic book *Noi: libro per i ragazzi* (We: A Book for Children), praised by Hawkes for its "adventurous, courageous spirit."[42] In the decade after the war, Rosa and Anna authored patriotic biographies of Risorgimento heroes.[43] Despite these renowned contributions to Italian children's literature and their almost sacred devotion to Italy, the sisters had their careers destroyed by anti-Semitism. Embittered by Fascist persecution, Anna died of poor health in 1940. Rosa found some solace in a circle of Jewish intellectuals that included her cousins Angiolo and Laura Orvieto, but then deportations began. Rosa survived by hiding in the house of a Christian friend for a year and a half until the Allies retook Italy from the Nazis.[44]

---

[38] Hawkes, *Before and After Pinocchio*, 139.

[39] Franco Laicini, "Ida Finzi," *Dizionario Biografico degli Italiani* 48 (1997), https://www.treccani.it/enciclopedia/ida-finzi_%28Dizionario-Biografico%29/.

[40] A third sister, Emilia Errera (1866-1901), also published children's books but died of tuberculosis before the war. Monica Miniati, *Italian Jewish Women in the Nineteenth and Twentieth Centuries* (New York: Palgrave Macmillan, 2021), 148-149. "Rosa Errera e le sue sorelle," http://www.letteraturadimenticata.it/Errera%20Rosa.htm.

[41] Paolo Paesano, "Rosa Errera," *Dizionario biografico degli Italiani* v 43 (1993), https://www.treccani.it/enciclopedia/rosa-errera_%28Dizionario-Biografico%29/. Vincenza Battistelli, *La moderna letteratura per l'infanzia*, 2nd ed. (Firenze: Vallecchi, 1925), 163-65, 180.

[42] Rosa Errera, *Noi: Libro per ragazzi* (Milano: Treves, 1919).

[43] Rosa Errera, *Manin* (Milano: Alpes, 1924) and Anna Errera, *Garibaldi* (Milano: Treviglio, 1928). Hawkes seemed to have known Anna personally. For her extended discussion of the Erreras see Hawkes, *Before and After Pinocchio*, 127-130.

[44] Ibid.

Almost one-third of the women authors discussed here came from families with a Jewish background.⁴⁵ The disproportionally high number of Jewish women publishing children's books needs further study. Partly this disparity reflects the higher literacy rates among Jews in Italy. In 1901, 97.6 percent of Jewish girls between six and fourteen could read and write (about the same rate as the general population in Britain).⁴⁶ Jewish traditions that emphasized studying scripture and valued academic learning may also have furthered female education in the post-ghetto era. Although many contemporaries considered a woman who published as little short of a prostitute (a scandalous "public woman"), writing for children seemed less transgressive. As one literary scholar explains, "the field of children's literature was one of the few spaces in which women could operate as major players without significant censure."⁴⁷ It has been difficult to find information about levels of piety and devotion among Jewish women writers, and most did not explore Judaism as a theme in their books. Most Italian Jews felt strongly attached to their nation and worked alongside non-Jewish women in all aspects of the war effort.⁴⁸

Fiction

Fictional stories provided another opportunity to explain the war to young readers while sending many of the same messages as the more didactic and prescriptive non-fiction publications. Ubertis Gray went beyond her informative expositions about little heroes of the Great War by creating imaginary worlds that enabled readers to understand the war. *Il romanzo di Pasqualino* (Pasqualino's Fantasy) featured toys crafted by wounded soldiers that come to life in the main character's dreams.⁴⁹ The story revolves around Pasqualino's experiences at the home front. His tutor spouts heavy-handed interventionist and prowar views, guiding Pasqualino to embrace nationalism

---

⁴⁵ Ida Finzi (Haydée), Laura Orvieto, Rosa and Anna Errera. Although Teresa Ubertis Gray (Térésah) is listed with other "*ebree*" in a 1938 Fascist list of authors to avoid, I have not found corroborating evidence that she was Jewish or of Jewish ancestry. It seems unlikely that she had Jewish roots given her husband's open anti-Semitism. Other notable Jewish women who wrote for children include Paola Lombroso Carrara, Eugenia Graziani Camillucci, Annie Vivanti Chartres, and Ermelinda Raimondi Zambonelli. Boero and De Luca, *La letteratura*, 174.
⁴⁶ Luisa Levi D'Ancona, "Modern Italy," *Jewish Women: A Comprehensive Historical Encyclopedia* (27 February 2009), Jewish Women's Archive, https://jwa.org/encyclopedia/article/italy-modern.
⁴⁷ Maria Truglio, *Italian Children's Literature and National Identity: Childhood, Melancholy, Modernity* (New York: Routledge, 2017), 134.
⁴⁸ Miniati, *Italian Jewish Women*, Chapter 5.
⁴⁹ Térésah, *Il romanzo di Pasqualino* (Firenze: Bemporad, 1917).

and recognize the essential sacrifices being made by the military. In her analysis of the story, Laura Gaudino sees Pasqualino as a "spokesman for national propaganda among other children," exhorting them to contribute almost as directly as prescriptive literature did.[50] Hawkes was unpersuaded by the author's attempt to combine "the real and the unreal" while commenting on "social and moral problems of that immediate period which are incomprehensible to the ordinary child."[51] Nevertheless, the use of fantasy made discussing the difficulties of war more palatable.[52]

In *La regina degli usignoli: Storia di una bambina belga* (Queen of the Nightingales: Story of a Belgian Girl), Ubertis Gray crafted something new: a female protagonist. Rosignoletta is an eight-year-old Belgian girl who transforms into a nightingale. At first, she is happy to be safe from the war, but the suffering she sees causes her so much distress that she puts aside her needs to seek help ending the violence.[53] Ubertis Gray's use of a female main character seems to arise not from a feminist desire to engage young girls or to expand the definition of who could experience and influence war. More likely, it was the young girl's vulnerability that made Rosignoletta an appropriately heartrending embodiment of Belgium. Her plight reinforced the case that Italy needed to intervene in the war because of the atrocities occurring there; staying neutral (in the kingdom of the nightingales or in Italy) was not a good option.[54] The book's graphic depictions of war, as Lindsay Meyers notes, reveal some ambivalence at the heart of the novel: "The war in this work is depicted as an invasive and impersonal machine" that "betrays a horror of modern warfare" absent in most other works of the period.[55] Overall, however, the book constructs a fantasy world that still delivered the clear moral judgement that the Great War was necessary and just. In the rest of her writing, Ubertis Gray followed the contemporary trend of telling war stories about boys that fostered a spirit of masculine sacrifice.

---

[50] Gaudino, *"Oh Fatina!,"* 42-47.
[51] Hawkes, *Before and After Pinocchio*, 134.
[52] Arpalice Cuman Pertile (1876-1958) framed a much more ambivalent war story about toys coming to life in *Ninetta and Tirintin* (Firenze: Marzocco, 1917). Cuman Pertile was a pacifist, and her books and poetry demonstrated a unique point of view for works coming out in the war years and immediately after. Boero and De Luca, *La letteratura*, 193-194 and Gaudino, *"Oh Fatina!,"* 90-104.
[53] Térésah, *La regina degli usignoli: Storia di una bambina belga* (Firenze: Bemporad, 1916). Gaudino, *"Oh Fatina!,"* 161 and Hawkes, *Before and After Pinocchio*, 133-134.
[54] Lindsay Myers, *Making the Italians: Poetics and Politics of Italian Children's Fantasy* (New York: Peter Lang, 2011), 96-97, 107.
[55] Myers, *Making the Italians*, 100.

A second example of centralizing female experience came from Maria Messina (1887-1944), who refashioned the Cinderella story into a wartime novel, *Cenerella*.[56] By placing a girl at the heart of the novel, Messina directly addressed female wartime experiences. She borrowed tropes from the fairy tale but replaced the romantic love story with one of devotion to family and country. Cenerella is a young Sicilian who does not join her mother and stepsisters when they leave for America and instead lives with an unworthy cousin as a servant in Naples. During the novel, her awareness of national identity grows as she contributes to the war effort. Eventually, she escapes her situation and loyally nurses her brother back to health after his stint as a prisoner of war. By the end, the siblings reclaim the family property in the countryside and happily reunite with their mother, who recognizes her lost daughter as a guardian of the hearth and a true Italian patriot.[57] Messina herself had emigrated from Sicily to Naples as a child, no doubt witnessing many of the same deprivations as her character experienced.[58] Although Cenerella is a true protagonist, who moves the plot forward with the choices she makes, her goal remained being a traditional caregiver.

Most books by women cast boys as central characters. Clelia Mila Carena attempted to make the war comprehensible to young readers in a realistic way with *Mentre il babbo é la guerra* (While Daddy is at the War). The story of six-year-old Renzo is fictional, but Carena underscored the war's bleak reality by dedicating the book to a real young man, "gloriously fallen" early in the war. That her own son was six when she wrote it and that she was an elementary school teacher helped her anticipate what young readers could handle. While the book recognizes wartime hardships, it preserves a hopeful tone. Renzo's father assures readers of the war's necessity, his mother, the importance of honoring the war dead. Renzo behaves admirably throughout the tale– befriending wounded soldiers, visiting a nursery for soldiers' children, collecting wool, and making "scaldaranci" (paper logs) to send to the Alpine troops to warm up their rations. Carena introduces two friends for Renzo, a Boy Scout and a refugee, who provide examples of different wartime experiences. At the end, Renzo's father returns home alive–with an amputated leg and a medal of valor. It is an archetypal war story, realistic without being gory or morose. Carena clearly supported the war but was also politically liberal. Her son, Massimo Mila, became a prominent antifascist, active in the

---

[56] Maria Messina, *Cenerella* (Firenze: Bemporad, 1918).
[57] Battistelli, *La moderna letteratura* 183-184 and Rita Cavigioli, "Minimal Departures: Female Mobility in Late Nineteenth- and Early Twentieth-Century Italian Children's Literature," *Quaderni d'italianistica* XXXV.2 (2014), 130-133.
[58] Gaudino, "*Oh Fatina!*," 89.

same group as Barbara Allason. He later recalled the "naïve nationalistic-Savoy enthusiasm" of his family, "naïve" in that it failed to anticipate the extremes of Fascism.[59] *Mentre il babbo* was Carena's only book.[60] It is significant for its blend of fiction and realism and because the author was a liberal patriot whose nationalism was not of the type easily co-opted by Fascism after the war.

Paola Baronchelli Grosson (1866-1954), publishing as Donna Paola, similarly presented the war to young readers through the eyes of a male character. She authored three juvenile novels following the adventures of Pippetto, a ten-year-old orphaned boy. Only the first volume was published during the war, but Baronchelli Grosson completed all three by 1920.[61] *Pippetto vuole andare alla guerra* (Pippetto wants to go to war) examines frustrations experienced by boys who were not old enough to go to war and feared missing out. As with Renzo in Carena's short novel, Pippetto modeled appropriate behavior, attitudes, and wartime contributions.[62] Today, Baronchelli Grosson is best remembered for two significant books arguing that wartime contributions should raise the position of Italian women.[63] Significantly, even a writer so attuned to the issue of women and war centered her series on a male protagonist and men's military roles.

Remembering the Great War in the Fascist Era

Books about the war appeared throughout the decade following the Armistice. Among the most popular was *Beppe racconta la guerra* (Beppe Recounts the War) by Laura Cantoni Orvieto (1876-1953). Like her cousins, the Erreras, Orvieto enjoyed great success in Liberal Italy with her books for children. She published *Beppe* in 1925 in the tenth anniversary of Italy's entrance into the

---

[59] Carla Cuomo, "Mila, Massimo," *Dizionario biograficao degli Italiani* 74 (2010), https://www.treccani.it/enciclopedia/massimo-mila_%28Dizionario-Biografico%29/.

[60] Her letters to and from her son while he was in jail for his Resistance activities came out posthumously, reprinted in Paolo Soddu, ed., *Argomenti strettamente famigliari: Lettere dal carcere, 1935-1940* (Torino: Einaudi, 1999).

[61] Donna Paola, *Pippetto vuol andare alla guerra* (Firenze: Bemporad, 1916); *Pippetto difende la patria* (Firenze: Bemporad, 1920); *Pippetto fa l'italiano* (Firenze: Bemporad, 1925). Olga Visentini followed the same route in *Primavere italiche: Romanzo d'attualità* (1915) which told the heroic tale of a boy who managed to get to the front lines only to die in the snowy Alps.

[62] For more on the importance of these books, see Mariella Colin, "La Grande Guerre vue par les livres pour les enfants (1914-1919)," *Chroniques italiennes* web17 (1/2010), 11.

[63] Donna Paola, *La funziona della donna in tempo di guerra* (Firenze: Bemporad, 1915) and *La donna della nuova Italia: Documenti del contributo femminile alla guerra (maggio 1915-maggio 1917)* (Milano: Quintieri, 1917).

war. Along with Salvator Gotta's *Piccolo alpino*, *Beppe* created the model for how the war was supposed to be remembered and understood by children in the postwar era.[64] The book is structured around Beppe, a chauffeur in contemporary Paris, and the stories he tells fellow servants of his wartime service. The conversational set up allows Beppe to describe details about the war from a personal point of view without sounding like a history textbook.

Beppe maintains that the war benefitted Italians. He describes, for example, a jovial mix of soldiers ("professionals, students, workers, and we emigrant Italians who returned home, to defend our land in the hour of danger") embracing the call to arms.[65] This view rejected the sense, growing in the 1920s across Europe, that a wasteful war waged by incompetent leaders had destroyed the younger generation. Instead, Beppe frames the soldiers as heroes and martyrs. When he finishes his long story examining the last victorious battle, he exclaims, "Four years of war, one year of passion! Everything is forgotten." He seems satisfied with the outcome, saying, "Here is our pain, our wounded, our heroes! Everyone in their place: the dead, in their war cemeteries, on Italian soil; everyone in their place, the living, for the greatness of Italy." Beppe thanks God "for having lived in these days."[66] Orvieto's positive view of the Italian war experience overlaps well with the ideals of the burgeoning Fascist state; note that Mussolini banned Ernest Hemingway's *A Farewell to Arms* for its portrayal of exhausted Italian soldiers who cared little for grandiose propagandistic messages. By assuming the identity of a male veteran (Beppe), Orvieto (a Jewish woman) found a way to participate in the national conversation about how to remember Italy's Great War experience.

Despite sharing similar views about the war, Orvieto's Jewish background made a permanent affiliation with Fascism impossible. Her husband (and cousin) Angiolo was a prominent writer who served as a leader in the Jewish community and worked with the regime in its early years.[67] Their son enrolled in the Fascist party after serving in the Great War and married a Catholic aristocrat; their daughter married the son of a prominent Fascist government

---

[64] Gotta's *Piccolo alpino*, originally published in 1926, remains the most famous and well-known Italian children's novel about the war, selling 600,000 copies in the twentieth century. It was re-released by Mondadori for a fiftieth anniversary edition in 1987. For other analyses of the book and its central importance, see Walter Fochesato, *La guerra nei libri per ragazzi* (Milano: Mondadori, 1996), 36-37; Antonelli, "Piccoli Eroi, "67-69; Boero and De Luca, *La letteratura*, 154-157; Francesca Orestano, "On the Italian Front: Salvator Gotta's *Piccolo Alpino* (1926)" in *Children's Literature*, eds. Paul, et al, 48-59.
[65] Orvieto, *Beppe racconta la guerra* (Firenze: Bemporad, 1925), 27.
[66] Orvieto, *Beppe racconta la guerra*, 284-285.
[67] Michele Sarfatti, *The Jews in Mussolini's Italy: From Equality to Persecution*, trans. John and Anne C. Tedeschi (Madison, WI: The University of Wisconsin Press, 2006), 68-69.

official. Enactment of the Racial Laws destabilized the family, who petitioned for exemption that asked for certain members be classified as "not pertaining to the Jewish race." Although their request was granted, they still had to go into hiding during German occupation. Luckily, they were protected by a Catholic priest whose efforts helped them escape deportation to concentration camps.[68]

Olga Visentini (1893-1961) penned another important postwar book, one of the few with female main characters: *La Zingarella e la principessina* (The Little Gypsy Girl and the Little Princess).[69] Like many women writers in this era, Visentini worked as a primary school teacher, and she enjoyed a prolific publishing career. Gaudino summarizes her oeuvre as consisting of "highly idealistic children's novels which exalted the value of God, family and fatherland."[70] In this book, Lidia, an eleven-year-old "Gypsy" (Roma) is orphaned when her patriotic grandfather dies. Facing the arrival of troops after the break at Caporetto, she becomes a refugee and befriends a two-year-old girl separated from her wealthy family. As they travel across northern Italy, they experience the hardships faced by the civilian population during the war: cold, hunger, isolation. On the one hand, this novel's girl-centered story broke the mold. The noted scholar of Italian children's literature Walter Fochesato called Lidia "active and vivacious, determined and autonomous." He praised Visentini's "restrained" and "calm" tone as she immersed the reader in the war.[71] But, as Rita Cavigioli has pointed out more recently, this book is a "gender-education narrative;" Lidia (like Messina's Cenerella) is really learning how to become a proper woman.[72] She must reject her street-performing background and impulse for self-preservation to learn to care for the lost little girl and be a good patriot. Visentini flourished in the Fascist era, publishing a seminal analysis of children's literature in 1933 and continuing to write novels that upheld conservative, Fascist values and collaborating with the famous children's author Salvator Gotta on a book promoting Fascist ideals of masculinity.[73]

---

[68] Maryks, *'Pouring Jewish Water,'* 177-187.
[69] Olga Visentini, *La Zingarella e la principessina* (Mondadori, 1926). For more on Visentini, see Boera and De Luca, *La letteratura,* 200-201 and Orestano, "On the Italian Front," in *Children's Literature,* eds. Paul, et al, 53.
[70] Gaudino, "*Oh Fatina!,*" 61.
[71] Walter Fochesato, *La guerra nei libri,* 47-48.
[72] Rita Cavigioli, "Minimal Departures," 134-135.
[73] Olga Visentini, *Libri e ragazzi* (Milano: Mondadori, 1933); Salvator Gotta and Olga Visentini, *Soldatini d'ogni giorno* (Milano: Baldini & Castoldi, 1938).

Conclusion

A search for publications that used the Great War as a backdrop to liberate Italian girls from conventional roles ended in failure.[74] As Cavigioli has also concluded, no Italian children's novels showed girls participating in the "national adventure" of the Great War or coaxed them into questioning traditional gender ideals.[75] Even women writers remained uninterested in pushing the boundaries of what girls could or should undertake. In the Great War and its immediate aftermath, Italian children's books took a patriotic, prowar stance that valorized soldiers and encouraged sacrifice. As the canon of children's wartime stories emerged in the decade and a half after 1918, Fascism limited the vista of writers and literary critics, both at home and abroad, to promote only books that echoed martial values and offered a positive spin on the war.[76]

In the decades since Fascism's collapse, Italian authors have continued to speak to children about the war, with each generation redefining social memory. A study of recently published Great War books concludes that current publications offer "a more balanced picture of the historical, cultural and political events" of the era.[77] Being able to place the war in one hundred years of context certainly has changed how young readers understand the grave situation that children faced in the 1910s, allowing room for more nuance and less overt nationalistic propaganda.

---

[74] Because of spatial limitations, I discuss here only some popular books by women. Other writers and editors who deserve attention include Jolanda Bencivenni (c1880-1965), Maria Bersani/Maribe (1883-1971), Milli Dandolo (1895-1946), Camilla Del Soldato (1862-1940), Enrica Grasso (1877-1967), Margherita Fazzini/Marga (no dates), Maria Vittoria Martinotti (no dates), Elvira Massetti-Moraldi (no dates), Lucia Petrali Castaldi (no dates), Maria Pezze Pescolato (1869-1933), and Annie Vivanti Chartres (1866-1942).
[75] Cavigioli, "Minimal Departures," 135.
[76] Early efforts to catalog wartime juvenile publications include Battistelli, *La moderna letteratura*; Sante De Sanctis and Francesco Valagussa, "Infanzia," *Enciclopedia Italiana*, 1933, https://www.treccani.it/enciclopedia/infanzia_%28Enciclopedia-Italiana%29/); Giuseppe Fanciulli and Guidotti E. Monaci, *La letteratura per l'infanzia* (Torino: SEI, 1928); Hawkes, *Before and After Pinocchio*.
[77] Marnie Campagnaro and Ilaria Filograsso, "Children, Soldiers and Heroes: The Great War in Past and Present Italian Children's Literature," *Libri & Liberi* 7.2 (2018): 223-246.

Section Two. Humanitarian Aid and International Solidarity

Chapter 5

The Armenian Genocide, Women Aid Workers, and World War I in the Middle East

Michelle Tusan
University of Nevada, Las Vegas

Abstract: World War I fundamentally changed the face of humanitarianism by legitimating new actors, discourses and alliances between Western-led aid projects and local communities. Nowhere was this truer than in the case of the woman aid worker during the Armenian Genocide. This chapter compares the work of two women who worked in the region and focused their efforts on assisting victims of genocide. Ann Mary Burgess, an English Quaker who started a mission in Constantinople to serve minority Ottoman Christians in the late 19th century, served thousands of mostly widowed women and orphaned children during the genocide and after. Zabel Yessayan, an Ottoman subject who was herself a victim of the Armenian Genocide, also served this community leading relief efforts among women and children throughout the Middle East. These women never met, but their stories, when read together, reveal important parallel histories of the gendered experience of aid work. Their work shaped how organizations delivered and understood the needs of especially female and child victims of war, genocide and famine. At the same time, the institutionalization of the humanitarian movement shaped their own choices and experiences as women living in a period of rapid gender and political transformation. This chapter decenters the experience of the white aid worker to focus instead on women-led aid networks run by Western and non-western women. It explores how diverse women who shared a common cause participated in modern humanitarianism as leaders, collaborators and disrupters.

Keywords: Ann Mary Burgess, Zabel Yessayan, Amenian Genocide, Humanitarianism, Famine, Middle East, Ottoman Christians, Quaker, World War I

***

Figure 5.1: Ann Mary Burgess, Studio portrait, c, 1910.

World War I fundamentally changed the way humanitarian aid worked.[1] New humanitarian organizations provided opportunities to focus on those who came to be understood as the most vulnerable victims of total war: women and children.[2] Nowhere was this truer than in the case of women who served

---

[1] Bruno Cabanes, *The Great War and the Origins of Humanitarianism* (Cambridge: Cambridge UP, 2014); Melanie Tanielian, *Charity of War: Famine, Humanitarian Aid, and World War I in the Middle East* (Stanford: Stanford UP, 2018); Keith Watenpaugh, *Bread from Stones: The Middle East and the Making of Modern Humanitarianism* (Berkeley: UC Press, 2015).

[2] Emily Baughan, *Saving the Children: Humanitarianism, Internationalism and Empire* (Berkeley: UC Press, 2012); 'Cultivating Internationalism: Save the Children Fund, Public Opinion, and the Meaning of Child Relief, 1919-24," in *Brave New World: Imperial and Democratic Nation-Building in Britain between the Wars*, Laura Beers and Geraint Thomas, eds. (London: Institute for Historical Research, 2012), 169-188; Edward Fuller, *The Right of the Child* (London: Gollancz, 1951).

displaced women and children in aid centers and refugee camps during resettlement campaigns after the Armenian Genocide. This chapter compares work done by two very different women on behalf of women and children in the Middle East during World War I. English Quaker Ann Mary Burgess started a mission in Constantinople serving Ottoman Christians in the Victorian period and continued work in the wake of the Armenian Genocide serving thousands of mostly widowed women and orphaned children. Zabel Yessayan, an Ottoman subject and victim of the Armenian Genocide, also served this community starting in the late nineteenth century and continued to work during and immediately after the war.³

Figure 5.2: Zabel Yessayan.

---

³ Other English spellings of her name include Esayian and Essayan.

These women never met, but their stories, when read together, reveal important parallel histories of women's role in professionalizing aid work in the international humanitarian movement. Their work influenced how aid organizations delivered and understood the needs of female and child victims of war, genocide, and famine. At the same time, the institutionalization of the humanitarian movement shaped their choices and experiences as women living in a period of rapid gender and political transformation.

This comparative frame shifts the focus of literature on gender and humanitarianism from stories of European and American missionary aid workers to women-led aid networks run by western and non-western women.[4] It poses the question: How can historians understand the implications of the gendering of aid work without knowing the full extent to which diverse women who shared a common cause participated in the business of relief work as leaders, collaborators, and disrupters?

These women, from very different backgrounds and places, found themselves serving the same community in a time of acute crisis. Christian minorities, long victims of discrimination and massacre in the Ottoman Empire, faced increasing pressure in the second half of the nineteenth century because of the Russo-Turkish War, European imperialism, and rising Turkish nationalism. The plight of this group—largely Armenians, Greeks, and Assyrians—garnered increasing international attention starting in the last third of the nineteenth century. Humanitarian aid for this community steadily found its way into the Ottoman Empire from British and, later, US and French sources.[5] Women played important roles, first in raising money to support humanitarian enterprises and later in distributing aid. The transformation of women's roles from fundraisers to aid workers had roots in the Victorian period, when gender norms were changing and philanthropic service became identified primarily with women.[6] Deep diplomatic and cultural connections between Britain and the Middle East made Ottoman Christians an obvious target of women's humanitarian activism during this period. Britain considered itself the guardian of Christian minority communities after the

---

[4] Lori Ginzberg, *Women and the Work of Benevolence* (New Haven: Yale UP, 1992); Mary Taylor Huber and Nancy Lutkehaus, eds., *Gendered Missions: Women and Men in Missionary Discourse and Practice* (Ann Arbor: Michigan UP, 1999); Rhonda Semple, *Missionary Women: Gender Professionalism and the Victorian Idea of the Christian Mission* (Rochester: Boydell, 2003); Susan Thorne, *Congregational Missions and the Making of Imperial Culture in Nineteenth-Century England* (Stanford: Stanford UP, 1999).

[5] Michelle Tusan, *The British Empire and the Armenian Genocide* (London: IB Tauris, 2017).

[6] Frank Prochaska, *Women and Philanthropy in Nineteenth-Century England* (Oxford: Clarendon, 1980).

signing of the Treaty of Berlin concluded the Russo-Turkish War in 1878. This opened the door for humanitarian institutions and networks to thrive during the last third of the nineteenth century.[7]

Both English women like Burgess looking abroad to serve distressed Ottoman Christians and indigenous women like Yessayan serving their own ethno-religious communities in the Ottoman Empire found opportunities in the professionalization of women's humanitarian activity during WWI. Women aid workers navigated new worlds of possibilities for meaningful remunerative employment while facing challenges that limited their authority in those institutional frameworks. These challenges proved a common thread in Burgess' and Yessayan's experience as aid workers. They also shaped how relief functioned, especially for women and children, during WWI. Women aid workers played a central role in the administration of aid and advocacy work in the Ottoman Empire while navigating challenges that limited their authority.

Each woman faced her own particular set of challenges and opportunities. Yessayan, an Armenian educated in Europe and Ottoman subject, was limited by her nationality (she ceased to have one when the Ottoman Empire dissolved after the war) and status as a woman. At the same time, her role as a writer and intellectual educated in France broadened her influence in concrete ways. She was the quintessential insider/outsider and became a voice for Armenian women and children and for Armenian men searching for a homeland after the destruction of the Ottoman Empire after WWI. Ultimately her reach and authority were limited by questions concerning loyalties to national and international organizations and by unreliable financial resources. As an English Quaker, Burgess had more freedom due to her nationality and institutional support but also found her experience as an aid worker shaped by her gender.

Burgess and Yessayan belonged to a network of women seeking opportunities within the growing international humanitarian movement's patriarchal structure that saw them as helpers rather than agents of change. They relied on fundraising and institutional support, often from female-run organizations that focused on women and children. The power of these small organizations collectively providing aid for the war's civilian innocents influenced the charge given to women aid workers. Their labor in the field fundamentally shaped perceptions of what humanitarian aid should do and who deserved it in wartime. The figure of the woman and child together as a symbol of deserving objects of charity (due to their status as war victims) emerged as a centerpiece of regional aid campaigns that would influence the internationalization of aid under the leadership of the League of Nations.

---

[7] Michelle Tusan, *Smyrna's Ashes* (Berkeley: UC Press, 2012).

Burgess' Mission

Quaker activist Ann Mary Burgess' Friend's Mission in Constantinople was characteristic of Victorian women-run relief projects. Part of a larger movement founded to spread Quaker ideals across the globe, the Mission started in the late 1880s and played a key role in ameliorating the conditions of victims of the Hamidian massacres of the mid-1890s.[8] Friends in Britain funded "this body and soul saving work," which also enjoyed widespread support from other religious and secular aid organizations.[9] The massacres initially targeted the male population, leading to the mission's focus on widows and orphans. Along with two other English women, Burgess "stayed at the mission and undertook relief work among the suffering women and children, as bread-winners had become very scarce" after Armenian relief workers were forced to flee Constantinople. According to Burgess, she was both "mother and father" to those under her care who received wages and services in exchange for work at the mission. [10]

Burgess cultivated ties with secular philanthropic organizations and government institutions. The London-based branch of the International Organization of the Friends of Armenia set up operations in Eastern Anatolia in 1897. Established to assist massacre victims, it had its own network of patrons that Burgess used to support her work. Women made up twelve of the fifteen members of the Executive Committee; they also held the majority of positions on the General Committee. The organization was headed by Lady Frederick Cavendish, whose husband, Lord Frederick, was a Liberal MP and close associate of W. E. Gladstone. Contributions and organizational support came from the Quaker Cadbury sisters, Lady Henry Somerset, and a host of other titled ladies. Twenty-seven branches of the British Women's Temperance Association also donated to the general fund.[11]

These women made humanitarian aid work a career. Burgess cooperated with other philanthropists and aid organizations to publicize and raise much-

---

[8] They were named after Sultan Abul Hamid II (1876-1909), whose policies created the conditions for the mid-1890s massacres. By the time they ended in 1897, massacres had claimed between 80,000 to 100,000 Armenian lives. See Tusan, *British Empire and the Armenian Genocide*, 57- 58.

[9] "Medical Mission among the Armenians: Occasional Paper," March 21, 1896, Friends House Archive, London.

[10] The leader of the medical mission, Dr Dobrashian, fled to England with his family. See "Friends' Mission, Constantinople: Letter from A.M. Burgess at the Request of Many Friends and Supporters of the Mission," Friends House, London.

[11] Friends of Armenia Annual Reports, 1897-1902, British Library, London.

needed capital for her projects for Armenian widows and orphans.[12] She also used her connections with consular staff at Constantinople, attending embassy dinners in dresses made with material sent to her by supporters in England who recognized the value of cultivating political ties.[13] Burgess' network of philanthropists, businessmen, government consuls, and workers created a thriving industry that supported over 700 women workers and generated sales of £8,000-10,000 per year.[14] The British Consul in Constantinople helped defray start-up costs at the mission and supported it throughout its nearly three decades of existence.[15]

As conditions for the Armenian community worsened in the decades following the massacres, relief work took on a more urgent role in and around Constantinople. Burgess' Mission bridged the roles of political advocate and spiritual guide, helping "prisoners in obtaining their release, in visiting and caring for the sick, in clothing the naked and in feeding the starving ones around us."[16] The massacres of the mid-1890s made Burgess anxious to find a way to protect and offer long-term financial support for the primarily women and child survivors. "In the first weeks that followed this political out-burst of hate and fury, we could do little else besides giving out bread to women and children and listening to tales of woe," she recalled. She immediately began seeking ways to help women support themselves doing needlework, knitting, and "oriental embroidery" that Burgess sold on local and European markets.[17]

This so-called "industrial work" generated funds through the production and sale of artisan crafts by needy Armenians. Amid extreme uncertainty and social instability, Burgess' workshops were a place of calm and security. By the time WWI began, Burgess had completely transformed what began as a medical mission into a multifunction campus, including a meeting hall, schoolrooms, and workrooms built alongside living quarters and offices that

---

[12] The international character of this organization meant that these networks came to include both British and American philanthropic organizations. See *Friends of Armenia*, "Constantinople News," January 1920, ns 75; "Constantinople News," October 1920, ns 78.

[13] AMB to Miss Peckover, Constantinople, January 23, 1921, Friends House Archive 387/2/1, Ryan correspondence, Middle East Center Archive (MECA), St. Antony's College, Oxford.

[14] Ann Mary Burgess Obituary, Friends House Archive, London.

[15] "Fifty Years Among Armenians," 24.

[16] "Medical Mission among the Armenians: Occasional Paper," March 21, 1896.

[17] "Industrial Work, Constantinople: Letter from Ann M. Burgess," 1904, Friends House, London.

hosted events and morality plays. Burgess called the young women in the mission's care "her angels."[18]

Remarkably, Burgess continued aid work during and after the Armenian Genocide. Instigated in April 1915 by the Ottoman government, the genocide targeted Christian minority populations and killed well over a million people, primarily Armenians, Assyrians, and Greeks.[19] While the Ottoman government made attempts to requisition Burgess' buildings and close the school during the war, her political connections protected her until Turkish nationalists took over the government and forced her to flee to the Greek island of Corfu in 1922. Her stated mission to serve women and girls also played a role. While men and boys were targeted for extermination by the government, Armenian girls were not victimized in the same way. Those not forcibly converted and married to Muslim men were sent to Ottoman government-run orphanages. Burgess' service to widows and girls put her mission at less risk than if she had openly declared it her mission to help men and boys, many of whom nevertheless found shelter in the mission. In May 1915, she claimed the mission continued to employ three-hundred women, despite having run out of money.[20]

Burgess had served the Armenian community for nearly thirty years when news came of the signing of the 1918 Mudros Armistice between the Ottoman Empire and the Allies. Initially, she believed she could continue her industrial work uninterrupted while the Allies sorted out the details of the ensuing peace settlement. However, the fighting continued, sparking a massive refugee crisis. Instability in and around Constantinople included riots and an attempt by Turkish nationalists to burn her rug factory down in August 1920.[21] "We are living a life of strange cares," she wrote one supporter a year later. "All these great upheavals are the results of the war which still continues in this unhappy land."[22] Indeed, war continued for nearly five years beyond the initial

---

[18] "Friends' Mission in Constantinople: Appeal for Completion of New Buildings Fund and for Additional Subscribers," 1906, Friends House, London.

[19] Taner Akçam, *The Armenian Genocide and Ethnic Cleansing in the Ottoman Empire* (Princeton: Princeton UP, 2012); Raymond Kevorkian, *The Complete History of the Armenian Genocide* (London: IB Tauris, 2011); Ronald Suny, "*They Can Live in the Desert but Nowhere Else*" (Princeton: Princeton UP, 2015).

[20] Burgess to Mr Hurnard, May 31, 1915, Anne Mary Burgess Papers, 1914-1928, Friends House, London.

[21] "Circular Letter," August 2, 1920.

[22] Burgess to Miller, July 1, 1921. MSS 1030, AMB Papers, Friends House, London.

Armistice and was only finally resolved with the signing of the Treaty of Lausanne in 1923.[23]

The realities of the protracted conflict guided Burgess' activism. Balancing the needs of those in her employ and care took on new weight in the unsettled conditions of the war. "Hatred and desire for revenge is found on all sides," she recorded in a letter at the end of January 1921. "Hunger, cold, sickness and inadequate clothing in this period of cold weather is horrible."[24] By February, she claimed that 20,000 refugees had entered Constantinople, fleeing the Greek invasion of the Pontic coast, an advancing Red Army on the Russian borderlands, and Mustafa Kemal's nationalist army. "Here everything is against us," she conceded in July. "Strife is the order of the day."[25] By the time the British embassy informed her that she had to leave Constantinople for her own safety in November 1922, she had already decided to move the mission and her charges to Corfu. On this island where thousands of other refugees took shelter, the Greek bishop who visited Burgess' factory called it a "sacred place." She kept the factory going with the labor of refugees who received both a small wage and support from the Mission funded by profits from the sale of rugs around the world.[26]

Burgess' experience in Corfu strengthened her belief that women had an important role to play in the future of world peace. In a 1926 letter to one of her patrons, she wrote of women's ability to prevent war by encouraging children to reject militarism. She claimed to admire the Armenians' endurance of constant, traumatic violence, which strengthened her own pacifism.[27] Worry about the spread of anti-minority violence topped her concerns: "Since the Armenians are nearly all out of Asia Minor (Turkey)," she recorded, "other Christians are now falling into similar troubles."[28] She blamed the problems of "our orphan girls" on "sicknesses" resulting from "deportations and suffering and sights so

---

[23] The first attempt at peace failed with the Treaty of Sevres, signed by representatives of the Ottoman government in 1920. The rising power of the nationalists under the leadership of Mustafa Kemal rejected the authority of Ottoman representatives in Constantinople and forced the renegotiation of Sevres at Lausanne three years later. See Ryan Gingeras, *Fall of the Sultanat* (Oxford: Oxford UP, 2016).
[24] Burgess to Miss Miller, January 30, 1921, AMB Papers, Friends House, London.
[25] Burgess to Miller, July 1, 1921, AMB Papers, Friends House, London.
[26] Burgess reported annual sales of around 5,000 pounds. See Burgess to Miller, November 25, 1922, AMB Papers, Friends House, London.
[27] Burgess to Alterina Peckover, Corfu, February 24, 1926, AMB Papers, Friends House, London. Burgess continued her membership the Wisbech Peace Association and distributed pacifist literature to tourists and clients.
[28] Burgess to Peckover, October 5, 1925, AMB Papers, Friends House, London.

painful," which included "seeing relatives murdered."[29] Burgess understood these traumas as falling particularly heavily upon women refugees supported by her Mission's limited resources:

> The bed cover was given to [...] a widow woman whose son and husband, sister, nieces and nephews and relatives by marriage were murdered or died from the hardships encountered during the deportation. The poor thing has one daughter about nine years of age during the war [,] this child was driven over a hundred miles on foot over rough roads just as Turks ordered and drove the poor woman and child and killed the others.[30]

Burgess believed that peace would eventually come and understood her mission to women and children as integral to that project. After visiting a Turkish refugee camp which housed over 4,000 women and children, she wondered how nations could continue the "terrible bloodshed" brought on by continuous war.[31] Burgess' belief that consideration of women and children's needs would focus attention on the need for peace sustained her work at the Corfu mission through the 1920s.

Some Quakers worried that relief efforts focused narrowly on women and children failed to fully address the scope of the wartime crisis. Criticism centered on one of the biggest and most well-funded American aid organizations, Near East Relief. Marshall Fox believed that its focus on orphans ignored homeless adults, a concern he expressed in a report to the League of Nations Nansen Office. But the idea that child survivors of the massacres represented a "living remnant" that was the Armenian nation's future had already taken hold and guided current and future relief work efforts in the Ottoman Empire. Anglican Bishop Gore, who deployed this term, advocated for a united policy to bring the League of Nations, Save the Children, Lord Mayors Fund and Friends of Armenia together in the larger purpose of redeeming the Armenian nation. The establishment of schools and model villages later supported by these international organizations was, at its core, driven by the plight of child victims.[32]

---

[29] Burgess to Peckover, Corfu, Jan 16, 1926, AMB Papers, Friends House, London.
[30] Burgess to Peckover, Friends Mission c/o British Post Constantinople, Dec 8, 1921, AMB Papers, Friends House, London.
[31] Burgess to Peckover, (no exact date) 1921, AMB Papers, Friends House, London.
[32] Marshall Fox's report, entitled "Descriptive account of the first steps towards the housing of homeless Armenians in Lebanon and Syria," was included in the "Illustrated report of the work done through the Nansen Office, 1926- 1934," 5, Friends House, London.

Yessayan's Mission

Zabel Yessayan was born Zabel Hovhannisian in 1878, outside of Constantinople. As a female and member of the Ottoman Christian minority community, she had few local options for education after primary school. She left for Paris, one of the first young Armenian women to do so, to continue her education in 1895. Fear of violence during the Hamadian massacres motivated her father to send her abroad, where she studied literature and history and began her career as a writer. She penned articles in Armenian and French, including discussions of European feminism, the Woman Question, and the role of Armenian women in social life and charitable work. Soon after marrying painter Dikran Yessayan in Paris in 1900, with whom she had two children, she returned to Constantinople to continue her writing career.[33]

Yessayan's growing reputation as a public intellectual earned her a seat on the humanitarian fact-finding commission established by the Constantinople Patriarch to investigate the 1909 massacres in the southern Anatolian city of Adana. The book that resulted, *In the Ruins*, chronicled her time as investigator and aid worker. Published in 1911, it cemented her reputation as intellectual, aid worker, and activist. In it, she recalled working with the English Consul's wife, who had started a hospital to aid survivors. "She told us, at great length," Yessayan recalled, "the stories of the children whom she had under her care."[34] The book is filled with the stories of survivors, mostly women and children, under the care of Adana's English consul, Lieutenant Colonel Charles H. M. Doughty-Wylie, and his wife, Lilian. The experiences of women and children motivated Yessayan's most intimate recollections and her determination to investigate the massacres and give hope to survivors by promising to represent their needs and tell their stories. Yessayan understood massacre not as an event but a process that defined the experience of a people. As she wrote in the aftermath of Adana, "Those who had not been massacred were blamed for surviving; those who had taken up arms to defend their homes and besieged villages were condemned to death or long periods of detention."[35]

Cooperation with Adana's English consulate, and especially Lilian Doughty-Wylie, shaped Yessayan's early experience as an aid worker. Doughty-Wylie facilitated Yessayan's access to massacre victims who had taken shelter and were receiving treatment in the English hospital. Armenian participation in this kind of aid work was unprecedented. They had been prevented from

---

[33] Victoria Rowe, *The 'New Armenian Woman': Armenian Women's Writing in the Ottoman Empire, 1880-1915*, University of Toronto dissertation, 2000, 9-13.
[34] Zabel Yessayan, *In the Ruins: The 1909 Massacres of Armenians in Adana, Turkey*, trans. G.M. Goshgarian (AIWA Press: Watertown, MA, 2016), 33.
[35] Ibid, 3.

participating in aid work on behalf of Armenian victims of the Hamidian massacres because of the risk of reprisals by the Ottoman government. Yessayan and her Armenian aid workers found the English hospital a safe space to investigate the Adana massacres and help care for the wounded. One old man who lost his entire family and endured grave injury recognized how unusual it was for Yessayan and her team to do this work. Her presence proved a comfort to him and others being treated at the hospital who felt helpless in the wake of what one patient called the "catastrophe." A fellow Armenian aid worker explained their presence to the patients saying: "Your fate is our fate. The blows you endure fall on us, too. We are incapable of doing all that foreigners can; we lack the means and the money. But the same tears in our eyes, and the pain of the same spilled blood is in our veins. We are all children of a single family."[36] The suffering of massacre victims proved an inspiration to Yessayan, who came to see it as her mission to serve her own community through aid work in the coming years.

Cooperation with Lilian Doughty-Wylie gave Yessayan access to resources for survivors and the opportunity to record their testimony. This double burden of the indigenous aid worker—to help and document atrocity—fell heavily on Yessayan, who wrote *In the Ruins* in large part to record what happened in Adana. She recalled that, as she climbed the stairs with Doughty-Wylie and viewed the ruins of the city outside, she "inquired about a great many details." The English hospital, she learned, also served as a shelter for orphans seeking safety from the chaos. She relayed the stories of those being treated and protected in the hospital in heartbreaking detail. Lilian Doughty-Wylie told Yessayan that in the early days of the massacres, she nursed wounded and cared for children, trying to take names of those who came to hospital either for help or seeking missing children. "Only once did a mother find her child," she told Yessayan, "but it was too late: the child was already dead."[37] This mother's grief deeply affected Doughty-Wylie, who had thought she could not "feel any new emotion after all the sensations that I'd already experienced," according to Yessayan. She found this particular mother's cry "unforgettable, and the sound of it will live on in my memory."[38] Yessayan gives voice to Doughty-Wylie and her hospital work in order to represent complex attempts by survivors and aid workers to understand the destruction of family and community bonds after the massacres.

Aid work functioned for Yessayan not only in an immediate and ameliorative form. It also had an important role in the long-term healing of a nation and a

---

[36] Yessayan, *In the Ruins*, 39.
[37] Ibid, 34.
[38] Ibid, 35.

people who wanted their stories told. Her embrace of women's roles as activist intellectuals was most certainly influenced by her time in France. She viewed gender norms in terms of a hybrid sensibility that fused feminism with patriarchal values, writing widely on women's issues that included advocacy for increasing women's civil rights. Her novels and essays constructed her own version of the ideal New Woman: politically engaged but also intensely loyal to family and country. As the only woman included on the list of intellectuals to be rounded up by the Ottoman government on the eve of the Armenian Genocide on April 24, 1915, she understood her precarious status as a woman intellectual and Armenian nationalist. Escaping to Bulgaria to evade capture with her daughter, she eventually returned to the Ottoman Empire with the help of the British government, who supported her work by giving her shelter in Legation offices in Teheran.[39]

Wartime work put her in contact with Allied governments and regional aid organizations, which supported her political and humanitarian work. As a result of her writing and experience with relief work, she emerged as an internationally respected voice. One contemporary described her as "a cultured Armenian lady, an author and a patriot." She worked with prominent members of the British philanthropic community, including Rev. Harold Buxton, and petitioned the British government for support for Armenian causes with the help of Member of Parliament Aneurin Williams, chair of the British Armenia Committee in London.[40] Yessayan served on a committee working to rebuild Adana after the massacres. In September 1909, she submitted a request to the British Acting Vice Consul to open an "industrial work" center employing 100 widows.[41]

The Armenian National Delegation, headquartered in Paris, supported Yessayan's work in French-occupied Anatolia after the 1918 Armistice between the Allies and Ottoman Empire. She redoubled her efforts on behalf of Armenian causes, set up orphanages and schools, and continued to write.[42] The Armenian Red Cross, based in Britain, relied on Yessayan for reports on the humanitarian emergency in the Caucasus in the summer of 1918. Aid money went through Teheran, where Yessayan used it to fund projects. Emily Robinson of the British-based Armenian Red Cross explained, "We do not send help through missionaries or through any political committee: our

---

[39] Yessayan to Boghos Nubar, Teheran, September 12, 1918, Nubar Library, Paris.
[40] Undated letter from G. M. Gregory to (?). Nubar Library, Paris.
[41] The request was submitted on September 15. It is not clear if she ended up opening the site. See "Further Correspondence, 1909 Oct.-Dec.," The National Archives London, UK.
[42] Letter to Yessayan, from the Armenian National Delegation, January 10, 1920, Nubar Library, Paris.

object is to help Armenians to help themselves." Funding Yessayan's schools and work programs, along with her political involvement with the British Legation at Teheran, was one way to achieve this.[43]

Political advocacy for Armenia and Armenians necessarily intersected with work on behalf of refugees. In a letter from Teheran to Armenian leader Boghos Nubar in Paris, Yessayan reported the terrible situation unfolding in Baku in September 1918. "There is no precise information on the situation of the inhabitants of the city who are certainly between the fire and the sword," she wrote. The expected arrival of 3,000 refugees and orphans, mainly from the Russian borderlands, would make matters worse in a region where "the oil wells of the black village.... are on fire and it is in this infernal and hideous situation that probably live the large part of the population."[44] The presence of Armenian forces who had supported the Allies for seven months did little to improve the situation for "persecuted refugees of Urmia and Baku" who overwhelmed the region. Yessayan directed Nubar's attention "to the charge that I have assumed": collecting "photographs" and "official documents" chronicling "cruelties committed by the Turks on the Armenians of Turkey," which she left in Baghdad and Teheran, hoping they would capture the Allies' attention.[45] The British military authority allowed her to travel in the region and supported her work. In this way, she straddled the worlds of observer, advocate, and aid worker in the weeks before the Armistice between the Allies and the Ottoman Empire.

Her reputation as a trusted advisor and voice for refugees earned Yessayan a seat as Armenian representative at the Paris Peace Conference. At Versailles, she brought women's issues to the international stage.[46] Yessayan spoke to delegates about two main issues: women's sacrifices during the war and the repatriation of women and children absorbed into Turkish families during the war. In January 1919, she delivered an illustrated lecture entitled "The Role of the Armenian Woman During the War." She spoke on behalf of the Armenian National Delegation (AND) and focused on the war's devastating effect on women and children. In so doing, she helped shape a gendered discourse around the war victim. The victims she spoke about were female, young, and

---

[43] Emily Robinson to Nubar (Heenegent France), July 22, 1918, Nubar Library, Paris.
[44] Essayan to Boghos Nubar, Teheran, September 21, 1918, Nubar Library, Paris.
[45] Ibid.
[46] Lerna Ekmekcioglu, "The Armenian National Delegation at the Paris Peace Conference and the Role of the Armenian Woman during the War," https://blogs.commons.georgetown.edu/world-war-i-in-the-middle-east/seminar-participants/web-projects/lerna-ekmekcioglu-the-armenian-national-delegation-at-the-paris-peace-conference-and-the-role-of-the-armenian-woman-during-the-war.

perhaps most importantly, moral actors. Women, "in all countries," she asserted, had played a "valuable role" in the war, both publicly and privately. The moral character of Armenian women made it possible for them to survive the murder of their spouses, mass deportation, and often rape and long-term displacement. She emphasized the physical strength of those women who fought alongside men as evidence of their moral character rather than masculine military prowess. This ability to fight did not diminish the Armenian woman's femininity but confirmed her determination to protect the honor of her people. "The Armenian woman, perhaps more than the men," she argued, kept deep "in her pure and serious soul the sacred traditions of the race." The embrace of European learning and customs among women and girls in urban areas made them adaptive and independently-minded, which allowed them to band together as women to collectively work to help one another after being "thrown on the road to exile" during the genocide. Thus, those who could bravely fought alongside their husbands and brothers during the war.[47]

In March 1919, Yessayan made another contribution to the Conference in a "note" on behalf of AND, entitled "The Liberation of Non-Muslim Women and Children in Turkey." She argued that the kidnapping of hundreds of thousands of women and girls from the Armenian, Greek and Assyrian communities, their subsequent conversion to Islam, and what was called "absorption" into Muslim families constituted a problem that the international community had an obligation to address. Starting with the alleged selling of women and child deportees in markets and its consequences, Yessayan moved to a discussion of rape and the attitude of female victims, many of whom, she reported, committed suicide. She concluded with concrete suggestions regarding the repatriation of women and children, which centered on establishing "an international commission of women" who would consult with the Allied powers to help those she referred to as "slaves." This commission would build orphanages, create work opportunities, and set up health and special services for women and children, who she saw as the best hope for the renewal of the Armenian nation.[48]

This detailed plan put indigenous women in the region and diaspora in a central role. The International Commission she proposed would consult "Armenian Ladies of Russian Armenia, Constantinople, Smyrna and European colonies of Egypt and America." The evidence she collected of atrocities

---

[47] "Le rôle de la femme Arménienne pendant la guerre," *Revue des Études Arméniennes* 2 (1922) 121–38.

[48] Note from Yessayan to Armenian National Delegation: "The Liberation of Non-Muslim women and Children in Turkey," Paris, March 8, 1919, Nubar Library, Paris.

committed against women and children during the war, from oral testimony to photographs and eye-witness accounts, should form the basis of "onsite investigation" into the scope of the problem. Yessayan proposed a very specific program for this team of observers, consultants, and investigators who would, along with the commission and under the protection of the Allied occupation,

> Find minor children who have lost their maternal language the memory of their parents and their nationality, and who have been moreover terrorized by their darkness, and who often renounce being Armenian or Greeks...
>
> [Liberate] non-Muslim women and children...
>
> [Increase] the number of orphanages ...
>
> [Create] places for women to return from the house of Muslims until they are repatriated in their birth places.
>
> [Organize] a health service, to examine the women because many are unfortunately contaminated with dangerous and contagious maladies, and to group them as a result.
>
> Create a special service for walled up women.
>
> Organize workers to find work for women and adults.[49]

This program of renewing the Armenian, Greek, and Assyrian nations by reabsorbing women into the nation through internationally sanctioned aid work had the full support of the Armenian Delegation at Paris. Leader Boghos Nubar offered his endorsement of Yessayan's plan, calling her a "woman of letters and one of our most distinguished writers" who "collected herself" testimonies of the women and children she cited in her presentation. Emily Robinson was inspired by Yessayan and suggested to Nubar the formation of a "women's movement on behalf of women in Turkish harems with representative from Britain, France and the US in order to convince the delegation in Paris to take prompt action to deliver these our poor sisters in such terrible distress."[50] Robinson's use of the nineteenth-century trope of "poor sisters" trapped in "Turkish harems" showed the persistence of a gendered

---

[49] Ibid.
[50] Robinson to Nubar, April 2, 1919, Nubar Library, Paris.

language of western aid that continued to place British and Armenian women in an unequal power relationship.

Yessayan's presence at the Versailles Peace Conference signaled that she had successfully established her authority as an authentic representative for Ottoman Christian women and children. This had important consequences for her own career and the way the international community came to understand civilian war victims. Gendering the war victim as female elicited a powerful empathetic mode of understanding that translated into action. Aid workers had reason to focus their efforts on this group of women and child victims of genocide regularly referred to as "the remnant." Women and children had long been cast as sympathetic victims, resulting in their becoming the central subject of philanthropic endeavors. Nineteenth-century philanthropy, largely run by middle-class women, easily translated into this new context of post-war internationalism run for and on behalf of suffering gendered subjects.[51] Yessayan contributed to these understandings of women and children as the war's most vulnerable war victims by using the case of her own people and other persecuted Ottoman minorities at Versailles. Drawing on the language of humanitarian activism rooted in Europe's long history with minority protection in the Ottoman Empire, she offered a gendered reading of the consequences of total war for civilians.

Nevertheless, Yessayan soon discovered the limits of her authority. Emboldened by her success at Versailles, she embarked on a campaign to set up schools and orphanages in the Allied-occupied region of Cilicia in early 1920. Her proposal to AND initially received enthusiastic support: "With patriotic sentiments and the devotion that drive her," one representative claimed he was convinced that she would "render real service to our orphans and school in Cilicia."[52] AND granted her permission to commence this work, but Yessayan soon fell out with male aid workers who had other ideas about how to best run these institutions.[53] AND began to question her methods and accused her of spreading feminist ideas among her charges at the orphanages and schools.[54] On the international stage, the League of Nations eventually commissioned a committee to oversee the work that Yessayan argued was so necessary to help women. Yessayan was not on the committee, which consisted

---

[51] Troy Boone, *Youth of Darkest England: Working-Class Children at the Heart of Victorian Empire* (New York: Routledge, 2005).
[52] AND to Mr. Mihran Damadian, January 10, 1920, Nubar Library, Paris.
[53] AND to Yessayan, January 10, 1920, Nubar Library, Paris.
[54] *Les Arméniens: La quête d'un refuge, 1917-18*, Presses De L'Universite Saint-Jospeh (Paris, 2007), 73.

of two women and one man.[55] After the death of her husband, she returned to Paris in the early 1920s and later accepted an invitation from the Soviet government to settle in Soviet Armenia, where she wrote and lectured on French literature. In 1937, she was sent into exile in Siberia by Stalin, where she is said to have died in the early 1940s.[56]

Conclusion

Historians have studied the aid worker as an agent of change in terms of professional opportunities and paid employment for women. They also have examined the ways in which her authority in the field was used at the expense of those in her care, reinforcing a racial patriarchy that served the imperial project.[57] The stories of Burgess and Yessayan show that the presence of women in aid work was transformative in other ways as well. Networks of women divided by race, experience and purpose worked in a mutually reinforcing relationship with those who received aid, reimagining both the meaning and practice of distributing relief in fundamental ways. The moral, cultural, and political authority of the woman aid worker mattered in shaping discourses and institutions that determined the shape of international humanitarianism. Gendered codes of behavior and acceptable roles for women also transformed how humanitarian aid worked from an institutional and practical perspective. In short, it redefined the war victim (gendered female) and how aid was delivered.

In the end, women had the clearest authority when speaking about domestic subjects. This made them ideal advocates for children, widows, and young girls. Like Burgess, Yessayan argued that women were uniquely situated to renew the nation by becoming surrogate mothers to orphaned children. Women aid workers had less authority to speak on behalf of men. Adult males and, to a lesser extent, single women, existed in the shadows as war victims; young women and children became synonymous with the term "civilian

---

[55] "Deportation of Women and Children in Turkey and Neighboring Countries," *League of Nations Journal*, April 11, 1921, Geneva. The League appointed a three-person commission of inquiry: Miss Emma Cushman, nominated by Roberts College, Constantinople; Dr. Kennedy, nominated by the British High Commission; and Madame Gaulis, nominated by French representatives.

[56] Rowe, *The 'New Armenian Woman,'* 13.

[57] Margaret Higonnet et al., eds., *Behind the Lines: Gender and the Two World Wars* (New Haven: Yale UP, 1989); Kimberly Jensen, *Moblizing Minerva: American Women in the First World War* (Champaign: Illinois UP, 2008); Michelle Moravec, "'Till I Have Done All That I Can': An Auxiliary Nurse's Memories of World War I," *Historical Reflections/ Réflexions Historiques* 42.3 (2016) 71-90; Susan Zieger, *Uncle Sam's Army: Women in the American Expeditionary Force* (Ithaca: Cornell UP, 1999).

victim." It was not simply because genocide targeted the male population that made it more dangerous to help them. Aid to women and children administered by women aid workers was made acceptable and legitimated by a longer tradition of aid work in the European philanthropic tradition that intersected and was itself shaped by contact with indigenous women aid workers and networks.

Raising money specifically for young women and children became standard practice and only accelerated after the war. The wartime campaigns of Near East Relief explicitly focused on children rather than adults. Save the Children, started in 1919 in London by Eglantyne Jebb, focused on Armenian orphans and child war victims rather than adults as well.[58] The face of aid work and ideas governing who deserved aid came into clear focus. Ultimately, long-standing gendered understandings of women's cultural authority and public roles, formed in the nineteenth century, influenced the rules of the game when it came to delivering aid. Women aid workers redefined the war victim by age and gender by focusing their efforts on widows, young girls, and children, and by training them to support themselves. The gender-defined limits and possibilities under which women like Burgess and Yessayan found themselves helped establish the boundaries of a discourse about aid and aid work that remain with us today.

---

[58] Clare Mully, *The Woman Who Saved the Children: A Biography of Eglantyne Jebb* (Oxford: OneWorld, 2009).

Chapter 6

Guernica, Politics, and International Humanitarianism: Spanish Child Refugees in Britain and the Soviet Union

Sandra Trudgen Dawson
Berkshire Conference of Women Historians

Patrick José Dawson
University of Maryland, Baltimore County

Abstract: Britain, France, and Belgium chose to remain neutral when the civil war in Spain began in July 1936. Italy, Germany, and the Soviet Union agreed to non-intervention rather than neutrality. After the firebombing of Guernica in April 1937 by the Germans, neutrality began to unravel. The immediate response was to evacuate 33,000 Basque child refugees, 2,895 went to the Soviet Union and 3,862 went to Britain on humanitarian grounds. The attitude and policies of each government had a profound impact on the experience and treatment of the Spanish children in exile. While most of the children sent to Britain in 1937 returned to Spain by the end of 1938, those dispatched to the Soviet Union remained until after the end of WWII, and some stayed even longer. The Soviet Union carefully prepared and provided state aid and lavish care for the children, whereas the British government, reluctant to even allow the refugees into the country, refused state aid and insisted the children be supported by charities and private funds, which were often woefully inadequate. This chapter explores the politics behind the humanitarian intervention of Britain and the Soviet Union and the way this shaped the experiences of the children in exile.

Keywords: Guernica, firebombing, international press, humanitarianism, refugees, ninos, Soviet Union, Southampton, *colonias*, Basque, communist, republican

***

It was a Monday: market day in Guernica. For three and a half hours on April 26, 1937, the German Luftwaffe repeatedly firebombed the Basque town.[1] Those who tried to run away were immediately strafed by machine-gun fire. Sixteen-hundred people, one-third of the town's population, were killed or wounded in the deadly attack, and seventy percent of all buildings were destroyed. After the raid, fires continued to rage for three days. The international press reported the devastating attack and the terror it unleashed on the civilian population.[2] George Steer of the *London Times* claimed that "waves of German-type planes" flung thousands of pounds of "bombs and incendiary projectiles" on Guernica just as the "priest blessed peasants filling the town on market day."[3] Noel Monks, an Australian reporter covering the war for the *Daily Express*, claimed, "I was the first correspondent to reach Guernica, and was immediately pressed into service by some Basque soldiers collecting charred bodies that the flames had passed over." The sight was like nothing Monks had ever seen: "Some of the soldiers were sobbing like children. There were flames and smoke and grit, and the smell of burning human flesh was nauseating. Houses were collapsing into the inferno."[4] For supporters of the Republican government in Spain, the firebombing of Guernica was yet another example of the barbarism and callousness of fascism. In a powerful and moving piece, Pablo Picasso immortalized the destruction in an anti-war mural titled "Guernica."[5]

---

[1] Guernica (Gernika) was the capital of the Basque region in northern Spain. The raid was made by the Condor Legion, an adjunct of the Luftwaffe. The Condor Legion provided the Luftwaffe with the opportunity to develop and perfect tactics of aerial warfare that fueled Germany's blitzkrieg through Europe during 1939 and 1940. See Carlos Cabalerro Jurado, *The Condor Legion: German Troops in the Spanish Civil War* (Oxford: Osprey Press, 2013).

[2] Noel Monks, "Franco Bombers Wreck Town, Riddle Fleeing Mobs: Women Die Huddling in Shelter," *Daily Express*, April 27, 1937, 1; "Franco Atrocity Shocks the Whole World," *Daily Herald*, April 28, 1937, 1; "Hundreds of Civilians Die in Machine-Gun Fire: Fleeing Spaniards Mowed Down in Refuges," *Evening News*, April 27, 1937, 1.

[3] G. L. Steer, "Historic Basque Town Wiped Out; Rebel Fliers Machine-Gun Civilians," *London Times*, April 28 1937, 1. Steer also wrote a book about the Guernica attack, *The Tree of Gernika: A Field Study of Modern War* (London: Hodder and Stoughton, 1938).

[4] "The Bombing of Guernica, 1937," EyeWitness to History, http://www.eyewitnessto history.com/guernica.htm.

[5] Because of the painting, Picasso was regarded as an enemy of the Nationalist regime that eventually became the government of Spain. See Genoveva Tusell Garcia, "Picasso, a Political Enemy of Francoist Spain," *The Burlington Magazine* 166.1320 (2013): 167-172. Picasso's "Guernica" was first exhibited July 1937 in the Spanish Pavilion at the Paris International Exposition. The painting later toured the United States and other countries to raise money for the Republican cause.

The firebombing of the Basque market town was part of the civil war in Spain that began in July 1936 between a coalition of leftist groups and the Republican government on one side, and a coalition of right-wing groups led by the Nationalist military forces of General Francisco Franco on the other. Those on the left regarded the conflict as a battle between fascism and socialism. Those on the right saw the civil war as a fight for the Church and Christianity against the onslaught of godless communism. The British and other international presses underscored these perceptions of the conflict and chose sides.[6]

Guernica had no military importance. Indeed, the Basque government chose Guernica as a place of safety—far from the front and without military interest—to establish Basque language schools at the start of the war.[7] One of the most tragic consequences of the attack on Guernica was the large number of women and children who died. Eyewitnesses claimed mothers carrying babies and clutching the hands of children were targeted by bombers as they fled the town. The devastating raid was part of the Nationalist strategy to defeat the Republican-supporting Basque government. Xabier Irujo maintains that after Guernica, the "rebels' strategy of terror warfare left no safe place for children in the Basque Country during the war."[8] As the Nationalists, supported by the Germans and Italians, came closer to overwhelming the Basque forces, the government began plans to evacuate the children.

The Basque port of Bilbao was already full of refugees from the war, mainly women and children. When Franco's forces blockaded the port in March 1937, the food and medicine situation became precarious.[9] After the April 26 attack on Guernica, refugee numbers swelled as survivors reached the port, exacerbating the food insecurity. The Republican and Basque governments negotiated with Britain, Belgium, France, Switzerland, Denmark, Mexico, and

---

[6] Left-leaning papers included the *Daily Herald, Daily Worker,* and the *News Chronicle.* See, for example, "Democracy and the Empire are at Stake," *News Chronicle,* August 8, 1936, and "Tomorrow May be Too Late," *News Chronicle,* January 19, 1937. Right-leaning papers included the *Morning Post.* See "Spain," *Morning Post,* July 21, 1936, and "Unparalleled Horrors of Spanish Civil War," *Western Daily Press,* September 14, 1936, and "Spanish War Atrocities," *Coventry Evening Telegraph,* August 20, 1936, 1. Roman Catholic papers include *The Tablet* and *The Catholic Herald,* and journals *Dublin Review, Clergy Review,* and *Blackfriars.*
[7] The schools were part of the Basque Government *kastolak* (public Basque-language schools) established at the beginning of the war. Xabier Irujo, *Expelled from the Motherland: The Government of President Jose Antonio Agirre in Exile, 1937–1960,* trans. Cameron J. Watson and Jennifer Ottman (Reno: University of Nevada Press, 2012), 47.
[8] Irujo, *Expelled from the Motherland,* 47.
[9] Ibid, 45. The blockade was over by 23 April 1937.

the Soviet Union to accept child refugees from the conflict. Evacuation began in small numbers in late March and accelerated at the end of April 1937. Teachers volunteered and registered with the Ministry of Culture to teach refugee children abroad.[10] Of approximately 33,000 Spanish child refugees, 2,895 went to the USSR and 3,862 went to Britain.[11] The vast majority went to France and other European countries, and approximately 500 went to Mexico. For many of the children, this was a second or even third evacuation. From November 1936, the Republican government encouraged parents to send their children from the cities to *colonias* (colonies) in the east of Spain and later, to the north.[12] The *colonias* were residential schools or groups of children in private homes in areas perceived as safe from German and Italian bombs.[13] The firebombing of Guernica proved there were no safe havens for children in Spain.

This chapter explores the political and humanitarian grounds for the acceptance of refugee children from Spain as well as the preparation and reception of the exiles in Britain and the Soviet Union. The attitude and policies of each government had a profound impact on the experience and treatment of the Spanish children in exile. While most of the children sent to Britain in 1937 returned to Spain by the end of 1938, those dispatched to the Soviet Union remained until after the end of WWII, and some stayed even longer.[14] The Soviet

---

[10] Ibid, 50.

[11] Dorothy Lagarreta, *The Guernica Generation: Basque Refugee Children of the Spanish Civil War* (University of Nevada Press, 1984), xii. Approximately 1,000 adult Spanish Communists went to the Soviet Union and helped educate the Spanish child refugees. See Karl D. Qualls, "Defining the Ideal Soviet Childhood: Reportage about Child Evacuees from Spain as Didactic Literature," in *War and Childhood in the Era of the Two World Wars*, Mischa Honeck and James Marten, eds. (Cambridge: Cambridge University Press, 2019), 71-86. Over 400,000 adults also left Spain.

[12] On November 13, the Evacuation Office of the Republican government created a separate Comité de Axilio del Niño (the Committee for Child Aid) to assist child aid and evacuation. See Suan Sheridan Breakwell, "'Knowing How to Be a Mother': Parenting, Emotion and Evacuation Propaganda during the Spanish Civil War, 1936-1939," in *Parenting and the State in Britain and Europe, c. 1870-1950: Raising the Nation*, eds. Hester Barron and Claudia Siebrecht (Palgrave Macmillan, 2017), 207-230, 209.

[13] The *colonias* replicated the pre-war summer *colonias* where urban children were sent to improve their health. See Breakwell, "'Knowing How to Be a Mother,'" 213. There were also progressive schools like the *colonias escolares* that provided "safety" to evacuated children. See Juan Félix Rodríguez Pérez and Francisco Canes Garrido, *Las Colonias Escalares Municipales Madrilenas, 1910-1936* (Madrid: Universidad Complutense de Madrid, 2001).

[14] Approximately 1,500 refugees returned to Spain between 1956 and 1959. Some returned to the Soviet Union. Qualls, *Stalin's Niños*, 5.

Union carefully prepared and provided state aid and lavish care for the children, whereas the British government, reluctant to even allow the refugees into the country, refused state aid and insisted the children be supported by charities and private funds, which were often woefully inadequate.

Britain and the Basque Children

Britain, France, and Belgium chose to remain neutral when the civil war in Spain began in July 1936. Italy, Germany, and the Soviet Union agreed to non-intervention rather than neutrality. Mexico supported the Republican government and sent military assistance.[15] By November 1936, Nazi Germany recognized Fascist Spain and General Franco as the legitimate leader and provided airpower to the Nationalists. Italy's Mussolini followed and sent air strength to assist Franco.

After the publicity surrounding the destruction of Guernica, the cross-party National Joint Committee for Spanish Relief (NJCSR) in Britain launched a press campaign to bring the Basque children to Britain and safety.[16] At the same time, the Basque government lobbied Mr. Stevenson, the British Consul in Bilbao, for Britain to accept refugee children.[17] Prime Minister Stanley Baldwin reluctantly agreed to allow 2,000 children to come to Britain as a short-term humanitarian measure.[18] As a neutral power, the state refused to take financial responsibility for the evacuation and care of the children. Only private funds could be used for the children's education and welfare, and, in another nod to neutrality, only non-combatants of all political parties would be admitted.[19]

To ensure the refugees were politically inclusive, the non-partisan Basque Children Committee (BCC) formed on May 15, 1937, under the umbrella of the NJCSR. The committee included members of the Catholic Church, the Labour movement, the Quakers, Save the Children, the Salvation Army, and

---

[15] Mario Ojeda Reyah, *Mexico and the Spanish Civil War: Domestic Politics and the Republican Cause* (Eastbourne: Sussex Academic Press, 2015).
[16] The NJCSR formed in December 1936, chaired by Ellen Wilkinson, MP, and the Duchess of Atholl, to co-ordinate relief efforts for victims of the Spanish Civil War.
[17] Susana Sabin-Fernandez, "The Basque Refugee Children of the Spanish Civil War in the UK: Memory and Memorialisation," (Ph.D. diss., University of Southampton, 2010), 113. Bilbao is a port city in Basque Country.
[18] Tom Buchanan, "The Role of the British Labour Movement in the Origin and Work of the Basque Children's Committee, 1937-9," *European History Quarterly* 18 (1988): 155-174.
[19] Legarreta, *The Guernica Generation*, 101-102.

the Communist Party Spanish Medical Aid organization.[20] The BCC immediately began raising funds to support the 2,000 refugees.

Each refugee was required to have a medical examination before leaving Spain and another on arrival in Britain. Two doctors, Dr. Richard Ellis, and Dr Audrey Russell, arrived in Bilbao to examine the children. Ellis claimed groups of women were filling sandbags and "there were children everywhere."[21] The medical checks took place outside a bomb shelter, and on the first day, air raid sirens delayed them for hours. A few children verged on starvation, but most were healthy. Ellis noted that "{I}t was equally clear however, that many of the women had starved themselves to supply their children with food."[22]

The situation in Bilbao was desperate. Officials persuaded the British government at the last minute to allow 4,000 children to come to Britain. Josephina Stubbs and her sister arrived at the docks expecting to go to the Soviet Union. An unexpected air raid forced the girls and their father to come back later. When they returned, the next available ship was bound for Britain and so their destination changed.[23] It is unclear how many other children had the same experience. The port was attacked from the air as the refugees waited to embark and the ship was shelled as it left Bilbao. The fifteen-hour journey aboard the ship was harrowing. The *SS Habana* finally arrived at Southampton on May 23, 1937, with double the number of people expected, just eight days after BCC fundraising began. The 3,862 children were accompanied by 95 teachers, 15 priests, and 120 adult volunteers. Ellis described the miserable voyage: "Four thousand wretchedly seasick children crowded into an old boat whose very latrines are apt to regurgitate in sympathy, are not a pretty sight."[24] Fortunately, most of the children were exhausted and slept.

Dr Ronald Gibson and Dr Cobb were charged with organizing medical care for the children once they arrived at North Stoneham Camp, outside Southampton. Gibson arrived two days before the children arrived to find "an area of about forty acres of grass" with 120 pitched bell tents and three or four

---

[20] Sabin-Fernandez, "The Basque Refugee Children of the Spanish Civil War," 114. While the BCC claimed to be non-partisan, most of the members were ardent supporters of the Republicans and there was only one Roman Catholic member, who resigned after a few weeks.
[21] Richard Ellis in Yvonne Cloud, *The Basque Children in England: An Account of their Life at North Shoreham Camp* (London: Victor Gollancz, 1937), 19.
[22] Ellis in Cloud, *Basque Children in England*, 22.
[23] Susana Sabin-Fernandez, "The Basque Refugee Children of the Spanish Civil War in the UK: Memory and Memorialisation," 113.
[24] Ellis in Cloud, *Basque Children in England*, 24.

marquees, one labeled "Medico." There was no medical equipment or supplies and no-one knew how many children to expect.[25] The next day Gibson learned that 4,000 children, aged six to fourteen, would arrive the following day. A third doctor volunteered to assist Gibson and Cobb at the camp, and they immediately ordered medical supplies and set up a second treatment tent. At the last minute, Moor Hill, an empty house approximately six miles from the camp, was offered as a home for sick children. Gibson claimed the house was "in a bad state of repair, and the sanitary arrangements were totally inadequate for the forty patients and necessary staff that it was hoped to house there." Volunteers worked "hard to make it 'good enough'" by the time the children arrived. By the following day, the house had been spring-cleaned and there were beds for forty children. The sanitary arrangements, however, remained deficient.[26]

Before the children disembarked on Sunday, May 23, they were given another medical examination. Those with lice were sent to Southampton baths "where an army of volunteers" deloused them.[27] The Borough Hospital and the Borough Isolation Hospital received those identified as sick or contagious, and the rest went on buses to the camp. The BCC relied on volunteers and groups like the Boy Scouts to organize the camp. The last-minute addition of two-thousand extra children proved a challenge. The camp was chaotic and unprepared. Volunteers took four hours to serve the first meal. The pandemonium continued as thousands of sightseers surrounded the camp. There was a tent full of toys, but no one to distribute them.[28] Donated clothes were trampled on the floor of another marquee and the latrine system was woefully inadequate.[29] A visitor to the camp maintained that the leadership was poor, there was insufficient supervision, and food was insufficient.[30] Another visitor disagreed and claimed that although the children were "adequately fed," they were "constantly hungry," probably as a result of the food shortages in Spain.[31] "Adequate," and "good enough" seemed

---

[25] Ronald Gibson, "Four Thousand Basque Children: The Refugee Camp at Southampton," *The Lancet* 230.5958 (November 6, 1937) 1091-1096: 1091.
[26] Gibson, "Four Thousand Basque Children," 1091.
[27] Ibid.
[28] E.P. Harries, "Basque Camp, Eastleigh, Report," Basque Children's Committee: Minutes and Documents, 1937-1939, Trades Union Congress Archive, Modern Records Centre (hereafter TUC MRC), 292/946/39/111, 1.
[29] Harries, Basque Camp, 1937, 292/946/39/111, 3.
[30] Harries, Basque Camp, 1937, 292/946/39/111, 1-2.
[31] Letter from Mary Sutherland to Walter Citrine, May 28, 1937, Spanish Conflict Basque Children, 1937-1938, TUC MRC, 292/946/37/165, 2.

the most appropriate descriptions of the preparations and conditions provided for the children.

When heavy rains transformed the camp into a quagmire, the doctors feared an outbreak of disease.[32] Typhoid broke out within days.[33] To prevent the spread of disease, all the children were kept in medical quarantine for a month and received compulsory vaccinations before they were permitted to leave the campsite.[34] The cost of setting up the camp and maintaining it for the first five weeks was almost £11,000, a considerable amount of money raised from donations.[35] The temporary camp remained open until September, when the BCC found alternative accommodations for the children.[36]

The Catholic Church reluctantly took 1,200 children into numerous orphanages and convents. The Church hesitated because the accompanying priests were known Republicans opposed to Franco. Pope Pius XI supported the Nationalists in Spain and encouraged European Catholics to do the same. Furthermore, the BCC expected the Church to assume the cost of caring for the refugees, which rankled the Catholic hierarchy.[37] The Salvation Army agreed to house 450 refugee children in a hostel in East London. One of the young girls described the hostel as "all so big and dark, it seemed like a prison.... there was an awful smell...It was cold and overcrowded."[38]

A former evacuee remembers, "There was no heating, little, if any, adult supervision, and very little food. There was a lot of bullying and we were left to our own devices to survive."[39] A letter from a local resident close to the Salvation Army Hostel in Clapton reveals the lack of supervision. Mr. R. Welch

---

[32] Adrian Bell, *Only for Three Months: The Basque Refugee Children in Exile* (Earls Barton, Northants: Wrightsons, 2007), 27.
[33] Cloud, *Basque Children in England*, 28.
[34] Bell, *Only for Three Months*, 64.
[35] W. Munday, "Expenses of Camp at Southampton, 21 May-30 June 1937," dated July 10, 1937, Basque Children's Committee: Minutes and Documents, 1937-1939, TUC MRC, 292/946/39/82, 1-2.
[36] There were 450 children still at the camp at the end of August 1937. See "Report, Basque Children's Committee, 17 September 1937," Spanish Conflict Basque Children, 1937-1938, TUC MRC, 292/946/37/43, 9.
[37] Catholic Archbishop Hinsley claimed he was railroaded into caring for the refugees. Quoted in Peter Anderson, "The Struggle over the Evacuation to the United Kingdom and Repatriation of Basque Refugee Children in the Spanish Civil War: Symbols and Souls," *Journal of Contemporary History* 52: 2 (2017): 310.
[38] *Recuerdos: Basque Children Refugees in Britain*, ed. Natalia Benjamin (Oxford: Mousehold Press, 2007), 16.
[39] Anonymous, quoted in Sabin-Fernandez, "The Basque Refugee Children of the Spanish Civil War," 120.

claimed that the refugee boys played on the marshes quite happily every day. "Naturally the residents take them in and give them food and any clothing they have to spare," Welch claimed. However, he was very distressed to find that some of the boys had been beaten with a stick by one of the supervisors. Welch told a Salvation Army Officer about the beating and claimed the locals were "disgusted to see such treatment." Surely, wrote Welch, the children had "been through enough horrors in their own country without more added to it."[40]

The rest of the children were sent to seventy "colonies" (*colonias*) throughout the country. The colonies were housed in abandoned school buildings, churches, orphanages, and even stately homes, supported by funds from local Basque Children's Committees, who in turn received central funds from the NJCSR.

There were positive experiences, too. Hywel Davis notes that the refugees who found themselves in a colony that had structure to each day fared the best. In Cambria House, the refugees spent most of the day at school, taught by two Spanish and three British teachers. The children ate well and had only English food on Sundays. All others were Spanish meals supplied by grocers in Cardiff and prepared by a Spanish cook.[41] Cambria House held concerts where the children sang Basque songs and danced traditional Basque dances to raise money for the cause. Cambria House also had an extremely popular football team that played against local teams.[42] For the most part, this colony was a successful enterprise.

Fundraising was fundamental to the refugee experience. *Modern Orphans of the Storm* was a publicity film financed by the NJCSR and jointly produced by the Realist Film Unit and Victor Saville Productions.[43] The total running time for the film is just ten minutes and the main emphasis is the identity of the children as "Basque," their experiences in Spain as innocent victims, and their humanitarian rescue in Britain. The second film, *Save Spanish Children*, is a fifteen-minute film designed to raise awareness and funds for the relief work of the NJCSC.[44] "A final emotive sequence compares dead bodies in a Spanish street with happy smiling children" safe in Britain, graphically illustrating the

---

[40] R. Welch, letter to Trades Union Congress, 1937, Spanish Conflict Basque Children, 1937-1938, TUC MRC, 292/946/37/153, 1-4.
[41] Hywel Davies, *Fleeing Franco: How Wales Gave Shelter to Refugee Children from the Basque Country during the Spanish Civil War* (Cardiff: University of Wales Press, 2011), 61.
[42] Ibid, 62-3.
[43] *Modern Orphans of the Storm: The Story of the Refugee Basque Children* (1937), dir. Basil Charles Wright and Ian Dalrymple, Realist Film Unit and Victor Saville Productions.
[44] *Save Spanish Children*, NGO (1937), Marlborough, Wiltshire: Adam Matthew Digital.

very real danger of leaving the children to die in Spain.⁴⁵ Both *Modern Orphans of the Storm* and *Save Spanish Children* were fundraising films that shaped their content. All the images of the children appear passive. There is no spontaneity, maximizing the idea that the children are passive victims, not radical political beings, and thus worthy of British emotional and financial support.⁴⁶ In an even shorter film by British Pathé, *Basque Civil War Refugee Children Arrive at Southampton* (1937) the narrator claims the children "belong to neither side" in the war. Indeed, the film explains that the children were "snatched from a living horror" in the Basque area as the bombs fell, threatening to destroy them. As the film shows the children stepping down from the ship and then the buses in Southampton, the narrator explains that each child is medically examined and given an identity tag, suggesting they present no potential harm to Britain and belong to the family identifiable on the name tag. The Basque children, the film clarifies, are apolitical, innocent, and vulnerable victims of a war that has nothing to do with them, and thus they are worthy of British compassion.⁴⁷

Despite attempts to depoliticize the children, the Stoneham camp initially divided the refugees into political sections, including Basque Nationalists, Socialists, and Communists, to avoid any altercations.⁴⁸ At the same time, pro-Franco supporters in Britain called for the immediate repatriation of the children, particularly after the fall of Bilbao on June 19, 1937.⁴⁹ The Basque Children's Repatriation Committee (BCRC), a pro-Franco group chaired by the right-wing Arthur Wellesley, fifth Duke of Wellington, formed in 1937 specifically to exert political pressure and return the children to Spain.⁵⁰ Antonio Masaeda, head of Franco's Repatriation Service, also called for the children to come back to Spain. He claimed, "our sacred mission is to recover for God and Spain the souls of these children who have been poisoned for so

---

⁴⁵ Kevin Myers, "Englishness, Identity and Refugee Children in Britain, 1937-1945," Unpublished Thesis, Coventry University (2000): 121-122.

⁴⁶ Myers, "Englishness, Identity and Refugee Children," 125.

⁴⁷ *Tragedy of Civil War: Basque Civil War Refugee Children Arrive at Southampton* (1937), British Pathé.

⁴⁸ Yvonne Cloud, *The Basque Children in England: An Account of Their Life at Stoneham Camp* (London,
Victor Gollancz, 1937), 52.

⁴⁹ See *The Tablet,* May 22, 1937, 728, and *New Statesman and Review,* May 24, 1937, 1.

⁵⁰ The Duke of Wellington was the Chairman of the Basque Children's Repatriation Committee. Franco also demanded the children be returned to Spain. See Bell, *Only for Three Months,* 15. This was part of growing right-wing politics in Britain. See Matthew Worley, *Oswald Mosley, and the New Party* (London: Palgrave Macmillan, 2010).

many years by anti-Catholic and anti-patriotic ideas."[51] In other words, the children belonged to Spain, where the correct environment for malleable and educable children could create patriotic future citizens.

The first refugee was returned in July 1937.[52] By October, the Repatriation Committee of the NJCSR succumbed to pressure and agreed to allow 800 children to return under the auspices of the Apostolic Delegate at Bilbao, but only if they had documentation from parents supporting their child's return.[53] The Catholic Church in Britain supported repatriation and the children in their care were some of the first to return.[54]

Despite the increased pressure, the NJCSR received letters from some parents begging them not to send their children home. Food was scarce, and safety not guaranteed. The organization maintained that the refugees could not return to Spain without written consent from their parents or family members.[55] When Pope Pius XI asked Catholic officials all over Europe to push for the repatriation of child refugees, pressure increased. The newly appointed Bishop for the Basque region, Francisco Javier Lauzurica, set up a special committee for the protection of minors and encouraged parents to "immediately request the repatriation of all their children," who, he claimed, had been dragged from their homes and "taken in foreign ships far from their parents by these enemies of God and country."[56] Parents were blackmailed into luring their children home. For families with members in prison and sentenced to death, the process was easy. As the NJCSR attempted to assist in the process of repatriation, they discovered that many parents did not want their children to return but were afraid of the consequences of not urging them to come home. Many letters were written by parents under pressure by Spanish authorities. One boy received a letter to say that everything was now normal in Bilbao and that he should return to join the Black Arrow Regiment. The boy knew his father would never want him to join the Black Arrow

---

[51] Quoted in Peter Anderson, "The Struggle over the Evacuation to the United Kingdom and Repatriation of Basque Refugee Children in the Spanish Civil War: Symbols and Souls," *Journal of Contemporary History* 52.2 (2017): 311.
[52] "First War Refugee to Return: Basque Committee to Ensure Child's Safety," *The Nottingham Journal*, July 9, 1937, 16. The refugee was an unnamed girl who went to Ligo, Portugal, not Spain.
[53] "Report of Repatriation Committee" and "Report on Joint Meeting of the National Joint Committee for Spanish Relief and Basque Children's Committee on 28 October 1937," TUC, MRC 292/946/39/53, 2-3.
[54] Michael Alpert, "Humanitarianism and Politics in the British Response to the Spanish Civil War, 1936-9," *European History Quarterly* 14 (1984): 423-40.
[55] "The Basque Children," Letter to the Editor, *The Times*, January 29, 1938.
[56] Irujo, *Expelled from the Motherland*, 61.

Regiment and he excitedly pointed to a small tear in the corner of the letter. This, he explained, was a prearranged signal that the letter was false.[57]

Franco sent Father Gabana to Britain in September 1937 with a list of parents who, he claimed, wanted their children returned.[58] The list was inaccurate and most of the letters from the parents were typed. As few Spanish families had typewriters in their homes, the letters were immediately suspicious. Many of the children did not want to return home and most Basque parents were unable to care for their children in near-famine conditions. When Gabana visited one of the children's colonies, he told them that Franco and Catholic Spain wanted them to return. There was a general uproar, and when Gabana told the children that communists had bombed Guernica, the "indignation of the children was such that the envoy had to leave the colony hurriedly."[59] Nevertheless, by the end of 1938, less than 500 Basque children remained in Britain.[60]

Spanish Niños in the Soviet Union

At the very beginning of the Civil War, the official Soviet press published daily columns about the Spanish conflict as well as occasional campaigns to raise funds to assist the children. This, according to Karl Qualls, personalized the war and kept the plight of Spanish children in the forefront of the Soviet population.[61] The Soviet Central Committee planned to receive Spanish war orphans from early September 1936, shortly after the start of the conflict.[62] The official Soviet press suggested that Spanish children in war zones should be evacuated to the USSR as a humanitarian gesture to the innocents caught up in the conflict.[63] On November 24, 1936, with considerable pomp and ceremony, the Soviets opened the first home for foreign children just outside

---

[57] Irujo, *Expelled from the Motherland*, 62.
[58] Father Gabana claimed that parents wanted 900 children repatriated. See "Letter from Gladwyn Jebb to Betty Arne," "National Joint Committee for Spanish Relief, 30 September 1937," and "Basque Children's Committee Minutes and Documents, 1937-1939," Trades Union Archive, Warwick University, 292/946/39/61, 1-3.
[59]Irujo, *Expelled from the Motherland*, 62.
[60] Many Basque children returned after the fall of Bilbao to Franco's forces in July 1937. See Lagarreta, *Guernica Generation*, 211-221. 470 Basque children remained in Britain until the end of the Second World War. See Bell, *Only for three Months*, 9.
[61] Qualls, *Stalin's Niños*, 22.
[62] Daniel Kowalsky, *Stalin and the Spanish Civil War* (New York: Columbia University Press, 2004), 123-124. See also Josep Puigsech Farràs, "Catalonia in the Face of the USSR: Soviet Intervention in the Spanish Civil War, 1936-9, *Journal of Contemporary History* (2021) 1-23.
[63] Kowalsky, *Stalin and the Spanish Civil War*, 124.

Moscow. It was a renovated nineteenth-century palace, filled with toys and nourishing food.[64]

The child refugees went to the USSR in four separate groups, accompanied by adults who were overwhelmingly women.[65] Unlike the children sent to Britain, those who went to the Soviet Union were children of communist party members and most came from the working-class industrial areas of Asturias and País Vasco. All the children were supposed to be aged between five and fifteen years, but some were as young as three.[66] The official Soviet press depicted the children as both "victims of fascism" and "little heroes."[67] Unlike the press coverage in Britain, the children were not portrayed as passive or apolitical—they were anti-fascist heroes. The refugees arrived in the USSR in four groups, the first shortly after the start of the Civil War. Unlike the last-minute preparations for the refugee children in Britain, Soviet authorities planned carefully and very publicly for the children and used state money for their care. David Kowalsky argues that the Soviet Union used the Spanish children very successfully as propaganda. The very public relief efforts and fundraising for the refugees served to unite the Soviet population and divert attention from Stalin's military purges.[68] Soviet international humanitarianism was meticulously choreographed and carefully reported, elevating the USSR's image internationally. Kowalsky claims that in "general, foreign reception of the Kremlin's official version of the evacuees' upbringing was strikingly uncritical, even naïve."[69]

When a group of 1,610 Spanish children arrived in Leningrad from Bilbao on June 11, 1937, just days before the port fell to Nationalist forces, they were met with an enthusiastic welcome by thousands of Soviet well-wishers: "Soviet Pioneer children stood by carrying flowers, flags, and other gifts for the sea-weary youngsters."[70] There was patriotic music and singing. One child claimed the whole experience was "like reaching paradise after being in hell."[71] Enrique Undiano wrote home from Leningrad, "the Pioneers met us at the door with a band and flags and for two hours we marched with the Soviet

---

[64] There were five foreign children's homes in Moscow, Krasnovidov, Numovski, Pravda, and Petrovska. Other children were cared for in Leningrad, Crimea, and other parts of Ukraine. See Xabier Irujo, *Expelled from the Motherland*, 60.

[65] Karl D. Qualls, *Stalin's Niños: Educating Spanish Civil War Refugee Children in the Soviet Union, 1937-1951* (Toronto: University of Toronto Press, 2020), 18.

[66] Ibid.

[67] Kowalsky, *Stalin and the Spanish Civil War*, 124.

[68] Kowalsky, *Stalin and the Spanish Civil War*, 150-151.

[69] Ibid,147.

[70] Ibid, 129.

[71] Juan Rodriguez Ania, quoted in Kowalsky, *Stalin and the Spanish Civil War*, 129.

insignia on our sleeves."[72] Angeles Perez wrote excitedly about the music and the large Soviet flags, and the armbands given to the children by the "red guard."[73]

From Leningrad, most of the children took a fourteen-hour train journey to pioneer camps near Odessa in the Crimea where they were given toys and fed with large amounts of nutritious food and pampered by nurses, teachers and caring individuals who had learned Spanish in advance to supervise and assist the children to settle. Alfonso Ibañez Cobos wrote home about the food: "when we arrived they gave us soup then chicken and sweets. Later we had fried potatoes, more soup and chocolate and coffee."[74] Pilar Alvares wrote from Artek in the Ukraine about the pioneer camp: "Artek is situated on the black sea and what I really like is the happiness when we have bonfires on the beach."[75] The children only expected to be in the Soviet Union for a few months, and the excitement and appreciation in their letters home perhaps reflect this. The Soviet Union felt like a vacation destination.

Later in September, two more ships arrived in Leningrad with another 1,061 children. The journeys lasted over a week. The ordeal of evacuation and the "arduous journey across rough seas patrolled by German submarines made landfall in a peaceful city a pleasant change for many of the children."[76] Yet for one refugee, Arturo, the voyage was miserable. He wrote, the "conditions on the Chinese boat were horrible. We were all in the ship's hold vomiting. To eat we were always given rice and the rats in the ship were as big as cats."[77] On arrival, the children were taken for baths and issued new clothes and shoes. While many of the children wrote home happily about their crisp, new uniforms, others were distressed when their old familiar clothes were taken away. Their clothes and meagre possessions, as Qualls argues, were "sometimes the children's only tangible connection to home."[78] Yet most of the refugees appeared happy to receive gifts and attention. Julianna wrote to her family that when they arrived, "we were given chocolate cakes and many gifts. Then

---

[72] Enrique Undiano, letter from Odessa, quoted in ibid, 111.
[73] Angeles Perez, letter from Moscow, quoted in ibid, 127.
[74] Alfonso Ibañez Cobos, quoted in ibid, 107.
[75] Pilar Alvares, quoted in ibid, 124.
[76] Qualls, *Stalin's Niños*, 24.
[77] Arturo, quoted in "Immaculada Colomina Limonero," *Dos patrias, tres mil destinos Vida y exilio de los niños de la guerra de España refugiados en la Unión Sovietica* (Madrid: Ediciones Cinca, 2010), 25.
[78] Qualls, *Stalin's Niños*, 32.

we were taken to a room full of toys. There we undressed and bathed then doctors came and reviewed us."[79]

Many of the children were malnourished and sick. Children with infectious diseases like tuberculosis or rheumatic fever (the result of untreated scarlet fever or strep throat), were separated from the others and sent to sanatoria. By August 1937, 1,053 of the 1,498 niños in the Soviet Union were in sanatoria. The trauma of war, poor nutrition and separation from families was reflected in the refugees' health. Their medical treatment and care were paid for by the Soviet authorities. Isidro San Baudelio Echevarría wrote happily to his family about the medical treatment: "We are well in a sanatorium and they treat us very well, don't think about me because I am very content here and am getting fat from the butter because at breakfast they feed us bread with butter and cheese and coffee with milk or coco and rice with milk I cannot tell you all the things we have been given."[80]

The Soviets established special boarding schools for the Spanish children to be educated in the struggle against fascism. In the homes for foreign children, the children spoke Spanish, and lived with other Spaniards. The children's education followed the Spanish model with the exception that they learned Russian as a second language. From the very first, the children were educated in Soviet ideology. As Qualls claims, the Soviets saw the children as the future builders of a new communist Spain.[81] Unlike the children in Britain, those in the Soviet Union did not receive religious instruction from Catholic priests. Rather, they were taught that the Church and religion were part of the system of oppression. When Soviet teachers removed crucifixes, prayer books, and other religious items, this caused misery and grief for children whose communist families continued to maintain their Catholic faith. As one child recalled, "We missed everything... we missed our homeland, we missed our parents, we missed our religion, we missed a Spanish education, we missed everything because we were very little."[82]

The Soviet Union produced two films about the Spanish children, *Spanish Children in the USSR* (1937), prepared for the domestic market, and *New Friends* (1937), screened only in the Spanish Republic. Both films showed

---

[79] Julianna, quoted in ibid, 27.
[80] Isidro San Baudelio Echevarría, quoted in Enrique Zafra, *Los Niños Españoles Evacuados*, 107.
[81] Qualls, *Stalin's Niños*, 38.
[82] Quoted in Karl Quall, "Defining the Ideal Soviet Childhood: Reportage About Child Refugees from Spain as Didactic Literature," in *War and Childhood in the Era of the Two World Wars*, eds. Mischa Honeck and James Marten (Cambridge: Cambridge University Press, 2019), 71-86: 75.

footage of the carnage of war in Spain, the enthusiastic reception of the Spanish children, and finally, their ecstatic faces in the impressive accommodations, surrounded by toys. Unlike the films produced by Britain, these were not fundraising films—they were Soviet propaganda. One notable difference is that Soviet symbols and flags are part of the domestic film but are absent from the film screened in Republican Spain. Indeed, as Kowalsky notes, all Soviet films destined for Spain were devoid of references to the USSR to prevent the perception of Soviet interference in Spain.[83]

As part of their education and to learn about the USSR, the refugees were taken on excursions and learned speeches made by Lenin and Stalin. Pilar Alvares wrote from Moscow on January 13, 1938, "In Moscow we visited Lenin's mausoleum, a building that I liked very much. But more, I liked reading the speeches that Comrade Lenin gave."[84] José Fernández Sánchez also wrote from Moscow, "The monuments that I most like are the statue of Lenin in Red Square showing all the great power of the USSR. I also very much like the Kremlin, the Lenin Mausoleum and the Metro."[85] Others, like Enrique Undiano, wrote of his amazement at seeing women drivers of electric trams, both of which were very foreign to the twelve-year-old.[86] Indeed, the metro, trams, railroads, and airplanes amazed the children and encouraged them to consider engineering and other careers they had previously not known. The Spanish children were also invited to join the Young Pioneers and to participate in processions. They were made to feel part of something bigger in the Soviet Union and to expand their ideas for the future.

Unlike the refugees in Britain, Pope Pius XI and the Catholic Church had no way to pressure the Soviet leadership to return the children to Spain. At the end of March 1939, it became clear that Franco had won the war. The Spanish children remained in their boarding schools, but the educational system shifted to the Soviet model. They were no longer seen as foreign children. They were now future Soviet adults. When Nazi Germany invaded the Soviet Union on July 22, 1941, as the troops moved on Moscow, the Spanish children were quickly evacuated east. The new locations had not been prepared and lacked heating fuel, food, beds, and teaching supplies. The adults caring for the children left and moved into wartime production and military roles. The gracious living conditions and luxurious food supplies changed to resemble those of the Soviet population as it mobilized for war. The Spaniards now

---

[83] David Kowalsky, "The Soviet Cinematic Offensive in the Spanish Civil war," *Film History* 19 (2007) 7-19.
[84] Zafra, Crego, and Heredia, *Los Niños Españoles*, 123.
[85] Ibid, 127.
[86] Kralls, "Ideal Soviet Childhood," 79.

faced the same hardships, food shortages, and rationing as the Soviets throughout the war and the years beyond.[87]

Franco remained in power until his death in 1975. In 1956, Franco and the Soviet leadership reached an agreement to return the now-adult exiles to Spain. After almost twenty years in the USSR, many decided to remain in the USSR for their careers, families, or because they had no family left in Spain. Those who did return to Spain were suspected of being communists and were constantly under surveillance by Franco's secret police. Some were eventually forced back to the Soviet Union.[88]

Conclusion

Neither Britain nor the Soviet Union were officially involved in the Spanish Civil War. Nevertheless, both countries (and others) accepted child refugees from Spain as a humanitarian gesture in 1937 following the destruction of Guernica. The politics behind the international humanitarianism contrasted sharply, as did the planning, funding and care given to the children. In both instances, those involved in the care of the children understood their role as preserving the life of a vulnerable population. Yet, while the British went to great lengths to maintain the children as apolitical, the Soviets celebrated them as heroes in the fight against fascism. Their reception in the two countries reflected these ideas. In Britain, everything appeared last-minute, haphazard, and dependent on volunteers and private fundraising. The children's stay was meant to be temporary. The reception of Spanish children in the Soviet Union, on the other hand, was planned as part of a charm offensive to the Soviet people and the international community. The Spanish children became a useful propaganda tool to deflect attention from the Stalinist purges of the 1930s. At the same time, the children were valued, nurtured, and educated to return to create a Soviet-style Spain. When it was apparent that Franco would not be toppled anytime soon, the children in the Soviet Union were educated to become useful and loyal members of the USSR.

---

[87] Karl Qualls, "From Ninos to Soviets? Raising Spanish Refugee Children in House No. 1, 1937-1951," *Dickinson College Faculty Publications,* Paper 43 (2014).
[88] Irujo, *Expelled from the Motherland,* 64.

Chapter 7

One with the Wounded: American Nurses in the Spanish Civil War

Gina Benavidez
University of New Mexico

Abstract: This chapter explores the identities, values, and actions of American women in the Spanish Civil War. Overlooked in the plethora of histories of the (mostly) male Abraham Lincoln Brigade, the six dozen women who risked their lives in Spain to contribute towards the fight against fascism deserve to have their stories told. As the Spanish Civil War broke out and Franco generated outright support from Italy and Germany, Spain became the battleground between fascism and democracy. Thousands of volunteers made their way to Spain through the Communist-organized International Brigades or other organizations, including nearly three thousand American men and women. Most women worked as nurses, some as translators, and even one as an ambulance driver, both on and behind the front lines. Featured are Salaria Kee, one of the few African-American nurses to travel to Spain, Lini De Vries, who witnessed the Battle of Jarama firsthand, and Fredericka Martin, chief nurse of the American Medical Bureau. This chapter seeks to bring the experiences of these women and others to the foreground and place them firmly in the context of making history alongside their male counterparts.

Keywords: Spanish Civil War, International Brigades, American Medical Bureau, Salaria Key, Lini De Vries, Fredericka Martin, Nurses, Battle of Jarama, fascism, democracy, communist

***

In February 1937, in a schoolhouse-turned-hospital in Romeral, Spain, over two hundred wounded men lay on the floor on makeshift mattresses and stretchers. Ambulances had transported them to the hospital from a nearby battle. The air was filled with the sound of patients moaning in pain while doctors and nurses worked forty hours straight to keep them alive, administering anesthesia for surgery, removing bullet shards and fragments, and tending to gaping wounds. Watching her patients shudder in fear and pain whenever they heard planes overhead, American nurse Lini Fuhr felt nothing but revulsion: "I hated what I saw and the forces responsible for this suffering, anguish, and death," she wrote. "I hated the hand grenades, the shrapnel, the dumdum bullets, the machine guns, the mortar shells. I hated seeing the bleeding wounds, the living wounded, and the dead. A part of me died with everyone who fell. The wounded became a part of me."[1]

That night in particular burned into the memories of the American medical personnel. They had arrived in Spain just a few weeks earlier to offer their skills to the Spanish Republic as volunteers. The Republic, a democratically elected coalition government called the Popular Front, had been fighting a bitter civil war since a group of military generals had attempted a coup in July of the previous year. The war was tearing Spain in half as the liberal, progressive Republicans who backed the Spanish government fought the conservative, traditionalist Nationalists who supported the military.

The latter were the forces responsible for Fuhr's hatred and the wounded men. By the end of 1937, three thousand Americans had volunteered to go to Spain.[2] Some went to fight; others - doctors, nurses, and medical staff - offered to take care of the Republican wounded alongside the International Brigades organized by the Soviet Communist International (Comintern). Most of the volunteers were motivated by idealism: they believed that fascism had to be stopped in Spain to prevent a greater European conflict.

One such idealist, Lini Fuhr, was among the few American women to use her vocation as a volunteer in Spain. This chapter is about how Fuhr and other nurses who traveled to Spain with the American Medical Bureau in the spring of 1937 utilized their professional identities for transnational political activism. It contributes to current research that broadens understandings of women's political contributions between 1920 and the 1960s by recovering lost narratives of their work in the public sphere.[3] Given the historical prominence of suffrage in 1920 and the "second wave" in the 1960s, it is understandable that the intervening years are lesser explored by historians of feminist politics. Yet it

---

[1] Lini Fuhr, *Up from the Cellar* (Minneapolis, MN: Vanilla Press, 1979), 208.
[2] Giles Tremlett, *International Brigades: Fascism, Freedom and the Spanish Civil War* (London: Bloomsbury Publishing, 2020), 15, Kindle edition.
[3] Mary Trigg, *Feminism as Life's Work: Four Modern American Women through Two World Wars* (Rutgers University Press, 2014); Anya Jabour, *Sophonisba Breckinridge: Championing Women's Activism in Modern America* (Champaign, IL: University of Illinois Press, 2019); Martha Jones, *Vanguard: How Black Women Broke Barriers, Won the Vote, and Insisted on Equality for All* (New York: Basic Books, 2020).

was during the interwar years that welfare and public health movements, including nursing, emerged in the U.S. alongside more overtly radical activism for labor reform and women's reproductive health.[4]

Nursing provided American women the skills for a career that facilitated their participation in the defense of democracy outside their own national borders, in ways that recent scholarship has only begun to uncover. It soon became a recognized and respectable profession, giving women a unique perspective and position that they could use to advocate for the greater good. In addition, nursing provided not only an income to many young women but also a means to overcome working-class status and immigrant, racial and ethnic inequalities.[5] This chapter examines how three volunteer nurses were motivated to use their professional agency as a political tool. It posits that nursing provided a path to post-suffrage activism by providing women with firsthand experience of an international conflict in which their government refused to intervene.

Background to the Civil War

The civil war in Spain quickly escalated into a transnational conflict when the Nationalists, led by General Francisco Franco, requested and received assistance from Italy's Benito Mussolini and Germany's Adolph Hitler. Both recognized the opportunity to strengthen a fascist-leaning axis in Western Europe if Franco were to win.[6] Fascism, an ultra-nationalistic right-wing ideology that originated in Italy in the early 1920s, was also reflected in Hitler's National Socialist Party. Defined by brutal oppression and authoritarian dictatorship, fascism's insistence on persecuting minorities was cause for alarm across Europe.

---

[4] Fuhr, *Up from the Cellar*; Jabour, *Sophonisba Breckenridge*; Joan Roberts and Thetis Group, *Feminism and Nursing: An Historical Perspective on Power, Status, and Political Activism in the Nursing Profession* (Westport, CT: Praeger Publishing, 1995); and Barbara Melosh, "The Physician's Hand: Work Culture and Conflict" *in American Nursing* (Philadelphia: Temple University Press, 1982).

[5] For more on the history of American nursing, see Deborah Judd, Kathleen Sitzman, and G. Megan Davis, *A History of American Nursing: Trends and Eras* (Sunbury, MA: Jones and Bartlett Publishers, 2010); Susan M. Reverby, *Ordered to Care: The Dilemma of American Nursing, 1850-1945* (New York: Cambridge University Press, 1987); Roberts and Group, *Feminism and Nursing*); and Melosh, *"The Physician's Hand."*

[6] Robert Whealey, *Hitler and Spain: The Nazi Role in the Spanish Civil War, 1936-1939* (Lexington: University Press of Kentucky, 1989),7; Martin Clark, *Mussolini* (New York: Routledge, 2014), 230-1. See also George Esenwein and Adrian Shubert, *The Spanish Civil War in Context, 1931-1939* (London: Longman, 1995).

Republican Spain looked for help to counter the growing international alliance but with little luck. Great Britain's Parliament, more fearful of a Popular Front coalition government (which included Socialists and Communists) than a fascist Spain, refused to send arms.[7] France, on the other hand, with its recently elected Popular Front government, faced internal conflict: Prime Minister León Blum wanted to aid Spain, but the conservative French cabinet did not.[8] In September 1936, Britain hosted an international Non-Intervention Conference, where most European countries signed their declaration of neutrality. The agreement had little effect. There was no manner of enforcing the agreement or punishing violators. Nevertheless, it did prevent the Republic from receiving official foreign assistance.[9] The United States was not a signatory of the Non-Intervention Agreement, but the government also chose to maintain a policy of neutrality in the Spanish Civil War.[10]

President Franklin Roosevelt, "widely rumored to be sympathetic to the Republic," faced mixed popular support. In December 1936, he chose to approve Congress's declaration of a Spanish embargo, for which there was only one dissenting vote from the Senate and House combined.[11] Unlike Congress, the American public's response was divided, but more favorable toward the Republicans.[12] News coverage of the war was extensive but highly biased. Conservative support for the Nationalists emphasized the danger the "red" (Communist) Republican forces would pose if they won in Spain, while supporters of the Republic warned of the spread of fascism across Europe if Franco won.

The Soviet Union ultimately became the Republicans' most valuable ally by sending military equipment in exchange for Spanish gold and organizing the Comintern's International Brigades.[13] The Brigades were a fighting force composed of over thirty-five thousand international volunteers from nearly fifty countries that served as a vital boost of morale and manpower for the

---

[7] Anthony Beevor, *Battle for Spain* (New York: Penguin Books, 1982), 133.
[8] Whealey, *Hitler and Spain*, 15.
[9] Judith Keene, *Fighting for Franco: International Volunteers in Nationalist Spain during the Spanish Civil War, 1936-1939* (New York: Leicester University Press, 2001), 33-4.
[10] Beevor, *Battle for Spain*, 287.
[11] Mark Falcoff and Fredrick B. Pike, *The Spanish Civil War, 1936-39: American Hemispheric Perspectives* (Lincoln: University of Nebraska Press, 1982), 172.
[12] In February 1937 the public opinion Gallup Polls reported that 65 percent of Americans favored the Republican side, but by February 1938, the percentage increased to 75 percent. See "American Institute of Public Opinion-Surveys, 1938-1939," The Public Opinion Quarterly 3.4 (1939): 581–607.
[13] Ibid., 22.

Republicans.[14] Mexico's president Lázaro Cárdenas and his administration also sent twenty thousand rifles and cartridges in support of the Spanish Republic.[15]

The International Brigades proved to be an incredible force for the Republicans. By the end of 1937, there were over thirty thousand recruits, including nearly three thousand Americans.[16] The literature on the American Abraham Lincoln brigade focuses largely on male participation.[17] In the past few decades, scholars have begun to address the role of women in the conflict.[18] However, publications that include specific examples of American women volunteers are brief and scarce.[19] By drawing on published letters and memoirs, archival material, newspaper accounts, and other sources, this

---

[14] This estimated figure is based on Giles Tremlett's most recent survey of the International Brigades. Though the number of volunteers has varied in the past, usually settling around 40,000, Tremlett has chosen a more conservative number based on likely errors in record-keeping in the 1930s. Tremlett, *International Brigades*, 11.

[15] Mario Ojeda Revah, *Mexico and the Spanish Civil War: Domestic Politics and the Republican Cause* (Eastbourne: Sussex Academic Press, 2015), 75.

[16] Tremlett, *International Brigades*, 15.

[17] Peter N. Carroll, *The Odyssey of the Abraham Lincoln Brigade: Americans in the Spanish Civil War* (Stanford University Press, 1994); Arthur Landis, *Death in the Olive Groves: American Volunteers in the Spanish Civil War 1936-1939* (Paragon House, 1988) Arthur Landis, *The Abraham Lincoln Brigade a Definitive History of the American Volunteers Who Fought for the Spanish Republic 1936-1939* (Citadel, 1967). On the International Brigades, see Michael Jackson, *Fallen Sparrows: The International Brigades in the Spanish Civil War* (American Philosophical Society, 1994); Richard Baxell, Angela Jackson and Jim Jump, eds. *Antifascistas: British & Irish Volunteers in the Spanish Civil War* (London: Lawrence & Wishart, 2010); Richard Baxell, *British Volunteers in the Spanish Civil War: The British Battalion in the International Brigades 1936-1939* (Barcelona: Warren & Pell, 2007).

[18] See, for example, Roseanna Webster, "'A Spanish Housewife is Your Next Door Neighbour': British Women and the Spanish Civil War," *Gender & History*, 27:2 (August 2015) 397-416; Angela Jackson, *British Women in the Spanish Civil War* (London: Routledge, 2002); Frances Lannon, "Women and Images of Women in the Spanish Civil War," *Transactions of the Royal Historical Society* 6 (1991) 213-28; Mary Nash, *Defying Male Civilization: Women in the Spanish Civil War* (Denver: Arden Press, 1995); and Mary Nash, "Women in War: *Milicianas* and Armed Combat in Revolutionary Spain, 1936-1939," *International History Review* 15 (1993) 269-82.

[19] See Martin F. Shapiro, "Medical Aid to the Spanish Republic during the Civil War (1936-1939)," *Annals of Internal Medicine* 97 (1982); Frances Patai, "Heroines of the Good Fight: Testimonies of U.S. Volunteer Nurses in the Spanish Civil War, 1936-1939," *Nursing History Review* 3 (1995); Walter J. Lear, "American Medical Support for Spanish Democracy, 1936-1938," in *Comrades in Health: U.S. Health Internationalists, Abroad and at Home*, eds. Theodore M. Brown and Anne-Emanuelle Birn (Rutgers University Press, 2013); Carmen Cañete Quesada, "Salaria Kea and the Spanish Civil War: Memoirs of a Negro Nurse in Republican Spain," in *Black USA and Spain: Shared Memories in the 20th Century*, ed. Rosalía Cornejo-Parriego (New York: Routledge, 2020).

chapter illuminates these women's stories and documents their journey across Republican Spain. By focusing on the volunteers and their experiences in Spain, it suggests that nurses used their professional identities as leverage for political activism on the international stage.

Medical Bureau for Aid to Spanish Democracy

The Comintern began organizing volunteer units for the International Brigades in the fall of 1936. A group of New York City-based doctors with Communist Party affiliations formed an organization specifically devoted to the Spanish Republic's medical needs alongside these units.[20] By early November, the physicians formed the Medical Bureau for Aid to Spanish Democracy, or the American Medical Bureau.[21] Dr. Edward K. Barsky, surgeon at Beth Israel Hospital, was the head physician and Fredericka Martin, the head nurse of the unit. They began a recruitment drive and fundraising efforts to gather aid, medical supplies, and ambulances to go with them to Spain.

One recruit was Helen Freeman, a nurse from a middle-class Jewish family in New York, orphaned at a young age and raised by her aunt. Freeman recalls that her aunt and uncle, both Russian immigrants, were involved in the American Socialist movement and advocated for union organization. After graduating as a nurse from the Brooklyn Jewish Hospital, Freeman worked there for a year before volunteering for Spain. Her decision to go to Spain came after she attended a meeting at the New School in Manhattan to recruit medical personnel to volunteer for Spanish Democracy in late 1936. Many decades later, in an interview, Freeman said she believed her motives were a mixture of political and humanitarian ideals: "We knew this is [was] something we needed and wanted to do – that these people were in dire need of medical help."[22] Freeman was in good company, traveling with other volunteers from the Brooklyn Jewish Hospital who had similar backgrounds and knew each other. Freeman described her group as "all very young, idealistic, beginning to become politically aware."[23]

This description, as well as Freeman's upbringing, reflect the demographics of her fellow nurses in Spain, nearly fifty in total. Most of the women were

---

[20] Lear, *Comrades in Health*, 66.
[21] In total, the American Medical Bureau would send nearly 150 medical personnel to Spain, including "almost fifty nurses, some thirty physicians, and approximately sixty others." Lear, *Comrades in Health*, 67-8.
[22] Helen Freeman interview with Frances Patai, August 13, 1991, Frances Patai Papers, ALBA.131, Box 1, Folder 18, Tamiment Library/Robert F. Wagner Labor Archives, Elmer Holmes Bobst Library, New York University Libraries.
[23] Ibid.

young, trained graduates of nursing school with at least a few years of nursing experience - some with ten to fifteen years.[24] Many had working-class backgrounds, came from immigrant families (typically from Eastern Europe or Russia), and resided in the New York City metro area. About a quarter of the nurses were members of the Communist Party, and little over half were Jewish. Frances Patai, who interviewed a number of the nurses personally in the 1990s, believes that the women "were not unmindful of the fact that Jews had been singled out as recent victims of Nazism. Their words reveal that their history as an oppressed group informed their social conscience to fight against fascism because it exploited and repressed all people."[25] The men who joined the Abraham Lincoln Battalion tended to match this idealism and shared similar motivations.

There were also new trends in Progressive-era health care during this time. Coming from working-class backgrounds and training in urban hospital settings, it is likely that the nurses were also inspired by the early twentieth-century public health movement, which embodied innovative, radical, political ideas, as well as the tumult of the Great Depression.[26] Some, like Fuhr, had worked in public health, settlement houses, or as social workers, seeing firsthand the need for social reform, community programs, and health education.[27] The diverse experiences and identities of these women converged on their ideological and political desire to help create a better world by joining like-minded volunteers to assist in Spain. By mid-January, the American Medical Bureau was ready to send the first unit.

Journey to Spain

The first few weeks of the journey were filled with excitement, anticipation, and eagerness to begin work. On January 16, 1937, the ocean liner *Ile de France* left New York City, carrying nearly one hundred volunteers for Spain. Of these, sixteen formed the first American surgical unit and ambulance corps for Spain, including Dr. Edward Barsky, Fredericka Martin, Fuhr, and Freeman.[28] Also on board were four ambulances and twelve tons of medical supplies, to establish a

---

[24] Their ages ranged from twenty-one to forty-nine. Patai, "Heroines of the Good Fight," 69.
[25] Patai, "Heroines of the Good Fight," 85.
[26] Patai, "Heroines of the Good Fight," 83.
[27] For more on the public health reform movement within the history of American nursing, see Judd, Sitzman, and Davis, *A History of American Nursing*, 97-99 and Melosh, *"The Physician's Hand,"* 113-157.
[28] "Hospital Group Sails for Spain: Sixteen in Party Leave on the Liner," *New York Times*, January 17, 1937.

base American hospital on the Spanish front. Fuhr remembers staying on deck until the Statue of Liberty and American shores had disappeared. Then she focused her attention on the sound of the waves and "the fact that I was going to Spain to play my little part toward shaping a decent world."[29]

This was not Fuhr's first time seeing the Statue of Liberty. The daughter of Dutch immigrants, Fuhr last visited her mother's family in Holland in 1933, where she developed an uneasy sense of the imminent danger of fascism in Europe. As a young teenager, Fuhr worked in New Jersey's silk mills to help support the family instead of attending high school. Fuhr eventually found a job that allowed her to work as a telephone operator at night and attend nurse training during the day at New Rochelle Hospital.[30] After a brief marriage that resulted in both early widowhood and the birth of her daughter, Fuhr began work as a part-time visiting nurse in the mornings while attending high school classes in the afternoons to pursue a career in public health nursing.[31] Fuhr earned her degree and worked full-time to save money and enter Columbia's Teachers College in the fall of 1933. In Manhattan, she joined the League Against War and Fascism and the Communist Party. Fuhr believed the Party "met the needs of idealism, or humanism, and met my personal need to work as an idealist/humanist."[32] She continued to study at night while working full time: first with Margaret Sanger and the Birth Control Clinic in Manhattan, then as a social worker for the Hospital of Joint Disease.[33] When Fuhr heard the need for medical personnel in Spain, she first tried to convince other nurses to go. When none agreed, Fuhr volunteered to go with the first unit of the American Medical Bureau in January 1937. Though she felt that she had no right to go and leave her young daughter in the care of family, she also felt she "*had* to go!"[34] A week later, she left for Spain.

After seven days at sea, the ship arrived in Le Havre, France. The French greeted the Americans with smiles and cheers. The Popular Front government hosted a welcome dinner and overnight stay in Le Havre, then sent them to Paris the following day.[35] After spending three days in Paris attending a reception in their honor and purchasing additional supplies, the unit crossed the Pyrenees Mountains to reach Port Bou, Spain, a small town located along the French-Spanish border. Nurse Toby Jensky recalls that "the scenery on the

---

[29] Fuhr, *Up from the Cellar*, 190.
[30] Fuhr, *Up from the Cellar*, 65.
[31] Ibid., 127.
[32] Ibid., 157.
[33] Ibid., 163; 170.
[34] Ibid., 174.
[35] Fuhr, *Up from the Cellar*, 191-2.

way down was beyond words or descriptions – snow capped [sic] mountains – sparkling sea (Mediterranean) and gay colored grounds and villages."[36] After a joyful reception in Port Bou, the Republican government then escorted the unit to Barcelona in luxury cars.[37]

Barcelona

As the first American medical group to arrive in the buzzing city of Barcelona, the Spanish people treated the unit "almost as saviors." [38] The group spent their days marveling at Spain's beauty and lamenting the shadow Franco's war cast over the glorious city. The air was palpable with the cosmopolitan atmosphere of revolutionaries, foreign volunteers and journalists, and war refugees. The Republican government lavished the volunteers with attention, tours of the city and a welcome reception at the palace of Catalonian President Luis Companys.[39] The group spent five days at the Hotel Oriente, attended official events and dances, went sightseeing, and met other members of the International Brigade on leave.[40] In a letter home describing these early days, lab technician Rose Freed wrote, "what sufferings these poor people must have endured to display such gratefulness towards our puny aid!"[41] This suffering, or the realities of the war raging further in Spain's interior, was evident among the fringes of the city's glitz and glamor, as refugees poured in and almost tripled Barcelona's population of 1.5 million.[42] Still, the North and Eastern parts of Spain remained Basque and Republican strongholds that had not seen much fighting at that point in the war.[43]

The beautiful coastal climate, the warm welcomes, and the revolutionary spirit of the Spaniards infused the volunteers with a heightened desire to get to work.[44] Mildred Rackley noted that France, England, Scotland, Belgium, Sweden, Switzerland, and Canada had already sent vast numbers of medical personnel and equipment into Republican Spain despite the International

---

[36] Ray Harris to Sally, Albacete, February 27, 1937, in *From Spanish Trenches: Recent Letters from Spain,* ed. Marcel Acier (New York: Modern Age Books, 1937), 14.
[37] Harris to Sally, Albacete, February 27, 1937, 15.
[38] Rose Freed to Lou, Barcelona, January 31, 1937, in *From A Hospital in Spain,* ed. Medical Bureau to Aid Spanish Democracy (New York, 1937), 10.
[39] Hal Clark, "Lini Fuhr Is Back from Spain Where Fascists Bomb Hospitals," *Daily Worker,* New York, May 20, 1937.
[40] Harris to Sally, Albacete, February 27, 1937, 15.
[41] Freed to Lou, Barcelona, January 31, 1937, 10.
[42] Ibid.
[43] The Basque region was a semi-autonomous ethnic community and province in northern Spain that remained loyal to the Republican government.
[44] Ibid.

Agreement. "And now that we are here," she continued in a letter home, "all eyes are turned to America to see what she will do. We cannot disappoint them; the need is too great."[45] The volunteers recognized that they represented their country, if not official U.S. policy, as they provided aid and support to the Spanish Republic.

The volunteers traveled south to Valencia, the temporary capital of Republican Spain, where the government again "besieged" them with countless official receptions and welcomes.[46] In Valencia, however, there "the streets were filled with the reality of wounded and refugees from Madrid." [47] The medical unit was impatient to get to the front. In Valencia they met Dr. Norman Bethune, a Canadian doctor who later became famous for his mobile blood unit that allowed doctors to collect, bottle and deliver blood to transfuse immediately on the front lines.[48] They also experienced their first air raid and overnight bombing of the city and harbor.

From Valencia, the unit moved closer to the Madrid front. Gone were the comfortable touring cars and fancy receptions as they drove further inland and up to the central plains.[49] Fuhr describes the trip: "...we drove around huge bomb craters, as Albacete loomed ahead of us. As we entered the town, we saw walls half-standing, with bits of furniture hanging out defying gravity. Here there were more bomb craters that were fantastic and frightening."[50] The Americans had reached Albacete, the headquarters of the International Brigades. There they waited to find a suitable building for use as their front hospital. As the headquarters and supply depot for the Brigades, Albacete was a crossroads of nationalities, languages, and "nondescript clothing that passed as uniforms" for some of the Brigades members.[51] Brigades leaders taught the volunteers how to jump from cars and lie as low as possible if their ambulances were attacked.[52]

---

[45] Mildred Rackley to Medical Bureau to Aid Spanish Democracy, Port-Bou, Spain, January 1937, in *From A Hospital in Spain*, ed. Medical Bureau to Aid Spanish Democracy (New York, 1937), 6.
[46] Mildred Rackley to Bobbie, Valencia, February 8, 1937, in Acier, 11.
[47] Fuhr, *Up from the Cellar*, 197.
[48] Fuhr, *Up from the Cellar*, 198; Harris to Sally, Albacete, February 27, 1937, 15.
[49] Harris to Sally, Albacete, February 27, 1937, 15.
[50] Fuhr, *Up from the Cellar*, 200.
[51] Ibid., 202.
[52] Ibid., 203.

After a few days, the Brigades leaders woke the unit in the middle of the night to move all personnel and equipment to their new hospital location.[53] The team progressed towards the front lines in total darkness. After a long harrowing night of moving while on the lookout for enemy planes, including a mistaken stop in a nearby town, the unit arrived at Romeral. The building they were to use was a new schoolhouse, which the villagers had built themselves. The whole village helped prepare the structure for the medical unit: "We watched children and teachers moving out desks, maps and books…They offered it to us with great pride."[54] Nearly one month after their departure from New York, the Americans were ready to set up their first hospital in Spain.

Romeral and the Battle of Jarama

The schoolhouse at Romeral, soon known as the American Hospital, started as a simple two-story building with no electricity, plumbing, running water, or heat.[55] Dr. Barsky gave the medical unit exactly 48 hours to set up the facility in readiness for patients. The unit asked the local mayor for the village's cooperation to help prepare the fifty-bed hospital.[56] The villagers again threw their support behind the operation, working day and night to help the volunteers unload equipment and set up the building. Rackley recalls "we had dozens and dozens of men carrying out school desks and tables, the electricians were wiring the building for lights, the telephone service were installing two telephones…" At the same time, another crew unloaded trucks and opened crates while an "army of women" swept and washed floors.[57]

By the end of the second day, the hospital was ready. The day after patients rapidly arrived.[58] The nearby Battle of Jarama was an unsuccessful Nationalist offensive intended to cut off the road between Valencia and Madrid. The conflict lasted most of February, with heavy losses on both sides.[59] The American men of the Lincoln Battalion had just arrived in Albacete, where the Brigades leaders hurriedly trained them to be sent as reinforcements. The

---

[53] Mildred Rackley to Medical Bureau to Aid Spanish Democracy, Romeral, March 8, 1937, in *Madrid 1937: Letters of the Abraham Lincoln Brigade from the Spanish Civil War*, eds. Cary Nelson and Jefferson Hendricks (New York: Routledge, 1996), 238. See also J. Fyrth, *The Signal Was Spain: The Aid Spain Movement in Britain, 1936-1939* (Palgrave: London, 1986).
[54] Ibid., 205.
[55] Harris to Sally, Albacete, February 27, 1937, 16; Fuhr, *Up from the Cellar*, 205.
[56] Mildred Rackley to Medical Bureau to Aid Spanish Democracy, Albacete, February,1937, in *From a Hospital in Spain*, 12.
[57] Rackley to Medical Bureau, Albacete, [February, 1937], 12.
[58] Ibid.
[59] Beevor, *Battle for Spain*, 208; 214.

battalion bore the brunt of the battle because their inexperienced commander had ordered them into multiple attacks on what became known as Suicide Hill.[60] Some of the wounded came to the hospital at Romeral. Fuhr recalled that she cut through the clothing of boys she had danced with on her way to Spain.[61] By nightfall of the first day, there were nearly two hundred soldiers, many laid on the floor in makeshift beds as the unit stabilized, triaged, and treated patients as best they could. Many were shot through the skull, some through the chest, and many of them had "nasty abdominal perforations."[62] Most needed surgery. One night the electricity gave out in the middle of an operation, requiring Dr. Barsky to remove a shattered kidney by flashlight.[63] The unit worked quickly to treat the men, then, once they were stable, placed them on the ambulance train and sent them to lines further back for convalescence.[64]

The medical unit stayed in Romeral for two weeks after the Battle of Jarama ended, never knowing how many patients would arrive at one time or in what condition. After this initial "baptism by fire," the volunteers had transformed the school building into a functioning, orderly hospital with an unusually low mortality rate, according to Fuhr.[65] There were about fifty local Spaniards working alongside the Americans as drivers, cooks, assistant nurses, stretcher bearers, and launderers.[66] The building included an operating room, a linen room, a pharmacy, two kitchens, a laboratory, at least fifty patient beds on the top floor and three wards' worth of beds on the lower floor.[67]

Interestingly, while the makeshift hospital contained some familiar elements of American hospitals, the social and professional dynamics between the nurses and physicians shifted. Early twentieth-century hospital training required nurses to follow a strict hierarchical protocol that included opening doors for visiting physicians, standing up when they entered the room and maintaining attention in their presence "like soldiers on duty."[68] Looking back on their experience decades later, at least two of the nurses recalled the differences between working with male doctors in the United States and in Spain. While setting up the hospital, Fuhr joyfully remembered watching doctors "as they pushed and hauled like anyone else." This glee of

---

[60] Ibid.
[61] Fuhr, *Up from the Cellar*, 207.
[62] Rackley to Medical Bureau, Albacete, [February, 1937], 13.
[63] Ibid.
[64] Fuhr, *Up from the Cellar*, 208.
[65] Patai, "Heroines of the Good Fight," 90; Fuhr, *Up from the Cellar*, 211.
[66] Rackley to Medical Bureau, Albacete, [February, 1937], 13.
[67] Fredericka Martin to Anna, [Romeral, Spring, 1937], in *From A Hospital in Spain*, 17.
[68] Melosh, *"The Physician's Hand,"* 51.

hers came after years of having to wait on doctors and interns "hand and foot" in a subservient role.[69] Similarly, Freeman recalled that as a female nurse in an American hospital you had to let the doctor enter the elevator in front of you, "because he was God." In Spain, she said "you worked *together* with the doctor who accepted you as a person, with respect."[70] These nurses exercised more autonomy within their practice alongside male physicians compared to the rigid structure of the American medical system. This adjustment in hierarchies and gender identities allowed the Medical Bureau to function efficiently as a team to help their patients in dire circumstances.

Nevertheless, the working conditions at Romeral often proved difficult. Freeman described the makeshift hospital setting as "kind of primitive," as the women experienced intermittent lighting, did their laundry in the river, and made great efforts to keep things clean.[71] Fredericka Martin, the head nurse, displayed great frustration in a letter home about teaching the local Spanish women volunteers how to work as aides alongside the American nurses.[72] Most of the nurses picked up some basic Spanish to aid communication with the locals, but cultural differences between simple details like ironing standards and bedmaking proved difficult for Americans like Martin to see beyond. The nurses frequently implored the recipients of their letters home to send more American personnel and equipment. By mid-March, the Jarama front was secured and the unit was ordered to move closer to the lines to Tarancón, where three base hospitals were already in existence.[73]

Tarancón

Tarancón, roughly sixty kilometers northeast of Romeral, was a brief stop for the medical unit as they searched for another location to set up their next hospital. The American unit had traveled and functioned efficiently as a team in their own hospital for nearly two months. In Tarancón, they encountered a "tower of Babel" of international soldiers, medical personnel, and other front workers. Subject to frequent bombings, the town was the last place to get gasoline before arriving at the fronts near Madrid or Jarama. Lines of up to forty vehicles - trucks, ambulances, and others – waited at the station for gas.[74] There were three International Brigades hospitals within one square block of the gasoline station. Dr. Barsky secured a house, which the unit called

---

[69] Fuhr, *Up from the Cellar*, 206.
[70] Freeman, interview.
[71] Ibid.
[72] Martin to Anna, [Romeral, Spring, 1937], 19.
[73] Fuhr, *Up from the Cellar*, 211.
[74] Ibid., 214.

the American Casa, for the medical unit to eat and sleep together so they could remain a team despite differing assignments among the three hospitals.[75] Lini Fuhr oversaw Hospital No. 3, which she described as a "mess," with "not a window intact" because of recent aerial bombings. She had to put patients two to bed while medical staff of different nationalities attempted to work together and make sense of how to run the hospital. Fuhr's recollections suggest a persistent struggle to maintain order: "It seemed as if everyone wanted to be boss, even we Americans."[76]

Rose Freed worked at all three hospitals as a night charge nurse, giving medications, dressing wounds and doing rounds in the operating room.[77] One night while she was off duty, the Americans were hosting a birthday party for a doctor at the American Casa when they heard the roar of planes. Freed and two other doctors all ran the short distance to the three different hospitals, arriving just in time. Freed remembered, the "the crash – you cannot – never can anyone realize the horror of what seems like the earth opening beneath you – the light of the magnesium flare bomb to see if they struck right – then eight more crashes – then silence, too long, and shrapnel flying in all directions."[78] No Americans were injured. After checking the two other hospitals, Freed returned to Hospital No. 3 and found the Spanish nurses crying silently. "What right had I to be frightened, I who had just tasted what they have long lived through? ...whose fathers, brothers, sweethearts, and husbands died on the battlefields?"[79] She sent them all to bed and took over night duty alone.

In Tarancón, Fuhr often found herself chasing "runaways," patients who had escaped before they were properly discharged, toward vehicles waiting to take them back to the front, and coaxing or scolding them back to the hospital. "I had never heard of soldiers going AWOL toward the front," she wrote, "but these boys from many lands and from the many provinces of Spain wanted to fight, not lay on a hospital bed."[80] These anecdotes reveal a fierce devotion to the antifascist cause that the soldiers and the American nurses believed in. Despite the poor working conditions, the frustrations, the many hours on their feet, and the terror of bombers flying overhead, the nurses felt deeply that they were doing their part "helping these men who are fighting our fight against fascism."[81] Reminiscent of the revulsion that shapes Fuhr's recollections,

---

[75] Ibid., 214; Freed to Lou, Tarancón, March 20, 1937, in *From A Hospital in Spain*, 23.
[76] Fuhr, *Up from the Cellar*, 215.
[77] Freed to Lou, Tarancón, March 20, 1937, 21.
[78] Ibid., 24.
[79] Ibid., 23.
[80] Fuhr, *Up from the Cellar*, 216.
[81] Lini to Ida, Tarancón, March 15, 1937, 30.

Martin also believed that the patients were "a part of us. When they suffer, we suffer and learn to hate more."[82] By healing the sick and wounded soldiers so they could return to the battlefield, the nurses contributed to the struggle for democracy "for the Spanish people and the whole world." There was no doubt that the idealism and hope that had brought the nurses to Spain was strengthened and reinforced by what they saw and experienced by working in the hospitals. Their skills were valuable, needed, and essential.

Shortly after the bombing, Dr. Barsky located two isolated buildings near the front. He planned to use one for medical care and one for convalescence. Another medical unit was on its way from the States, and the Americans intended to integrate the arrival team and use their supplies to help outfit the new locations.[83]

Villa Paz

By the end of March, the medical unit moved to Villa Paz, located along the Madrid-Valencia Road. Villa Paz and its estate, the former summer palace of a member of the royal family, spanned twelve square miles and boasted dense foliage, a creek with waterfalls, a garden, and a swimming pool.[84] The former servants who lived nearby still maintained the palace and grounds. Both the second and third American medical units – leaving New York in mid-March and mid-April, respectively – joined the volunteers at Villa Paz. The team and the new arrivals used the additional equipment to set up a huge ward with over a hundred beds and more in the making.[85] The ward was reportedly so large that Dr. Barsky put up signs on the walls to guide the medical staff.[86]

One of the new arrivals was Salaria Kea, who gained attention and acclamation for her role as the only female African American nurse to volunteer in Spain. [87] Growing up with two brothers in Akron, Ohio, Kea excelled in sports

---

[82] Martin to Anna, Romeral, Spring, 1937, 21.
[83] Fuhr, *Up from the Cellar*, 219.
[84] Adam Hoschchild, *Spain in Our Hearts: Americans in the Spanish Civil War, 1936-1939* (Boston, MA: Houghton Mifflin Harcourt, 2016), 135; Rose Freed to Lou, [Villa Paz], April 20, 1937, in Acier, ed., *From Spanish Trenches*, 27.
[85] Freed to Lou, [Villa Paz], April 20, 1937, 27.
[86] Ibid.
[87] In May 1938, a pamphlet entitled *A Negro Nurse in Republican Spain* was sponsored and published by the Negro Committee to Aid Spain and the American Medical Bureau and North American Committee to Aid Spanish Democracy. This third-person account describes Kea's childhood and experience in Spain. This, alongside a personal memoir housed in the Tamiment Library archives which Carmen Cañete Quesada says has been identified as the source for some of the first-person quotations in *A Negro Nurse*, has proven controversial. Specifically, some of the information does not line up with certain

and school while facing everyday racism. Despite being the valedictorian of her graduating class, three local nursing schools in the Midwest rejected her on account of her race before she was accepted at the Harlem School of Nursing.[88] After graduation, she worked briefly at Sea View Hospital on Staten Island before returning to Harlem Hospital, experiencing difficult working conditions at both. Only four of twenty-six hospitals in New York accepted Black graduate nurses at the time.[89] If hired, these nurses were usually assigned "undesirable tasks in unsafe conditions," such as Kea's duty to oversee tuberculosis patients at Sea View and an understaffed maternity ward at Harlem Hospital.[90] Living and working in Harlem in the 1930s allowed Kea to participate in Black activist-sponsored events such as "lectures and discussions on civic affairs, local, national, and international."[91] In 1936, Kea found an opportunity to volunteer as a nurse to aid victims of the Ohio River Valley flooding. The American Red Cross rejected her, and told Kea that the color of her skin "would make me more trouble than I'd be worth to them."[92] Instead, she volunteered to go to Spain. "It seemed so funny, me being turned down in a democratic country and then allowed to go to a fascist one," she commended in a later interview.[93] Though she was willingly accepted by the American Medical Bureau, her experience in Spain was not free from racial discrimination.

---

perceived historical "truths," resulting in a questioning of the validity of both the pamphlet and Kea's memoirs. As this chapter is intended to be an entry point into the experience of American women in the Spanish Civil War, I focus on secondary sources and newspaper articles that document elements of Kea's life rather than exclusively on primary sources until further research can be done. For more on the controversial nature of these documents and her work on recovering Kea's historical voice as a representative of a highly marginalized group in the 1930s United States, please see Cañete Quesada, "Salaria Kea and the Spanish Civil War: *Memoirs of A Negro Nurse in Republican Spain*," in *Black USA and Spain: Shared Memories in the 20th Century*, by Rosalía Cornejo-Parriego, ed. (New York: Routledge, 2020), 113-33.

[88] "Each letter read 'We have no provision for training colored nurses.'" As quoted in Darlene Clark Hine, *Black Women in White: Racial Conflict and Cooperation in the Nursing Profession 1890-1950* (Bloomington & Indianapolis: Indiana University Press, 1989), 137.

[89] Ibid., 138.

[90] Quesada, "Salaria Kea and the Spanish Civil War," 119.

[91] *A Negro Nurse in Republican Spain,* New York: The Negro Committee to Aid Spain with the Medical Bureau and North American Committee to Aid Spanish Democracy, 1938.

[92] Blake Green, "The Angels of the Last 'Pure War'," February 10, 1977, *San Francisco Chronicle*, 22.

[93] Kea, as in Green "The Angels of the Last 'Pure War,'" 22.

The racial integration of white and black troops in the Abraham Lincoln Battalion, the first of its kind in an American military unit, has long been touted as an example of liberal progressivism. However, recent studies have begun to challenge this image with sources that describe racial tensions and incidents among Americans in Spain.[94] Salaria Kea's experience was no exception. She described at least two incidents of racial prejudice at the hands of her white comrades.[95] At the time, Kea represented a marginalized group of Americans living under Jim Crow laws in the United States who believed fighting fascism would improve the lives of those under oppression, including themselves.[96] This was the perspective shared by Kea and other African Americans who supported the Republic despite the racial tensions present. Kea became a popular figure in Spain, frequently described in glowing terms during her time at Villa Paz by her fellow coworkers and patients alike.[97]

Most of the medical staff's descriptions of Villa Paz consist of its beauty and the camaraderie shared among the staff and patients. Anne Taft wrote how the medical unit had "been able to establish a really beautiful and efficient hospital."[98] Rose Freed shared her memories of one evening in the garden when the nurses, doctors, patients, and Spanish friends were "sitting and listening to the enticing music being played by Victor, our chauffeur, on his electric victrola."[99] Although the bright moonlit night cast a slight shadow of fear "even in the happiest of moments" (by lighting the way for enemy bombers), the medical team remained comforted by the shared camaraderie.[100] Through difficult working conditions and the hardships of war in a foreign country, the women of the American Medical Bureau felt valued and justified in their participation.

Conclusion

Most members of the American Medical Bureau unit stayed in Spain until November 1938, when the Republican government sent all international volunteers home. Lini Fuhr returned to the United States in the summer of 1937 and went on a speaking tour to raise funds for the Republican war effort.[101] Helen Freeman returned home on emergency medical leave after

---

[94] See Quesada, "Salaria Kea and the Spanish Civil War."
[95] Quesada, "Salaria Kea and the Spanish Civil War," 126.
[96] Ibid., 1.
[97] Quesada, "Salaria Kea and the Spanish Civil War," 120.
[98] Anne Taft to T.-, Villa Paz, July 15, 1937, in Nelson and Hendricks, *Madrid 1937*, 249.
[99] Freed to Lou, Villa Paz, April 20, 1937, 28.
[100] Ibid.
[101] Fuhr, *Up from the Cellar*, 233.

suffering a fractured skull and arm in a bombing attack.[102] Salaria Kea was also furloughed home in 1938 after an injury during a bombing raid. She joined activist Thyra J. Edwards on an ambulance tour to raise money and send medical supplies to Spain.[103] Once back in the U.S., many of the volunteers pivoted from nursing to transnational political activism and fundraising. Many of these voices were not acknowledged until, at the height of the McCarthy-era Red Scare, the Federal Bureau of Investigation harassed nurses and other Spanish Civil War volunteers.[104]

American women's participation in the Spanish Civil War offers valuable insight into the antifascist movement of the interwar years. American women were not apolitical actors. The women of the American Medical Bureau used their professional identities as nurses to fight fascism on the international stage. As they followed their political and ideological convictions across the Atlantic, the nurses felt that their skills were needed and contributed to the antifascist cause. Events like the Spanish Civil War shed light on the transnational politics women actively participated in and supported in the post-suffrage era.

---

[102] Freeman, interview.
[103] Gregg Andrews, *Thyra J. Edwards: Black Activist in the Global Freedom Struggle* (Columbia, Missouri: University Press, 2011), 109.
[104] Lear, *Comrades in Health*, 77; Freeman, interview; Fuhr, *Up from the Cellar*, 243-309.

Chapter 8

Standing in Solidarity: British Women and the China Campaign Committee, 1937-1945

Mark J. Crowley
University of Utah

Abstract: Following the invasion of Nanjing by Japanese forces in 1937, an event that saw the beginning of the Second World War in China, the British trade union movement expressed horror and explored ways by which they could help. The speed and scale of the Japanese advance had left thousands dead and millions displaced and/or wounded. This action, branded as Fascist by British trade union leaders, spurred the movement into action. The head of the British Trades Union Congress, Walter Citrine, now mentioned the necessity for the trade union movement to respond to the plight of its Chinese comrades to help in their hour of need – a call also taken up by Lady Astor, a senior female trade unionist. This saw the creation of a new group, the China Campaign Committee (CCC), which explored methods by which financial aid and practical assistance could be provided to China. While the efforts of the CCC on the British Home Front were noteworthy as a form of reducing the levels of British money arriving in Japan through consumption (initiated through the boycott movement), it is through the initiatives pursued as a means of providing direct assistance to Chinese citizens that their success was most deeply felt. This chapter examines the instrumental role played by women in raising funds (through a series of specially organized events) and their collaboration with Chinese women to provide assistance to China in their time of utmost need.

Keywords: Nanjing, Second World War, Trades Union, Walter Citrine, China Campaign Committee, China, Japanese Occupation, Lady Astor, Boycott, Consumption

***

Introduction

When Imperial Japan invaded Manchuria in July 1937, the British Trades Union Congress (TUC) quickly established the China Campaign Committee, chaired by Lady Astor.[1] The Committee was comprised of trade unionists and politicians. Many, like Astor, were women who desired to assist Chinese victims of Japanese aggression. The TUC response was not reflected in the actions of the British government that was most intently focused on events in Europe. While the horrors of conflict played out in China, the British government remained hopeful that Neville Chamberlain's policy of appeasement would hold strong in Europe. Nevertheless, with the expansionist policies of both Benito Mussolini and Adolf Hitler, this looked increasingly unlikely. The spread of fascism in Europe meant that, for many, Britain and its empire became a refuge for those escaping persecution. It was here that the British government's attention was dedicated, especially in relation to refugee children.[2]

While British government officials were acutely aware of developments in Europe, they knew less of what was happening and causing massive humanitarian concerns in China. Following the Japanese invasion of the Chinese city of Nanjing in December 1937, the trade union movement was particularly vocal in raising concerns about the humanitarian crisis.[3] The China Campaign Committee implored the British government to assist China, while also exploring ways they could help. The unions saw the conflict in China in the same way it viewed the war in Spain—as a fight against fascism.[4] When the civil war in Spain began in 1936, trade unionists joined the fight against the nationalists and in support of the Republican government.[5] Hundreds of unionized British coal miners, many from Wales, left their homeland to fight with the international brigades against what they considered to be the fascist advance in Spain.[6] Unions also gave funds to and

---

[1] Alastair J. Reid, *United We Stand: A History of Britain's Trade Unions* (London: Allen Lane, 2004).
[2] Sandra Trudgen Dawson, "Refugee Children and the Emotional Cost of Internationalism in Interwar Britain," *Journal of British Studies* 60 (2021) 115-116.
[3] Iris Chang, *The Rape of Nanking: The Forgotten Holocaust of World War Two* (New York: Basic Books, 1997).
[4] Tom Buchanan, "'Shanghai-Madrid Axis'? Comparing British Responses to the Conflicts in Spain and China, 1936–39," *Contemporary European History* 21.4 (2012): 534.
[5] Tom Buchanan, *Britain and the Spanish Civil War* (Cambridge: Cambridge University Press, 1997).
[6] For a detailed analysis, see Hywel Francis, *Miners Against Fascism: Wales and the Spanish Civil War* (London: Lawrence & Wishart, 2012).

raised money for the National Joint Committee for Spanish Relief (NJCSR) to assist refugees and give medical aid.[7]

Just as the unions raised funds and supported the Republican side in Spain, they supported China against an expansionist and seemingly fascist Japan. In a style like that adopted by coalminers' unions to support Republican Spain, the China Campaign Committee asked members and citizens to dedicate whatever resources they had at their disposal to help Chinese victims of fascist aggression. Trade union women played a significant role in the formation and the work of the China Campaign Committee in its efforts to educate the public, raise funds, and galvanize a movement to boycott Japanese goods. Using similar methods to those that raised funds for Spanish, German, and Czech refugees, trade union women were the grassroots activists in efforts to bring attention to the horrors of war, the plight of women and orphaned children, and the need to fight fascism in all its forms any way possible.

While the international movement to assist the Spanish republican government has garnered scholarly attention, the work of the China Campaign Committee has been largely overlooked.[8] This chapter examines the committee, the campaign, and the campaigners who continued to pay attention to the plight of the Chinese from 1937-1945.

The China Campaign Committee

The Imperial Japanese Army captured the key Chinese city of Nanjing in December 1937. The speed and scale of the Japanese advance in China left thousands dead and millions displaced and wounded.[9] News of these events spurred the trade union movement into action. The head of the British Trades Union Congress, Walter Citrine, argued that the British trade union movement needed to respond to the plight of its Chinese comrades in their hour of need.

TUC support for China was not new. As Tom Buchanan notes, the interest in China among the British left had developed over several decades. Notable figures such as ethical socialist Richard H. Tawney visited China in the 1930s. He returned and commented on the poverty and lack of infrastructure in the

---

[7] The National Joint Committee for Spanish Relief was a voluntary umbrella organization formed in late 1936 by Ellen Wilkerson MP and the Duchess of Atholl MP to aid the Republican government in Spain. See Jim Fyrth, *The Signal Was Spain: The Spanish Aid Movement in Britain, 1936–39* (London: Lawrence and Wishart, 1986).

[8] This has, in part, been examined by Arthur Clegg in his study, "Aid China, 1937-1949: A Memoir of a Forgotten Campaign," *Science and Society* 56.1 (1992), but more research is needed to understand the scope of the CCC's activities, especially the role of women.

[9] Jonathan Henshaw, Craig A. Smith, and Norman Smith, eds., *Translating the Occupation: The Japanese Invasion of China*, (Vancouver: University of British Columbia Press, 2021).

country. Tawney's revelations partly explain the affinity of the trade union movement with China, and the desire to assist the victims of Japanese aggression in what turned out to be the start of the Second World War in Asia.[10] Military assistance like the international brigades that went to Spain in 1936 were not feasible, as the distance between Europe and Asia was immense and the journey too time-consuming. Nevertheless, unions explored other ways to help their Chinese comrades. The conflict in China was regarded as equally important as the war in Spain. Buchanan notes, "the two conflicts [Spain and China] often seemed to be viewed through bifocal lenses, especially in the left-wing press."[11] Both conflicts revealed the very real threat of the spread of authoritarianism and fascism.

The establishment of the China Campaign Committee almost immediately after news of the Japanese invasion signaled the importance given to the situation by the unions. Nancy Astor, American-born socialite and the first elected woman in Parliament, led the efforts to form and develop the China Campaign Committee.[12] At first, Astor tried exerting political pressure through speeches in the House of Commons and meetings with senior government officials to influence government policy towards China. In representing the China Campaign Committee, she argued that significant diplomatic and economic moves needed to be taken against Japan. Despite Astor's formidable presence in Parliament, her speeches gained little traction amongst policymakers. One of Astor's requests, that Britain loan money to China, was taken up by Lord Plymouth in December 1938. The House of Lords debated a loan to China to assist the Chinese as they battled Japanese aggression. Astor and the Committee maintained pressure on Parliament to ensure the loan was granted to provide material relief for the millions of Chinese refugees caused by the Japanese invasion.[13]

Parliament's lukewarm response to the requests for more assistance to China led the China Campaign Committee to explore other ways to garner wider grassroot support that would inflict economic damage on the Japanese for their actions in China. One of the first roles of the committee was to raise funds and explore ways to provide practical assistance. Elite women like Astor

---

[10] Tom Buchanan, *East Wind, China, and the British Left, 1925-1976* (Oxford: Oxford Scholarship Online, 2012), pp. 1-6.
[11] Buchanan, "Shanghai-Madrid Axis,'" 534.
[12] Lady Astor was elected to Parliament in 1919 after the extension of the franchise to women over the age of thirty. Adrian Fort, *Nancy: The Story of Lady Astor* (London: St. Martin's Griffin, 2014).
[13] China Campaign Committee Information Letter No 4, January 8, 1939, SWCC MNA.NUM/L/20/110.

often chaired fundraising committees in the interwar years. Their names and their connections made these women particularly useful and successful fundraisers. Women's committees within the China Campaign Committee also worked to organize a range of grassroots fundraising events. These included meetings and lectures about the situation in China, articles about the conflict in local and national newspapers, and the involvement of churches. Local parish churches were encouraged to organize fundraising bazaars and fetes, and to hold special prayer sessions for the Chinese. Committee members also raised awareness about the war in China. Union members, often women and children, gave out leaflets in their communities or assisted the committee in mass mailings.

As a response to the conflict and to show solidarity with their Chinese comrades, the China Campaign Committee launched a Christmas campaign in 1938 to boycott Japanese products.[14] The aim was to stop British consumers from buying Japanese goods. These included silk scarves, children's toys and food products. The Christmas campaign focused efforts on women as consumers. Indeed, women, especially wives, were perceived as those responsible for purchasing food and other household products for the family.[15] In the boycott campaign, the Committee portrayed women to be key consumers who, once educated, would ensure the maximum effectiveness of the boycott. Social class was also a consideration. The interwar years saw the rise in the importance of working-class consumers and the idea that the home was the site of "domestic efficiency" and women were "household consumers and managers."[16] Women, then, were deemed essential to the success of the Christmas boycott campaign.

In response to the campaign, consumers pointed out that it was difficult to distinguish between Japanese goods and other foreign products, since labels did not indicate the country of origin.[17] The China Campaign Committee recognized the issue and campaigned in Parliament to amend the

---

[14] China Campaign Committee Information Letter No 4, January 8, 1939, SWCC MNA. NUM/L/20/110.
[15] Erika Rappaport, *Shopping for Pleasure: Women and the Making of London's West End* (Princeton: Princeton University Press, 2000). In the 1930s, marketing to men became popular. See Paul Deslandes, "Selling, Consuming, and Becoming the Beautiful Man in Britain: The 1930s and 1940s," *Consuming Behaviours: Identity, Politics, and Pleasure in Twentieth-Century Britain*, eds. Erika D. Rappaport, Sandra Trudgen Dawson, and Mark J. Crowley (London: Bloomsbury, 2015).
[16] Sandra Trudgen Dawson, "Working-Class Consumers and the Campaign for Holidays with Pay," *Twentieth Century British History* 18.3 (2007), p. 286.
[17] China Campaign Committee Information Letter No. 4, January 8, 1939, WCC, MNA. NUM/L/20/110.

Merchandise Marks Act—a nineteenth-century law that required goods to note whether they were made in Britain or elsewhere. The law did not specify the country of origin but simply labeled goods as "foreign." The China Campaign Committee called for goods to be labeled with the country of origin to ensure consumers could avoid purchasing Japanese products.[18]

Despite the setback, the Committee continued to work diligently to remind consumers to be more discerning in their choices of gifts for Christmas. In a letter to supporters in December 1938, the China Campaign Committee warned parents, "Beware! Christmas toys may be dangerous playthings." The danger came about because the "money you spend could be used for bombs to fund Japanese bombings of China." The Committee implored consumers to purchase "artificial silk because real silk is made in Japan. Help China by refusing to buy Japanese goods."[19]

The Committee didn't only direct their campaign to parents. They also targeted British children who were reminded that they were more fortunate than their Chinese counterparts. In an open letter to children, the committee highlighted the difficulties and traumatic nature of war: "We are wiring a Christmas letter to you on behalf of the thousands of parents and children in China who are suffering hunger, pain and death." While enjoying the season's festivities, the Committee asked British children to think of others: "When you are enjoying presents, parties and Christmas pudding, will you think of the children of China who have nothing?" The letter asked children to give to the campaign: "Will you give some of the money you have to spend to the China Campaign Committee to send to China to buy food for the hungry and homeless children and pay for medicine and bandages for their fathers who are badly wounded?"[20] In this campaign, British children were expected to show empathy for others in need and contribute their Christmas money.[21]

The boycott appeared to be successful. By late December 1938, the China Campaign Committee reported that Britain now had an adverse trade balance with Japan. Exports to Japan fell by 21.4 percent and imports from Japan were down 35.2 percent.[22] The Committee's goal was to modify consumer habits

---

[18] Ibid.
[19] China Campaign Committee Information Letter from Mr G. Hardy, December 9, 1938, SWCCC MNA.NUM/L/20/110.
[20] China Campaign Committee Information Letter from Mr G. Hardy, December 9, 1938, SWCCC MNA.NUM/L/20/110.
[21] Children were often involved in fundraising for other children. See Dawson, "Refugee Children."
[22] China Campaign Committee Information Letter from Mr G. Hardy, December 9, 1938, SWCCC MNA.NUM/L/20/110.

and reduce the imports of raw materials for peaceful industries (cotton, wool, and timber) from Japan by 30 percent. Committee members hoped that, eventually, these reductions could be enshrined in legislation and that Japan be officially regarded as a hostile nation by Parliament.

There was also evidence that the boycott was having an impact on the Japanese economy. Japanese media reported economic changes to its citizens. The monthly bulletin of the Mitsubishi Research Bureau claimed that "adverse business conditions, the boycott movement and the relatively high prices of export goods were the main causes of reductions in the export trade" (emphasis in the original). The Japanese government was forced to take 300 million yen from its 800-million-yen reserve to fund the import of raw materials and address the decline in foreign trade. To stave off citizens' concerns, Japanese propaganda reassured the people that its gold reserves were enough to prevent inflation. In response to this propaganda, the China Campaign Committee advised the British public that the gold reserves would only be a temporary solution.[23] The Committee urged supporters to remain resolute and stand shoulder to shoulder with China and watch as the crisis deepened rapidly for Japan.

The perceived success of the initial boycott campaign encouraged the Committee to pursue additional boycotts. On February 23, 1939, the committee began a campaign in London imploring British people not to buy Japanese silk.[24] It was formally launched after an informational meeting and a film show. Tickets for the boycott launch were priced at 6d, and all funds raised were donated to China. Five thousand gas-filled balloons were released, each with pledges attached stating a commitment not to buy Japanese products.[25] The new boycott campaign also included some new strategies formulated by the women of the Committee. The result was a strategic framework for all supporters to follow. At the London event, attendees and supporters were asked, upon pledging their support to this cause, to adhere to three basic principles. First, they would be required to buy and wear a badge which explicitly stated their commitment to boycott Japanese products, and to encourage others to do so. Second, they were asked to sign and return the boycott pledge provided upon payment of the attendance fee. Finally, attendees and supporters were asked to purchase a shoppers' guide, compiled

---

[23] China Campaign Committee Information Letter from Mr G. Hardy, December 9, 1938, SWCCC MNA.NUM/L/20/110.
[24] China Campaign Committee Information Letter No. 4, January 8, 1939, SWCCC, MNA.NUM/L/20/110.
[25] China Campaign Committee: No Silk Spring Boycott Campaign, January 8, 1939, SWCCC, MNA.NUM/L/20/110.

by the China Campaign Committee, which provided detailed guidance on how to avoid Japanese products. The guide provided detailed information on products that originated from Japan and stated that all supporters should avoid purchasing these products and encourage others to boycott the goods.[26] Until Parliament changed the Merchandise Marks legislation, the guide helped supporters distinguish Japanese goods from other imports. The success of this strategy and effort helped the Committee to coordinate a national boycott across Britain.

One of Astor's original requests to Parliament, that Britain loan money to China, was taken up by Lord Plymouth in December 1938. The House of Lords debated a loan to China to assist the Chinese as they battled Japanese aggression. The Committee saw its role as maintaining pressure on Parliament to ensure the loan was granted to provide material relief for the millions of Chinese refugees caused by the Japanese invasion.[27]

The Committee also recognized the importance of media in galvanizing public support. In January 1938, just six months after the Japanese invasion of China, the Committee created a newspaper, *China News*, eliciting the assistance of experienced media personnel to help with disseminating their message to a wider audience. Author and social commentator J. B. Priestley edited the paper. Priestly had a wealth of experience that gained wider attention for the Committee and its work.[28] In his first editorial, Priestly addressed readers directly by noting: "it isn't easy for us in the west to visualize what is happening in China today, how in the midst of war and suffering these brave people are building up new industries, rebuilding their universities, determined that their lives and long civilisation shall not suffer."[29] Nevertheless, the aim of *China News* was to address the lack of information and educate members of the British public about what was happening in China and the important work of the China Campaign Committee.

China News was published weekly and contained articles written by missionaries, Chinese leaders such as Chiang Kai-Shek, the head of the Chinese Co-Operative movement Rewi Ali, and Dr Robert Lim, a man once famed as "the greatest doctor in China" and now the Head of the Chinese Red Cross.[30] The articles covered several themes, including the growth of

---

[26] China Campaign Committee Information Letter No. 4, January 8, 1939, SWCCC, MNA.NUM/L/20/110.
[27] Ibid.
[28] Priestly served multiple roles in radio and the press during the Second World War.
[29] China Campaign Committee: No Silk Spring Boycott Campaign, January 8, 1939, SWCCC, MNA.NUM/L/20/110.
[30] China Campaign Committee, June 12, 1939, SWCC, MNA/NUM/L/20/111.

education, reconstruction of industries, emancipation of women, and the building of cooperatives in West China. Some of the articles included vivid descriptions of the suffering of Chinese civilians under Japanese occupation that were often harrowing. Many focused on the fate of Chinese women and children. Many children lost their fathers, and some were orphaned by the war. Issues of *China News* were priced at 1d per copy or 9d for 12.

Messages concerning the suffering of the Chinese population, particularly women and children, were communicated directly to some of the British elite. In November 1938, Sir Robert Ho Tung, an influential Hong Kong businessman and philanthropist in British Hong Kong (and friend of the Churchill family) wrote to Clementine Churchill, wife of the future Prime Minister, enclosing a gift of tea in preparation for Christmas. At a time when the British were still digesting the seemingly good news from the appeasement negotiations secured by Chamberlain in September 1938, the realities of war and the dangers of fascism were already abundantly clear to those in Hong Kong. Tung's concerns and fears were clear. He wrote, "China is passing through a terrible ordeal. Living though we are in the security of a British Colony, we are still daily in contact with all the evidence of the cruelties of modern warfare."[31] He continued, "Refugees, wounded soldiers, wounded civilians and pauperized merchants have been pouring into this little island refuge from all parts of China."[32] Trade had all but ended and this just added to the misery of thousands unable to find the most basic goods. The whole conflict appeared "futile" to Tung, who hoped for peace in the West and the East.[33]

In January 1939, Japanese Prime Minister Prince Koneye resigned (and subsequently took a place on the Privy Council). His replacement, Kiichirō Hiranuma, spelled the intensification of brutality against the Chinese. It was the China Campaign Committee who first identified the dangers of this political change and argued that the British government needed to respond, both to help the Chinese, who had already been subjected to two years of Japanese aggression, and to shore up Sino-British relations in response to the growing (and now global) threat of fascism. The Committee argued that the Government should focus on three priorities.[34] First, an embargo needed to be placed on all Japanese products in accordance with the decision of the League of Nations reached in September 1938. This would cut off essential

---

[31] Robert Ho Tung to Mrs Churchill, November 1938. Churchill Archives, Cambridge University (hereafter CHAR) 1/324/2-3.
[32] Ibid.
[33] Ibid.
[34] China Campaign Committee Information Letter No. 4, January 8, 1939, SWCC, MNA. NUM/L/20/110.

finances to Japan and reduce the available capital to fund its war machine. The Committee noted that in January 1939, twenty-eight London boroughs and thirty provincial areas now fully boycotted Japanese goods.[35] Secondly, the Committee urged the British government to provide a long-term loan to the Chinese government, both to assist those who had been left destitute because of Japanese atrocities and to aid the Chinese military with weaponry to fight Japanese forces. And finally, the Committee maintained that Anglo-US relations should be deepened and that both countries should present a unified response to Japanese aggression. The Committee also believed Britain and the United States should develop a strategic plan on how Western allies could aid the Chinese, in the face of increased Japanese aggression and threats to their sovereignty, to secure a speedy conclusion to the war in Asia.[36]

Evidence of increased Japanese brutality came to the China Campaign Committee. On June 21, 1939, a missionary in China sent a telegram outlining the atrocities occurring in Nanjing. The missionary "witnessed terrible bombings… deliberate ruthless attempts destroy, burn, terrorize. Civilian, cultural, business area of capital laid waste." According to the missionary, there were no "important military results. Chinese morale unimpaired but suffering of people is appalling. Hundreds trapped in fires." The missionary "saw scores of charred bodies." The hospitals worked ceaselessly "receiving streams of wounded without sufficient water, light, medical supplies. Two crowded hospitals destroyed. Hundred thousand homeless."[37] The missionary was an eyewitness to the misery of war and the sufferings of the Chinese at the hands of the Japanese.

The China Campaign Committee wanted to provide direct assistance to the Chinese. Responding to telegrams and articles in the *China News*, Committee members campaigned to support the countless children orphaned by the war in China. As early as May 1939, Committee members believed the best way to raise awareness of the war in China and raise funds to assist victims was to send speakers from the China Campaign Committee's headquarters in London to visit all areas of Britain to give speeches about the plight of the Chinese.[38] The Committee appealed to union members for support in raising the necessary capital and asked them to offer accommodation to visiting speakers. The plight of children was central to this drive. Two unions—the Civil Service Union and the Association of Women Clerks and Secretaries—

---

[35] Ibid.
[36] China Campaign Committee, May 1, 1939, SWCC, MNA/NUM/L/20/111.
[37] China Campaign Committee, June 21, 1939, SWCC, MNA/NUM/L/20/111.
[38] Ibid.

launched the "Adopt a Chinese Orphan" scheme.[39] Unlike other refugee campaigns, this scheme would not require a British family to actively take care of a Chinese child.[40] The child would remain in China and be relocated to a safe place. The adoption was purely a financial commitment for impoverished orphaned children in China. The scheme was originally recommended as a policy for London branches of the unions, where it was enthusiastically supported. In response to the union scheme, several girls' schools and women's colleges adopted children whose parents had been killed by the Japanese. In their appeal for additional volunteers, the Association of Women Clerks and Secretaries advised their members that they would be required to write a letter to the Secretary of Peace and Democracy in London. Shortly afterwards, they would receive a photo of the adopted child who would be maintained in a home in China.[41]

Building on the success of the "adopt a Chinese orphan" scheme, the China Campaign Committee wrote to its members in July 1940, expressing their desire that members collaborate to ensure that July 7, 1940, could be organized as "China Day" across the nation. July 7 was the anniversary of the Japanese invasion of China. Aside from raising money for the victims of war in China, it was hoped that a strong expression of solidarity among the population would ensure that the feelings of the British public concerning their attitude towards Japan would be made clear. This would demonstrate to the British government that the British people did not want a deal to be secured with Japan at the expense of China. The unions made clear their position vis-à-vis Japan and wanted to ensure that the government responded more positively with assistance to China.[42]

Despite the war in Europe, the China Campaign Committee and its numerous female activists worked to ensure continued attention was afforded to China. Communiques sent to the China Campaign Committee revealed the atrocities meted out by the Japanese army against Chinese soldiers and civilians. Telegrams and letters also revealed that the slaughter was continuing apace, possibly with greater intensity than before. Since the invasion in July 1937, over a million Chinese had been killed, and sixty million were homeless

---

[39] China Campaign Committee: No Silk Spring Boycott Campaign, January 8, 1939, SWCCC, MNA.NUM/L/20/110.
[40] In the 1930s, the British public were asked to house refugee children from Spain, Germany, and Czechoslovakia. At the outbreak of war on September 3, 1939, the British public were also required to house thousands of children from British cities. See Dawson, "Refugee Children," and John Welshman, *Churchill's Children: The Evacuee Experience in Wartime Britain* (Oxford: Oxford University Press, 2010).
[41] China Campaign Committee, May 1, 1939, SWCC, MNA/NUM/L/20/111.
[42] Ibid.

and thus refugees in their own country. A telegram from a missionary to the China Campaign Committee concluded on an optimistic, albeit fatalistic note: "China is struggling for her freedom under a Christian leader, whose prayers are giving him strength to continue his struggle for an honourable peace."[43] In response, the China Campaign Committee pledged to lobby local British churches to use July 9, the anniversary of the outbreak of the war in China, to be observed as "China Sunday." Churches were asked to donate the money collected in their offerings to the China Campaign Committee to raise funds for China.

In 1941, a statement by Madame Chiang Kai-Shek, the wife of the Chinese leader, conveyed the horrifying stories of the experiences and challenges faced by pregnant Chinese women at the hands of the Japanese.[44] The headline of the article in the *China News* read, "Mothers to be terrorized by air raids!"[45] In the article, Madame Chiang Kai-Shek observed the raids in Chungking, "Not only were 6000 lives lost in the first two raids.....but over 2000 shops and homes were destroyed in the city and over 200,000 people have so far evacuated the place."[46] The article notes that the Japanese had used poison gas against pregnant women, and that the British government continued to fail in its obligation both under the nine-power treaty and the covenant of the League of Nations to protect China, instead offering protection for Japan even though it had occupied China. The China Campaign Committee argued that if Britain joined with the Chinese in resisting the Japanese, this would also weaken the fascist forces in Italy, Germany, and Spain, since they claimed that these governments had collaborated with the Japanese to facilitate the spread of fascism. In making this plea, the Committee sought to make the correlation between the support of China to the defeat of fascism globally.[47]

The first major state visit to Britain by Chinese officials during wartime occurred at the beginning of 1943.[48] The British ambassador to China, Sir Horace Seymour, accompanied by members of the China mission, Dr Wang Shih-Chieh and Dr W C Chen, counsellor at the Chinese Embassy (and educated at London and Cambridge), and other delegates arrived in London

---

[43] China Campaign Committee, June 12, 1939, SWCC, MNA/NUM/L/20/111.
[44] For more on Mme. Chiang Kai-shek, see Hannah Pakula, *The Last Empress: Madame Chiang Kai-shek and the Birth of Modern China* (New York: Simon & Schuster, 2009).
[45] United Aid to China Fund: Chinese Mission to the UK organised for January 1, 1943, SWCCC/MNB/PP/20/N/7.
[46] Ibid.
[47] Ibid.
[48] United Aid to China Fund: Chinese Mission to the UK organised for January 1, 1943, SWCCC/MNB/PP/20/N/7.

on January 1, 1943.[49] In honor of the Chinese visit, Britain held a "Flag Day" on which Britons were encouraged to purchase small Chinese flags to show solidarity with the Chinese. At the lunch organized by the China mission and accompanied by its members, Dr Han Li-Wu claimed, "we have seen with our own eyes how you people have sweated and toiled, have faced dangers and emerged triumphant."[50] He said that they would return to China with positive stories about the British people. They would recognize the large donations, but also the thousands of small donations by ordinary people. People who had "warm hearts but few words."[51] He later commented, "it will be a picture of a heroic and friendly people that we shall take back with us."[52] After his return to China, Dr Wang, in a letter to Lady Cripps, summarised their visit by noting, "I must say that, until after my arrival in London, I did not realise the scope and efficiency of the work which you are leading in aiding China. The details I learned from your office yesterday impressed me profoundly.[53]

The details he referred to were given to the Chinese delegation by British officials who explained that fundraising events helped the British public to embrace Chinese culture. This was evident in the adoption of Chinese festivals throughout Britain. As the aid effort increased, so too did the scope of the celebrations and events that took place during Chinese festivals on British soil. The double tenth festival, celebrated on October 10, included special concerts scheduled in London. The largest was a performance by the London Philharmonic Orchestra at the city's Royal Albert Hall on October 10, 1943. Other events included the hosting (in London) of amateur boxing tournaments (raising £700), poetry readings (raising £90), and a Chinese market selling traditional Chinese food and ornaments (raising £1200). In the pipeline was a screening of Lawrence Olivier's film *A Demi-Paradise* in the Odeon Theatre, Leicester Square. £3000 worth of advanced ticket sales were recorded in fifteen minutes by the deputy chair of the China Campaign Committee's Ladies Committee, Lady Dalrymple-Champneys. She praised the local organisation of the China Campaign Committee, who now boasted 242 working parties nationwide.

As a result of these various events, significant financial sums were raised and sent to China.[54] Irene Ward MP, a prominent member of the China Campaign

---

[49] Ibid.
[50] United Aid to China Fund, January 31, 1944, SWCCC/MNB/PP/20/N/7.
[51] Ibid.
[52] Ibid.
[53] Ibid.
[54] United Aid to China Fund – Letter to Irene Ward, October 20, 1943, SWCCC/MNB/PP/20/N/7.

Committee, received a letter on October 20, 1943, from Mr C. S. Cheng at the West China Union University at Chengtu. In it, he expressed his gratitude for the contribution of the China Campaign Committee and requested that Ward act as a messenger for the Chinese in Britain to express their gratitude for their contributions. He wrote, "News comes now and then from that side of the world that the British people, rich and poor, old and young have been so generously responding to the call of the united aid to China fund by making unstinted contributions to the best of their ability." This was especially when the donations came from "disabled people, pensioners, workmen and schoolgirls and boys." Cheng claimed that the "friendship already existing between the peoples of Britain and China has gone far in laying a foundation for post-war cooperation between these two countries." While Cheng expressed his appreciation as an individual, he maintained that it was shared by "all my countrymen." Thus, Cheng implored Ward to "bring this sense of gratefulness of the Chinese people to the people" of Britain.[55]

By November 1943, China had received over £155,000 in less than one year from various sources. This was a large sum at the time, and such was the level of donations, the previous custom of allocations being made by Mme Chiang Kai-shek with the British ambassador Sir Horace Seymour was replaced with the appointment of an advisory committee formed by Chiang Kai-shek under chairmanship of Dr Wang Chung-hui, Secretary General of the National Supreme Council. Chug-hui was educated in the UK and was a barrister. Under his leadership, a new scheme that became known as "factories for families of deceased soldiers" was formed. Here, families and widows were trained to work, and when proficient, they become employed. This initiative was developed in response to the millions of families that had lost a male breadwinner. Many women, poorly educated and with few skills, received needed employment training under this scheme. The successful development of the initiative led members of the Chungking Women's Association to write to the China Campaign Committee in Britain. The Chinese association recognized the work of women in Britain, which was also fighting fascism in Europe and Asia. The association addressed "our dear British sisters" who are also "engaged in a heroic fight." The Chinese women declared, "Your glory is ours and the freedom for which you strive is ours too." They recognized the perseverance of their British counterparts which, they claimed, "set us a great example." They expressed their gratitude to British women from the "bottom of [their] hearts." The letter went on to say that the achievements in Britain "provide excellent models for us and your great spirit and courage add to our

---

[55] United Aid to China Fund – Letter to Irene Ward, October 20, 1943, SWCCC/MNB/PP/20/N/7.

own, taking us one step further on the way." The Chungking women were "grateful" for the "example of faith and courage."[56]

Mme Chiang Kai-Shek also expressed her gratitude for the work of the China Campaign Committee. On behalf of herself and her husband, she wrote to Lady Cripps on December 31, 1943, to express their "sincere appreciation" for all the efforts of the Committee, "not only on behalf of securing practical aid for China's relief, but also for your excellent work in bringing about better understanding between our two great countries." She continued, "We realise the value and importance of educating the peoples of both Great Britain and China in our common aspirations and needs, especially in bringing home to them that fundamentally we both are peace-longing nations and want a better world for ourselves and others."[57]

Indeed, the numbers reveal the extent to which the China Campaign Committee supported the efforts in China. In 1943 alone, £3000 in total was sent to China from Southampton, with £977 coming in honor of the double tenth festival. An additional £750 was raised in Sheffield. In the period since the outbreak of the war in China, £125,000 had been sent, and was divided between famine relief and the Red Cross in various ways. £15,000 had gone directly to the Red Cross for aid and relief work, with £15,000 specifically designated for famine relief. An additional £15,000 had been donated to the newly established refugee children national association, most stemming from the "adopt a Chinese Orphan" scheme. A further £10,000 was given to Chinese provinces to improve their national health administration. Another £10,000 was given to a new charity, "Friends of the Wounded." This fund assisted anyone helping a friend or relative injured by Japanese attacks. The remaining funds were divided among the Chinese Industrial Co-Operatives and the families of wounded soldiers, who received direct financial payments.[58] The distribution of funds from Britain was originally administered by Mme Chiang Kai-Shek and the British Ambassador Sir Horace Seymour. By 1944, there was a change in policy. Mme Chiang Kai-Shek formed an advisory committee under chairmanship of Dr Wang Chung-Hui, Secretary General of the Chinese National Supreme Council. A British-educated official and qualified Barrister, he was seen as a good choice for this appointment. Under his leadership, a new scheme, "Factories for Families of Deceased Soldiers," was established,

---

[56] United Aid to China Fund – Letter from Chungking Women's Association to the CCC, November 1943, SWCC/MNB/PP/20/N/7.
[57] United Aid to China Fund – Letter from Mme Chiang Kai-Shek to Lady Cripps, December 21, 1943, SWCC/MNB/PP/20/N/7.
[58] United Aid to China Fund, October 31, 1943, SWCCC/MNB/PP/20/N/7.

providing training for widows so that they could ensure their financial independence in the absence of a breadwinner at home.[59]

By January 1944, the support of the China Campaign Committee was evident and real results were apparent in China. On the invitation of the Chinese government, Lady Seymour and her husband Horace, the British ambassador at Chungking, accompanied Irene Ward MP to visit one of the many centers established with the assistance of money from the China Campaign Committee. The main destinations for the visit were the Wounded Soldiers Rehabilitation center and Mme Chiang Kai-Shek's "warphanages" at the gorge of the Chialing river, fifty miles from Chungking. The "warphanage" housed 350 children. The building itself was an old temple, and while there was very little space, the work it was performing was vital for these displaced children. Upon arrival, the British delegation were met by a band, and the children stood to attention. All were well-trained, with girls dressed in overalls and pink blouses, and boys in scout uniform. The superintendent was, according to Lady Seymour, "a woman of personality and charm." The children liked her, and they all received three meals a day—porridge, rice and vegetables with some gravy, and rice and vegetables. As part of their stay, the children helped with housework, grew vegetables, and kept pigs. They also received an education. The best students went on to middle and secondary schools. The others went to work in factories under supervision. Some of the boys were trained as assistant cooks for the foreign army and air forces stationed in China. According to the delegation, the women in the centers appeared devoted to their work. The rehabilitation center for wounded soldiers and civilians was the first of its kind in China. Set on 300 acres with bamboo and plaster buildings, men were trained in agriculture and produced some of their own food, in addition to making straw sandals, bamboo furniture and umbrellas. These products were made in an adjacent factory. The China Campaign Committee donated £5000 to the rehabilitation center.[60] The delegation returned to Britain convinced that the work of the China Campaign Committee had made a difference in the lives of many Chinese men, women, and children.

Conclusion

When the Second World War ended in the Pacific, the collaboration and ties between the British trade union movement and the Chinese did not cease. While the nature of the relationship changed, the bond between workers and the people remained. When Mao Zedong took power in the post-war period,

---

[59] United Aid to China Fund, January 31, 1944, SWCCC/MNB/PP/20/N/7.
[60] United Aid to China Fund, 31 Jan. 1944. SWCCC/MNB/PP/20/N/7.

visits by British trade unions from the coal mining industry helped to build international solidarity between the industries of the two nations, and to share ideas about occupational health. Throughout the years of the Second World War, the efforts of the China Campaign Committee and the United Aid to China Fund gave sustenance to many in China. While the evidence shows that the leaders of this very significant group were women from the British elite, the role of women as grassroots organizers was crucial to the success of the China Campaign Committee. Furthermore, the willingness of women consumers to embrace the boycott initiative served not only to exert pressure on Japan, but also gave some much-needed support for the Chinese. The China Campaign Committee provided information to the British public about the atrocities in China, which received less attention in the British press during the war years. The Committee also provided tangible support to the Chinese in their time of need. What is significant about this group is that it was not only led by women, but its success was due to the organizational and fundraising efforts of British women.

Section Three.
Consumption and Conflict

Chapter 9

Indoctrinating Dinners: Feeding Ideology to the Hungry during the Franco Dictatorship in Spain, 1937-1948

Suzanne Dunai
Southwestern Oklahoma State University

Abstract: This chapter examines aspects of the everyday interactions that vulnerable Spaniards had with the Francoist state as it claimed territory during the Spanish Civil War (1936-1939) and its aftermath. Using sites of state-sponsored food charity of a lens, I identify how food-insecure Spaniards coped with the economic and social limitations of their postwar realities, and how the ideologies of the Francoist state fell short of expectations when implementing food relief policies.

Spanish society was divided between "winners" and "losers" when the dictator Francisco Franco solidified his power and enacted a new form of social stratification within Spanish society. Despite the promotion of traditional family values by Francoist ideology, the economic and social reality of the war and postwar tore Spanish families apart, specifically for those on the losing side. With the Spanish families on the losing side of the war was systematically punished, the authoritarian Francoist state intervened to create a surrogate family, providing housing, childcare, and even food according to the traditional values of a Spanish home. Relying upon governmental records, the chapter examines how the Franco regime attempted to recreate the familial dinner table within the public dining halls of its Social Aid program. A deeper reading of these sources reveals aspects of acquiescence, non-conformity, and resistance—all of which signal forms of political engagement—by socially-vulnerable, marginalized patrons in the consumption of their daily meals at these state-run sites of food relief. Failure of the Francoist state to control ideological messaging and practices within its site of food relief reveal the limitations of the Francoist regime to control the Spanish population in the practice of everyday life and help to elucidate new aspects of historical agency within dictatorial societies.

Keywords: Food charity, Spanish Civil War, FET-JONS, Authoritarian dictatorship, Francisco Franco, Social Aid Program, Francoist ideology

***

During the Spanish Civil War (1936-39) and the early years of the dictatorship of Francisco Franco Bahamonde, food was in scarce supply, so the Spanish state used food as leverage to manipulate the population to conform to specific cultural and social values. This chapter analyzes how the politics and culture of food relief programs shaped Spanish diet and society during the time of political, economic, and social upheaval known as the "hunger years." The *Auxilio Social*, or "Social Aid" program, provided food charity for women and children during the Spanish Civil War and acted as the coercive component of the regime's food policy. Understanding how food was distributed through government-run dining halls helps elucidate the reconstruction of Spain's urban society after the civil war and the impact of Francoist repression in shaping modern Spanish food culture. This chapter examines how the Franco regime used food to try to control Spain's resources and dictate the experiences of daily life as well as the way ordinary Spaniards adapted to the consequences of war and dictatorship through food survival strategies and limited food choices.

Food aid for Spaniards during the consumer crises of the 1930s and 1940s was structured in a way that coerced vulnerable populations, particularly women and children, to conform to the ideals and practices of conservative Spaniards while suppressing the ability for this marginalized demographic to secure food through their own means. The food charity program "Social Aid" was founded and operated by the far-right coalition of political parties formed during the Spanish Civil War, the *Falange Española Traditionalista y de las Juntas de Ofensiva Nacional Sindicalista* (FET-JONS). Social Aid exploited its status as a branch of the Franco regime to gain access to Spain's food supply and coerce Spaniards with limited resources to adopt FET-JONS model behavior in exchange for daily meals. Praying before a meal or singing fascist songs in food lines were a few of the demonstrative behaviors that were required in exchange for food.

Desiring to fulfill a paternalistic role in Spain by making women and children dependent on the Francoist state while maintaining strict surveillance of daily practices as intimate as eating, the Franco regime, through Social Aid, aimed to restructure the Spanish family meal with Franco as the head of the family. Historian Ángela Cenarro found that Spanish children who received charity from Social Aid were made to internalize both their sin and their subordination within the Francoist charity structure.[1] The habitual rituals performed at Social Aid dining halls aimed to indoctrinate women and children with the beliefs and practices of conversative Spain. These extreme and coercive measures, according to social historian Antonio Cazorla-Sanchez, meant that Spanish families only sought state charity as a last resort, choosing to rely on traditional family networks instead.[2] Still, for many Spaniards who faced the difficult choice between submitting to the Francoist state or going hungry, they chose to submit their bodies and minds to the FET-JONS in exchange for food.

Spain's working-class families, particularly women and children, were targeted by the Social Aid program for two reasons. First, the Franco regime blamed the working classes for the leftist politics of the Second Republic. As historian Michael Richards notes, Spain's urbanization and its accompanied growth of working classes were seen as a huge threat to the Francoist order,[3] so the subordination of this demographic was essential in order to achieve a "total victory" in the civil war. Second, the families of the working classes—women and children of meager resources—were the most vulnerable in the aftermath of the civil war and most in need of humanitarian relief. Many of the state initiatives specifically targeted the working-class families in order to transform them into model families in Franco's Spain. The totalitarian ambitions of the regime required the conversion of hearts and minds to the FET-JONS cause, and daily meals and eating practices were a viable way to subdue, indoctrinate, and train the Spanish population. Thus, Social Aid was developed to meet the real needs of vulnerable Spaniards, fulfilling Franco's military campaign promise to provide Spaniards with bread. Yet the program was implemented in such a way that it coerced working-class Spaniards to adapt to the regime's moral codes.

Social Aid was first launched as "Winter Aid" (*Auxilio de Invierno*) by Javier Martínez de Bedoya and Mercedes Sanz Bachiller who modeled their relief program according to Nazi Germany's *Nationalsozialistische Volkswohlfahrt* (NSV).[4] Their efforts evolved into *Auxilio Social* (Social Aid) in May 1937, when it became clear among conservative leaders that permanent and long-

---

[1] Ángela Cenarro, *Los niños del Auxilio Social*, (Madrid: Espasa Calpe, 2009), 28.
[2] Antonio Cazorla Sánchez, *Fear and Progress: Ordinary Lives in Franco Spain, 1939-1975* (Malden: Wiley-Blackwell, 2010), 70-71.
[3] Michael Richards, *A Time of Silence: Civil War and the Culture of Repression 1936-1945* (Cambridge: Cambridge University Press, 1998), 129.
[4] Ángela Cenarro, *La Sonrisa de Falange: Auxilio Social en la guerra civil y en la posguerra* (Barcelona: Crítica, 2006), 42.

term relief was going to be needed in the conquered territories.[5] Social Aid had a prominent relief role during the civil war and many international humanitarian agencies continued to channel resources through the organization at the end of the war, further legitimizing both the organization and the Franco regime within the international community. Although the Red Cross, the Rockefeller Foundation, and various national governments provided humanitarian aid to Spain, the international humanitarian networks designated Social Aid as the best conduit for humanitarian relief for Spain's urban population, thereby channeling their resources through the FET-JONS program. Likewise, the Catholic Church, Spain's traditional outlet of humanitarian relief in times of crisis, partnered with Social Aid by providing staff and locations for food distribution. Logistically and financially, Social Aid was considered nationally and internationally to be the only relief organization prepared to handle food distribution in the aftermath of the war. Thus, Social Aid gained humanitarian hegemony at the end of the civil war both domestically and internationally, further solidifying its position as part of the Franco regime.

Ultimately, the organization failed to completely coerce hungry Spaniards into following their prescribed model of urban eating. Corruption within the organization itself, such as dining hall directors who forged ledgers to sell food on the black market, acted to undermine the mission of the organization. More commonly, those who were empowered by their role in food distribution were apathetic to the hunger and plight of impoverished families. Apathy and ineptitude plagued the organization and kept it from achieving efficient charity administration. Spaniards who relied on charity from the organization were supposed to conform to the ideals of the FET-JONS in exchange for food. Many Spaniards ignored the rules and exploited bureaucratic blind spots in its food distribution. Forms of resistance to coercion were seen in the daily consumption of meals. Some Spaniards remained silent during prayers or patriotic songs rather than verbally support the institutions of the party or the Church. Others were picky about the food they received or hid food to eat at home or share with others. Many patrons remained indifferent to the values promoted by the organization, submitting to the performative demands of Social Aid as a survival strategy to acquire food without internalizing Francoist morality. Ultimately, the Social Aid program failed to subdue and indoctrinate Spanish urban families.

Every aspect of Social Aid was meant to be coercive for the patrons. The FET-JONS party determined who qualified for food, where food would be distributed, decorated the dining halls to promote state values, and cooked and served the food in a manner that reinforced the goals and values of the state.

---

[5] Ibid., 7.

The whole process was intended to model social dynamics for the Francoist state that relied on patronage and paternalism. Yet, from the chaos of the civil war and the extreme scarcity that lingered in its wake, food provisioning by Social Aid and the FET-JONS largely failed to prescribe and create a new Spanish society. Instead, many of the political divisions, opportunisms, and apathies of the civil war continued throughout the hunger years.

Earning Eligibility to Eat

The path of coercion employed by Social Aid began with requests for aid. Spaniards were categorized as male, female, youth, adult, elderly, diabetic, pregnant, student, or veteran. Each group qualified for different forms of relief according to how their demographic group was valued by the FET-JONS. Children were eligible to receive food from the child dining halls (*comedores infantiles*), while older teens received food if they attended one of the party trade schools or were members of the college student union (SEU).[6] Adults in severe economic hardship could solicit family assistance from the community kitchens (*cocinas de hermandad*), and mothers could receive special foods during pregnancy and breastfeeding through the Mother and Child program (*madre y niño*).[7] Initially, veterans who fought for Franco in the Spanish Civil War were eligible for food from Social Aid until a separate veteran program was established (*Camisas Viejas*).[8] Social Aid created demographic hierarchies that determined who received access to food and who did not. Rigid bureaucracy complicated access to food. Spaniards were forced to complete extensive paperwork for each individual requesting assistance.[9] The application process was a form of power exercised over the Spanish population where the benefactor selected who was worthy or unworthy of their charity.

To gain access to food from the dining halls, families completed an application form at the local office of the Social Aid located in each provincial capital. The application had to provide verification through census records that they were residing in the same neighborhood as the site of charity *before*

---

[6] *Labor realizada den 1944* (Madrid: Sección Femenina de FET y de las JONS, 1945).
[7] "Datos que nos han sido facilitados por la administración de esta elegación provincial, solicitados por ese departamento central" Madrid, 26 de marzo de 1940. Auxilio Social: Delegación Provincial, Madrid, Departmento Auxilio de Invierno. Archivo General de Administración. Fondo Auxilio Social, Caja 3 (122) 2180.
[8] Archivo General de Administración. Fondo Auxilio Social, Caja 3 (122) 2180.
[9] "Solicitud de asistencia en cocina de hermandad" Auxilio Social. Archivo General de Administración, fondo Auxilio Social. Caja 3 (122) 1686 BIS.

the war began.[10] With so many neighborhoods bombed and burned throughout the war, many families had to flee to other areas where buildings and utility lines were still intact. Refugees from the countryside did not qualify for relief within cities and Spaniards could not transfer eligibility from one neighborhood to another. Municipal records kept by Republican authorities were destroyed during the war, further complicating the process and leaving many Spaniards, particularly orphans and widows, without proof of pre-war residency. Without the ability to prove their residency, they were deemed ineligible for food charity through the Social Aid program. Often, only ecclesiastical records remained to validate a family's residency in a neighborhood. These records excluded secular Spaniards who left the church during the religious freedoms of the Republican period, children who were never baptized, or women who had civil marriages instead of religious ceremonies. With a reliance on Catholic records to assess eligibility, The Social Aid program systematically punished Spaniards who deviated from the conservative culture valorized by the FET-JONS and then the Franco regime.

For families who were able to gather the necessary census records to prove their food eligibility, the next step in the application process was to explain the economic, health, and political situation to justify their need for food aid. Those who were illiterate needed additional help writing their petition and were unable to verify what was written on their behalf. The last part of the form required the signature of the solicitant to affirm that they agreed with the social justice measures of Franco's Spain. If families did not sign and agree with the measures of the regime and the Social Aid, they would not receive the much-needed food. Child registration for the meal program differed slightly. The form required that a priest sign to confirm the child's baptism, first communion, and confirmation depending on their age.[11] In both cases, Spaniards needed to meet the religious and political expectations of Social Aid and, by extension, the Francoist state to qualify for food charity. Those who did not meet the political or religious requirements went hungry.

Once the application was submitted, a representative from Social Aid inspected the home of the solicitant to assess the family's moral character and write a report that verified the family's economic need. A family had to open their private space to the surveillance of a state official in order to assess their family values and morals to determine their aid. If enrollment into one of the

---

[10] "Carta circular" Auxilio Social (departamento central de Auxilio de Invierno) Madrid, 16 noviembre 1940. Archivo General de Administración. Fondo Auxilio Social, Caja 3 (122) 1686 BIS.

[11] "Solicitud de Ingreso en Comedor Infantil". Archivo General de Administración. Fondo Auxilio Social, Caja 3 (122) 1686 BIS.

relief centers was granted, Spaniards became completely reliant on the community kitchen for their daily provisioning of food. A family's rationing coupons were suspended while they received Social Aid as to limit eating alternatives.[12] This policy was adopted to curb Spaniards from eating at dining establishments and then selling their rations on the street for money or luxury goods. It made working-class families completely dependent on the dining halls for their daily meals, limiting their already restricted food choice through ration cards.

In theory, Social Aid could have supplied all of the needs of the family and taken over the difficult duties of women to provide meals for their families. In practice, the program created new challenges by removing the ability of Spaniards to buy their own food. Some kitchens and dining halls provided patrons with enough food for the entire day, permitting them to collect food to cook at home for their families, but most did not. This meant Spaniards had to travel to their assigned center twice a day and eat their meals segregated from their families at the dining facilities.[13] The relief of the Social Aid was intended to help with provisioning food for families in need, but the structure of the bureaucracy was intimidating, coercive, and overwhelming for many impoverished Spaniards.

Sites of Food Charity

Once Spaniards were sorted into their indicated relief center, most had to physically travel to their assigned dining facility each day. By the end of 1939, Social Aid divided the province of Barcelona into 10 districts with a total of 112 child cafeterias and 113 brotherhood kitchens. Some of the facilities served a double purpose for children and adults by serving staggered meals. The city was occupied by 207 sites.[14] The intent of dividing cities and towns into feeding districts was to improve the efficacy of food provisioning and to increase access to food distribution centers. On paper, each city was divided to provide relief to hungry populations in each neighborhood. In practice, food distribution through Social Aid proved much more complex than drawing lines on a map.

---

[12] "Falange Española Tradicionalista y de Las JONS: Auxilio Social, El Delegado Nacional" Madrid, 24 de febrero de 1943: Camarada Jefe del Departamento Central de Auxilio de Invierno. Archivo General de Administración, fondo Auxilio Social. Caja 3 (122) 2180.
[13] "Comedor de ancianos, Martínez Campos 18 (distrito de Santa Engracia) Auxilio Social- Departamento Central de Auxilio de Invierno" Madrid, 1 dic 1939 (ano de victoria). Archivo General de Administración. Fondo Auxilio Social, Caja 3 (122) 1704.
[14] "Relación de Asistidos y Raciones Servidas" Provincia de Barcelona, 1939. Archivo General de Administración, fondo Auxilio Social. Caja 75/25493, carpeta 20.

The Social Aid institutions took an important Spanish tradition—mealtime with the family—and reconfigured the custom within its walls of surveillance and coercion. Their goal was to instill traditional, conservative values to those whose beliefs, actions, and eating habits were not aligned with the ideology of the Francoist state.[15] Parents were separated from their children in the division between community kitchens and the child dining halls.[16] Instead of mothers cooking and serving the meal to family members, this intimate act was performed by Falangist volunteers. While the FET-JONS valued the Spanish family unit and promoted family life in its propaganda, its implementation of food provisioning through Social Aid divided families and negated the party's own doctrine. The FET-JONS claimed that children should be with their mothers, but some mothers were deemed unfit to adequately care for their children.[17] Falange members and volunteers perceived themselves as better able to raise children and provide meals than their working-class parents. The way Social Aid targeted working-class families for their charity program and then divided parents from children suggests the party deemed working-class families as unfit for Franco's Spain.

With few exceptions, entrance to the dining facilities of the Social Aid program meant that Spaniards entered sites of political indoctrination. The buildings and spatiality of the charity institutions were designed to glorify God, country, and the FET-JONS party. Within each dining center, the power politics of the regime were acted out in the provisioning of a meal. Each dining room operated by Social Aid was required to have a portrait of the Caudillo Francisco Franco, a portrait of José Antonio Primo de Rivera (the founder of the Falange party), plus an image depicting the infant Jesus in child dining halls or a crucifix in adult dining halls.[18] The emblem for Social Aid, a menacing hand clutching a dagger, was displayed on cars and uniforms, reinforcing its militaristic roots in the Spanish Civil War.[19] The Social Aid integrated connections between the victory of Franco in the Spanish Civil War, the religious crusade, and the FET-JONS political movement.

Irregular food relief through Social Aid was exacerbated by its conscripted labor force, which did not necessarily care about the ideology or values of the

---

[15] Cenarro, *Los niños del Auxilio Social*, 133.
[16] Ibid., 133.
[17] *Auxilio Social y el problema demográfico español, 1939-1950* (Madrid: Sección Femenina, 1950), 26.
[18] "Menaje necesario para un comedor infantil de 50 plazas". Archivo General de Administración. Fondo Auxilio Social, Caja 75/25494, carpeta 22.; "Inventario General de la Institución: comedor universitario del SEU" Calle Beneficencia, 8 Madrid. 2 Julio 1944. Archivo General de Administración. Fondo Auxilio Social, Caja 3 (122) 1660.
[19] *Franco in Barcelona*, 15.

FET-JONS or the Franco regime. Those who worked in the kitchens to cook, clean, and serve food were expected to be cheerful and represent the mission of Social Aid and the Franco regime. Employment with Social Aid required a background check, and only those with a history of activism for the FET-JONS were awarded high-paying positions as director of the charity institutions. Otherwise, Social Aid relied heavily on "volunteers" conscripted from the Women's Section's Social Service program, which was a six-month program required for all women aged seventeen to thirty-five that was comparable to required male military service during the dictatorship.[20] Women who wanted to apply for a passport, driver's license, or work permit had to complete three months of volunteer work, and many were assigned to volunteer in the Social Aid dining halls. Up to 60% of Social Aid workers were conscripts from the Social Service program.[21] As their labor was required and unpaid, many goals —such as a happy workforce and attitude of service—were not met.

Many of the workers in the dining facilities cared little for policies or hygiene, and even less for FET-JONS ideology and mission. Those who received charity from Social Aid had greatly varying experiences. In some cases, the volunteers provided extra food to those in need, or let their friends or family skip the line.[22] In other cases, the volunteers disregarded the needs of patrons and treated them poorly, threatening to report them to the police, and at times becoming physically violent to the women in line.[23] There was a spectrum of experiences and interactions between those who gave charity and food access and those who had to conform to those in power to receive daily meals. In one community kitchen, a volunteer did not take the tickets of those in line, meaning that the patrons with whom she interacted could return multiple times for meals that day. In the same institution, another volunteer was tasked with distributing bread with the meal, but saved the rolls for herself, essentially stealing food from people in need.[24] Since there was no

---

[20] Kathleen Richmond, *Women and Spanish Fascism*, 17.
[21] "Organizaciones Actuales. Instituciones." Madrid, 29 de julio de 1939. Archivo General de Administración. Fondo Auxilio Social, Caja 3 (122) 1686 BIS.
[22] "Cocina de Hermandad 2, Calle águila 22 (Distrito Latina) Madrid; 22 noviembre de 1939 (Año de Victoria)" Auxilio Social- Departamento Central de Auxilio de Invierno. Archivo General de Administración. Fondo Auxilio Social, Caja 3 (122) 1704.
[23] "Ref. Cocina de Hermandad 4, Calle Cervantes 36 (Distrito Congreso) Madrid, 14 Noviembre de 1939" Auxilio Social: Departamento Central de Auxilio de Invierno. Archivo General de Administración. Fondo Auxilio Social, Caja 3 (122) 2272.; *Franco in Barcelona*, 15.
[24] "Ref. Cocina de Hermandad 4, Calle Cervantes 36 (Distrito Congreso) Madrid, 14 Noviembre de 1939" Auxilio Social: Departamento Central de Auxilio de Invierno. Archivo General de Administración. Fondo Auxilio Social, Caja 3 (122) 2272.

consistency between locations or daily practices, there was no uniform indoctrination or coercion of the patrons.

While the workers did not always reflect the values of the Franco regime, the actual dining and kitchen spaces also failed to reflect conservative Spanish values. One inspector reported, "The facility finished its renovations two months ago, but the dining hall still lacks chairs, tables, electric lights, and tablecloths. Furthermore, many dishes in the kitchen are broken so that the cooks cannot cook to the capacity needed for the children."[25] The lack of dishes, chairs and tables did not deter hungry children from eating. One inspection noted that children simply gathered on the floor to eat their meals because of the lack of tables and chairs.[26] The most desperate Spaniards suffered the worst experiences, often risking proper hygiene and disease for food. In general, the poorer neighborhoods endured negligent care and indifference to their daily suffering.

The indoctrination of space through Catholic and FET-JONS regalia suffered as well. Some inspections found that facilities did not display the ideological items of the regime, such as the portrait of Franco. Directors claimed that images of Franco, along with food and decent dining furniture, were all in short supply. One child dining facility in northern Madrid "...lacked crucifix and photographs of Franco and Jose Antonio, leaving the children to pray and sing to a blank wall.[27] Although the intent of the hunger relief programs was to feed Spaniards a Francoist discourse within a regime-controlled space filled with ideological symbols, these objectives fell short in the social chaos of the Civil War and its aftermath.

Eating State Food

The final step in the process of charity administered by Social Aid was meal service to the patrons. As Lara Anderson has noted in her recent work on the cooking culture of Francoism, the regime utilized key ingredients in a

---

[25] "Ref: Comedor Infantil 5, Calle Ventorrillo 14 (Zona 1 distrito de la Inclusa) Madrid, 25 septiembre de 1940"

[26] "Informe sobre a visita de inspección realizada el dia 31 de enero de 1949 al jardín maternal de Bravo Murillo" Auxilio Social, Delegación Nacional Madrid: 2 de febrero de 1949. Archivo General de Administración. Fondo Auxilio Social, Caja 75/25492, Carpeta 6.

[27] "Ref: Comedor Infantil 2, Calle Santa Engracia 154 (Zona 4 Chamberí) Madrid, 25 de enero de 1940". Archivo General de Administración, fondo Auxilio Social. Caja 3 (122) 1704. "Rfr: comedor infantil 3, Calle Galieleo 14 (zona 4 distrito Universidad) Madrid, 10 de febrero 1940. Archivo General de Administración, fondo Auxilio Social. Caja 3 (122) 1704.

nationalization process to standardize Spaniards and their diet.[28] Social Aid attempted to standardize the meals served so that individuals in their categorical group (child, pregnant mother, college student, or adult) received the same meal as everyone else. The national delegation for Social Aid imposed standardized recipes for meals that all charity dining halls were supposed to follow. Nevertheless, variation was inevitable as cooking styles and quality of ingredients varied at each institution. Still, a closer look at the official menu of Social Aid, and the variation from that menu, provides insight into how broadly the Spanish government attempted to regulate eating habits, and how the practice of everyday life dissolved aspects of that power dynamic.

Recent academic interest in the connection between authoritarian Francoist policy and food culture of the time has focused on the nationalization, standardization, and indoctrination of aspects of Spanish food culture during the dictatorship. As mentioned previously, the state and party, represented by Social Aid, replaced the family in the provisioning of daily meals, creating a new form of family with its own culture and traditions. Each meal nationalized Spaniards who attended the program, generating a singular Spanish food culture over regional or international variations. The practice of eating corralled Spaniards into a food culture of austerity, forcing the needy into a cheap, monotonous, and bland diet. Social Aid further herded Spaniards into congregational feeding, ignoring personal taste and preference in the making of a meal. Taken together, these three attributes of Social Aid's food program acted to reinforce the new power dynamics of the "culture of victory," dictated by Franco, the Church, and the FET-JONS party.[29]

To nationalize the Spanish diet, Social Aid selected key ingredients promoted by the Franco regime to be part of the national Spanish diet. Anderson explains that rice and oranges were praised during both the dictatorship of Primo de Rivera and Franco as foods that embodied Spain's national character. Their preparation and consumption demonstrated participation in the nation-building processes of these dictators.[30] Social Aid reinforced the efforts of the Spanish government to instill national pride in rice consumption through serving it in several of its establishments on an almost weekly basis. In the community kitchens, rice in fish soup and rice in

---

[28] Lara Anderson, *Food and Francoism: Food Discourse, Control & Resistance in Franco Spain* (1939-1959) (Toronto: University of Toronto Press, 2019), 28.
[29] For more on the theory of the development of Franco's "culture of victory" in the aftermath of the Spanish Civil War, see Carlos Fuertes Muños, *Viviendo en Dictadura. La evolución de las actitudes sociales hacia el franquismo* (Granada: Editorial Comares, 2017).
[30] Anderson, *Food and Francoism*, 33.

fish stew were common meals.[31] Rice was used as an inexpensive filler, which was often mixed with meat, potatoes, chickpeas, cod, or tuna. [32]

Oranges were another nationalized food served by Social Aid, but since oranges were considered a dessert and therefore a luxury item, they were largely reserved for attendees in the diabetic dining halls, the student dining halls, and the prenatal programs.[33] Despite the scarcity of many foods during the 1940s, Spain enjoyed a surplus of oranges harvested from their groves. Yet, the government used its orange production as economic levrage, selling Spanish oranges on the international market for a quarter of the price of California or Florida oranges.[34] Spain's ally of the time, Nazi Germany, took advantage of Spain's cheap orange prices and close political ties, buying up 64.29 percent of Spain's orange supply in 1939.[35] There were not enough remaining oranges to feed all Spaniards, so only those with special privilege and priority from the regime received oranges as part of their meal. As the example of oranges demonstrates, privilege and participation in the regime's initiatives was divided within the nation-building project in the early Franco dictatorship.

The mass distribution of food through the charity meant that meals were prepared in large quantities, often with little regard for health and safety standards. Many Social Aid locations in Madrid reported that they served hundreds of meals in a matter of hours for both lunch and dinner. The amount of food, labor, and time to cook for such large quantities meant that quality went by the wayside. The mismanagement of the dining centers produced such low quality that some meals were inedible. Nevertheless, hungry people were expected to be appreciative of the food that they received. Some meals served Social Aid can only be described as a punishment to the patrons inflicted by the FET-JONS party and the Franco regime. Yet patrons were not permitted to protest or complain. One inspection of a community kitchen in the

---

[31] "Cocinas de Hermandad". Archivo General de Administración. Fondo Auxilio Social, Caja 75/25494, carpeta 22.
[32] "Comedor Infantil: Comidas compuestas". Archivo General de Administración. Fondo Auxilio Social, Caja 3 (122) 2154.
[33] Centro Diabéticos (Chamberí, zona 4) C/General Martínez Campos, 36- 21. Archivo General de Administración. Fondo Auxilio Social, Caja 3 (122) 1665.; "Ref: Comedor Infantil 1, Concepción Arenal 1 (Distrito del Centro) Madrid, 4 de diciembre de 1939" Auxilio Social: Departamento Central de Auxilio de Invierno. Archivo General de Administración. Fondo Auxilio Social, Caja 3 (122) 2250.; "Hogar Ciudad Universitaria". Archivo General de Administración. Fondo Auxilio Social, Caja 3 (122) 1666.
[34] M. Pérez Urruti, *España en números: Síntesis de la producción, consumo y comercio nacionales, 1940-1941*, (Madrid: M. Aguilar, 1942,) 40.
[35] Ibid., 40.

neighborhood of Chamberí reported that a rat fell into a vat of soup that was nevertheless served to patrons.[36] Rats also entered food storage areas and nibbled on bread that was later served at a children's dining facility in the central Madrid neighborhood, causing widespread diseases among the vulnerable children.[37] There was no question that rodents carried diseases and were a threat to public health. By serving food contaminated by rats, Social Aid risked spreading disease within working-class neighborhoods. Yet the rodent-infested food was served anyway to the impoverished working classes within the city. One possible motive was that the directors of the dining hall did not want such large quantities of food to go to waste. If the volunteers stopped serving contaminated food, there would not be enough for the hungry population. Ultimately, however, the decision to continue serving contaminated food suggests that the Social Aid workers did not care about the health of those in need. Rather, they believed impoverished Spaniards should and would be happy with any food, despite the quality or contamination.

Food shortages contributed to the poor quality of food served by the Social Aid program and variability to the dining hall menus. Food shortages and economic stagnation in the 1940s affected the program's ability to secure and distribute food to the growing need. The Francoist state failed to supply the funds needed to cover all the costs of the relief operation.[38] Many private benefactors to the charity experienced donor fatigue at the end of the war even as the hunger and poverty continued into the 1940s. Children were served rice and lima beans, often without any form of oil, seasoning, or bread to accompany the meals.[39] Social Aid reports reveal that administrators knew how much the children hated lima beans, but they directed institutions to serve them often for both lunch and dinner.[40] Some children refused to eat

---

[36] "Ref: Cocina de Hermandad 2, Santa Engracia 116 (Distrito Chamberí) 2 diciembre 1939; Auxilio Social- Departamento Central de Auxilio de Invierno". Archivo General de Administración, fondo Auxilio Social. Caja 3 (122) 1704.

[37] "Ref: Comedor Infantil 1, Calle Concepción Arenal 1 (Distrito del Centro) Madrid, 7 de Diciembre 1939" Auxilio Social: Departamento Central de Auxilio de Invierno". Archivo General de Administración. Fondo Auxilio Social, Caja 3 (122) 2250.

[38] Cenarro, *La sonrisa de Falange*, 51.

[39] "Ref: Cocina Infantil 1, Calle Bravo Murillo 125 (Zona 4, Distrito de la Universidad) 9 de mayo de 1940" Auxilio Social: Departamento Central de Auxilio de Invierno. Archivo General de Administración. Fondo Auxilio Social, Caja 3 (122) 1704.

[40] "Ref: Cocina Infantil 1, Calle Bravo Murillo 125 (Zona 4, Distrito de la Universidad) 9 de mayo de 1940" Auxilio Social: Departamento Central de Auxilio de Invierno. Archivo General de Administración. Fondo Auxilio Social, Caja 3 (122) 1704.; "Ref: Comedor Infantil 2, Calle Ramon y Cajal 18 (zona 2 Distrito Congreso) Madrid, 16 enero 1940" Auxilio Social- Departmento Central de Auxilio de Invierno. Archivo General de Administración. Fondo Auxilio Social, Caja 3 (122) 2272.

the monotonous and bland food, while others suffered greatly from hunger and resorted to eating plants and nuts found outside the charity institutions.[41] While there are documented cases of Spanish children becoming sick from such foraged food, there were also documented cases of children developing severe gastritis from the food they ate at the Social Aid dinning-halls.[42] One account reported that a cook erroneously used motor oil instead of olive oil in a recipe and poisoned a hungry child.[43] Spaniards who participated in food charity not only sacrificed individual taste. Sometimes they sacrificed their physical health also.

While the official menu for Social Aid suffered from monotony and poor-quality ingredients, some of the problems with the food were due to local variability in the foodways and poor management. Lack of proper ingredients, lack of education or communication of the recipes, or personal motivations and opportunism by the directors or volunteers led to unsafe food.[44] Those who relied on hunger relief surrendered choice and accepted the reliance and provisioning of the FET-JONS. Often, food arrived spoiled, underweight, or improperly preserved. One internal report on potato provisioning found that of the 400kg of potatoes needed at the Cervantes community kitchen, 161kg were rotten. For one child dining hall, 30kg of the necessary 47kg of potatoes were rotten. The inspector noted this level of waste was normal for many other child dining halls.[45] To accommodate these shortages, patrons were either served rotten potatoes or smaller portions. Fish that was going bad was double-fried to mask the unsavory flavor of spoiled seafood.[46]

Opportunism by Social Aid staff abounded, and those reliant on charity were at their mercy. At the child dining facilities, staff routinely ate better meals than those served to the needy children. Many children suspected that

---

[41] Ángela Cenarro, *Los Niños del Auxilio Social* (Madrid: Espasa Calpe, 2009), 180.

[42] "Acuso recibido a tu oficio número 108, de fecha 8 del corriente." Archivo General de Administración. Fondo Auxilio Social, Caja 3 (122) 2180.

[43] "Ref: Comedor Infantil 4 (Distrito del Centro) Madrid 27 de noviembre de 1939" Auxilio Social: Departamento Central de Auxilio de Invierno. Archivo General de Administración, fondo Auxilio Social. Caja 3 (122) 2250.

[44] "Madrid, 12 de junio de 1944. Camarada Jefe del Departamento Central de Abastecimiento". Archivo General de Administración, fondo Auxilio Social. Caja 3 (122) 1658.; "Auxilio Social: Delegación Nacional" Madrid, 24 de septiembre de 1942. Archivo General de Administración, fondo Auxilio Social. Caja 3 (122) 2180.

[45] "Ref: Información sobre suministro de patatas" Madrid, 16 noviembre de 1939 Auxilio Social- Departamento Central de Auxilio de Invierno. Archivo General de Administración. Fondo Auxilio Social, Caja 3 (122) 1704.

[46] Centro Diabéticos Martínez Campos, 36 (Chamberí zona 4) clase adultos. Archivo General de Administración. Fondo Auxilio Social, Caja 3 (122) 1664 BIS.

the adults stole their rations.[47] Other staff exploited their access to food for their own consumption or to sell on the black market, leaving patrons with smaller meals or missing key ingredients needed for a balanced diet. One community kitchen recorded 40kg of fish in its ledger, but an inspector weighed the amount as 60kg. When the inspector asked the director, he stated that the additional fish was reserved for the staff.[48] In another case, a director of a child dining stole 11kg of sugar in one week for herself. When caught, she dismissed the theft as "only a teaspoon or two for her personal use."[49] Black marketeering, forgery of the pantry ledgers, and hoarding were all too common among the Social Aid workers who exploited their access to state food.

In theory, meals served by the Social Aid were at specific times to regulate travel to the dining facilities, to determine when patrons gathered in groups to receive rations and when they ate. The set mealtimes essentially pushed Spaniards into the urban public spaces at feeding times or cast them back to their homes and private life after the meals. The Franco regime regulated that dining establishments could only serve lunch before 2:30 pm and dinner before 9:30 pm.[50] Social Aid kitchens were included in this regulation.[51] Self-reporting from the directors of the Social Aid hunger relief programs claimed that meals were available from 12 pm until 1:30 pm for lunch and around 8 pm for dinner.[52] Mealtime regulation was intended to prevent patrons from forming long lines or roaming the city streets after dark. If meals were served late, female aid workers risked walking the streets alone in the dark, which would have raised questions about their morals and could lead to arrest or attacks.[53] Punctual meals were important to Social Aid, but once again, expectations were curbed by the reality of food and labor scarcity during the 1940s.

---

[47] Cenarro, *Los niños del Auxilio Social*, 183.
[48] "N.R. Cocina de Hermandad 3, Marqués de Zafra 12 (Congreso) Madrid, 31 agosto 1939" Auxilio Social: Departamento Central de Auxilio de Invierno. Archivo General de Administración. Fondo Auxilio Social, Caja 3 (122) 2272.
[49] "Ref Comedor Infantil 1, Calle Silva 6 (zona 2 centro) Madrid, 30 abril 1940" Auxilio Social: Departamento Central de Auxilio de Invierno. Archivo General de Administración. Fondo Auxilio Social, Caja 3 (122) 1704.
[50] Tomás Espuny Gómez, *Legislación de abastos: Exposición metódica de las principales disposiciones vigentes*, (Tarragona: Imprenta de José Pijoan, 1942), 376-377.
[51] Cenarro, *La Sonrisa de Falange*, 102.
[52] "Cuestionario". Auxilio Social. Archivo General de Administración, fondo Auxilio Social. Caja 3 (122) 928.
[53] "Me comunica la Jefe del Comedor Universitario...". Archivo General de Administración, fondo Auxilio Social. Caja 3 (122) 1658.

In practice, eating times were very irregular at the dining halls. One inspector noted that when he stopped by at 1 pm to assess the food distribution, the cook was still peeling potatoes, not even cooking them or plating them yet.[54] Other institutions ran out of food within 30 minutes and left hundreds of registered working-class families without food.[55] As it was common for kitchens to run out of supplies and the risk of hunger was so great, Spaniards preferred to wait in line rather than come later and risk being turned away. One inspector commented after visiting a community kitchen in the Hospicio neighborhood about the "continuous spectacle of unpleasant lines that begin to form [in front of the community kitchen] at one in the morning until four in the afternoon.[56] Many orphaned children had nowhere to go in between meals, so they loitered around the charity facility, creating "gangs of vagabond children" as one observer put it.[57] Dinner was also later, sometimes not beginning until 9:30 pm and some were reported as late as 10:30 pm.[58] Spaniards were subjected to the operating times of the Social Aid, regardless of the time it took them to travel to the dining center or the times in the day that they were hungry.

Conclusion

The Social Aid program was designed as a coercive tool of the Francoist state to monitor and control the everyday eating habits of needy Spaniards. The organization regulated when people ate, what they ate, and the quantities they ate. While feeding the vulnerable populations of Spain's cities fell under the guise of charity, the meals were not given freely and required significant coercion and adaptation to the mission of the FET-JONS and the Francoist state. Some Spaniards, desperate to fill their bellies, conformed to some of the demands of Social Aid. Others presented small examples of non-conformity or resistance to the program's mission, despite the domineering power dynamic of the charity dining halls. In practice, Social Aid failed to live up to the grand

---

[54] "Ref. Cocina de Hermandad 3, Comedor Infantil 3 (Márquez de Zafra 12), Cocina de Hermandad 5 (O' Donell 57), Cocina de Hermandad 4 (Cervantes 36), Comedor Infantil 2 (Ramon y Cajal 18), Gutemberg 10 Congreso" Madrid, 28 Octubre 1939. Archivo General de Administración. Fondo Auxilio Social, Caja 3 (122) 2272.
[55] "Cuestionario". Auxilio Social. Archivo General de Administración, fondo Auxilio Social. Caja 3 (122) 928.
[56] "Informe 12" enero 1939. Cocina de hermandad 2, Calle Gongora 5. Archivo General de Administración, fondo Auxilio Social. Caja 3 (122) 1704.
[57] Correspondencia. Madrid, 25 de febrero de 1943. Archivo General de Administración. Fondo Auxilio Social, Caja 3 (122) 2180.
[58] Archivo General de Administración. Fondo Auxilio Social, Caja 3 (122) 2212.

ambitions of its mission because of a lack of adequate government funding and corruption by its local administrators and conscripted volunteers.

Spaniards adopted new patterns in their daily routines, particularly cooking and eating, due to the circumstances of the repressive dictatorship and the material limitations of international isolation and war. The process of acquiring and consuming daily meals was significantly altered in that many Spaniards were forced to rely on the food distributed by the Francoist regime through the Social Aid program that forced a ritual of affirmation of state policies and values in exchange for daily meals. With coercion applied to every aspect of the meal—eligibility requirements, geographic limitations to dining halls, indoctrinating décor within the facilities and the nationalized meals served—women and children felt the repression of the new dictatorship on a daily basis.

The way Spaniards interacted with food—either through discourse, policy, popular culture, or the eating of a meal—provides a unique window into how individuals and communities react to larger governing bodies and cultural institutions. In the case of Spaniards living under the Franco dictatorship, the analysis of food charity and through the Social Aid program demonstrates how the state imposed restrictive and coercive food practices on the Spanish population. The FET-JONS proposed totalitarian aims to control Spain and its resources. Food was particularly important during the dictatorship because of its scarcity. Chronic famines during the 1940s and constant consumer-good shortages in cities meant food was in short supply and many Spaniards felt the pangs of hunger. The food policy of the Francoist state determined who had access to food and who did not, rewarding those who conformed to state ideology while punishing those who resisted with hunger. Yet this chapter also illustrates the way Spaniards responded to food policies and food cultures imposed on urban society. Thus, the performance of eating and not eating, and the discourse surrounding the production, distribution, and consumption of certain foods, reinforced or contested the ideological or political boundaries of the repressive dictatorship.

Chapter 10

Women, Children, and "Slow Starvation" in Occupied France

Kenneth Mouré
University of Alberta

Abstract: The Vichy regime that governed France under the German Occupation 1940-1944 stressed the importance of the family as "the very foundation" of French society. It declared it would build a stronger France with a "new moral order" based on order, hierarchy, paternal authority, and the return of women to the home to raise children in traditional families.

During the Occupation, many families did strengthen their connections with relatives and communities. But this was fostered by lived experience, in collision with Vichy rhetoric, and in opposition to Vichy policies. Vichy's food regime of "slow starvation" increased women's responsibilities in providing for their families, their public roles in food acquisition, and promoted the evasion of state controls as necessary to feed families and raise children.

Keywords: Vichy France, occupation, food controls, patriarchy, food policies, family, women, children, blackmarket

***

When France fell in June 1940, First World War hero Marshal Philippe Pétain declared that France had lost the war because decadence had sapped national strength: "Less strong than twenty-two years ago, we also had fewer friends, too few children, too few arms, too few allies." In July, as head of state in Vichy, he claimed that Vichy family policies would restore a healthy and strong France, with abundant children and secure families as the foundation for national renewal. "The family," Pétain wrote, "is the essential cell; it is the very foundation of the social edifice. It is on this we must build; if it weakens, all is lost; so long as it holds, all can be saved."[1] In place of the Third Republic's revolutionary call for "Liberty, Equality, Fraternity," Vichy offered "Work, Family, and Fatherland" with the family as central to a nation based on order, hierarchy, and paternal authority.

Four years later, as the well-armed allies of Free France landed on the beaches in Normandy to end the German Occupation and Vichy rule, Vichy's family policy lay in shambles. It was underfunded, conflicted in its policy goals and methods, and its claims to improve moral and gender order had fallen victim to the imperatives of lived experience in Occupied France. Police and prefects lamented the decline of morality and the indolence and criminal propensities of a younger generation that lacked a moral compass. Four years of occupation, in their view, had damaged youth morale and state of mind, posing a threat to order in France after the war. France needed moral reconstruction, not just economic, to repair the damage of the Vichy years.[2]

Vichy's program for the family was traditional and paternalist, wishing to restore a mythic world of secure families with mothers at home raising children while fathers provided income, authority, and discipline. This vision collided with the facts of existence under German occupation. Despite the artificial and temporary peace after the armistice with Nazi Germany in June 1940, French families lived under conditions of war, with many fathers absent, families separated, and essential goods in scarce supply. The economy of penury under German occupation and the low amount of rations allowed to French citizens meant that finding sufficient food became the primary concern for most families. This chapter surveys the experiences of women and children as they dealt with food shortages and improvised to obtain needed goods. Lived experience rather than Vichy ideology did strengthen family ties and cooperative action. It did so not thanks to, but in opposition to, the New Order Vichy had promised.

Vichy's Family Program

Along with Vichy's agenda in the slogan "Work, Family, and Fatherland," Pétain's attribution of the French defeat to a list that included having "too few children" made families and raising children a core objective for Vichy's

---

[1] Maréchal Pétain, "La politique sociale de l'avenir," *Revue des Deux Mondes* [Sept 1940], 114-15.
[2] Archives Nationales, Paris [AN], 72AJ/384, Col. Meunier, "Synthèse pour la période du 15 décembre 1944 au 15 janvier 1945," February 12, 1945, is one of many such reports. The concerns for moral decline are explained in Mouré, *Marché Noir: The Economy of Survival in Second World War France* (Cambridge : Cambridge University Press, 2023), 197-99, 222-27.

restoration of France. Concerns for France's low birth rate had preoccupied governments since the French defeat by Prussia in 1870, and Vichy brought to power a constellation of individuals who drew on pronatalist, Catholic, and conservative ideas to promote families as the foundation for a healthy nation. The family as a social unit was seen as the essential building block for a nation no longer divided and weakened by false notions of equality, democracy, individualism, and greater freedoms for women. But every element of "Work, Family, and Fatherland" was compromised by the German occupiers and by Vichy administrators' belief that collaboration would enable the National Revolution to restore a traditionalist, hierarchical, paternalist, and authoritarian France. Work was underpaid, with wages fixed in a period of rising prices, and it was increasingly organized to support Germany's war effort. Despite Vichy propaganda as to its importance and the new laws to restrict women's employment and promote childbearing, the family was increasingly in danger of starvation. The fatherland, with Pétain as its heroic military leader, operated ever more evidently as a puppet state serving German interests rather than French.[3]

The Vichy agenda for the family offered more discriminatory rhetoric against women for taking on roles outside motherhood than positive developments to promote healthy families. Responsibility for the family was in the hands of the Ministry of Family and Youth from July 1940, but was passed to a Secretary for Health in the Ministry of the Interior, and then to a Secretary for the Family and Health in February 1941, which then became the Secretary for Health in May 1942.[4] Vichy rhetoric and legislation focused initially on removing women from the workplace and measures to contain the "plagues" it saw as threatening the life of the family: alcoholism, prostitution, and abortion. Vichy policies would return women to "the place that nature assigned to them"—the home.[5] Family allowances paid for each child (beginning with the second) had begun in 1932, and Vichy broadened family eligibility for the allowances. Vichy recognized the contribution of mothers in re-establishing Mother's Day in 1941 as an official holiday on the last Sunday

---

[3] On the importance of collaboration, see the key contributions of Robert O. Paxton, *Vichy France: Old Guard and New Order, 1940-1944* (New York: Columbia University Press, 1972) and Philippe Burrin, *France Under the Germans: Collaboration and Compromise*, translated by Janet Lloyd (New York: The New Press, 1996).
[4] Christophe Capuano, *Vichy et la famille: Réalités et faux-semblants d'une politique publique* (Rennes: Presses universitaires de Rennes, 2009), pp. 50-53.
[5] Sarah Fishman, *We Will Wait: Wives of French Prisoners of War, 1940-1945* (New Haven: Yale University Press, 1991), pp. 42-45; quote from Georgette Varenne, *La Femme dans la France nouvelle*, 1940.

of May. This recognition provided more window-dressing than useful support.[6] The inconsistencies, contradictions, and weaknesses of Vichy policies for motherhood and the family are nowhere more evident than in the problems of food supply.

Vichy's food rationing regime was implemented in September 1940. It was the product of poor planning in preparation for war, supply disruptions in the summer of 1940, and German pressures for a national rationing system. They had assumed a long, defensive war, with access to imports from Allies and the empire in the long path to ultimate victory. Some preliminary measures were imposed in early 1940, and planning began for a national system based on individual ration cards. Defeat in 1940 produced chaos, with more than eight million people fleeing the German advance in "the exodus" and food supply disrupted by the transport chaos and by some local authorities (especially prefects of French departments) who forbade the transport of food out of their region, anticipating shortages. Prefects and municipal authorities used temporary measures to allocate limited food supplies. The invading German forces seized control of food warehouses and transport infrastructure, and divided France into occupation "zones" with tight restrictions on transit between them. In July and August, the Germans required the creation of a national rationing system before they would release stocks of food from warehouses. Against French protests, the Germans insisted on ration levels that imposed slow starvation: adult rations of 350 grams of bread per day, 360 grams of meat per week, 500 grams of sugar per month. Adult rations thus gave less than 1300 calories per day, well below the League of Nations basic level of 2400 calories for an adult. French rations were the lowest in occupied Western Europe, although higher than the rations in Eastern Europe.[7]

---

[6] Muel-Dreyfus titles her section on this Vichy initiative, "The Imposition of Mother's Day." See Francine Muel-Dreyfus, *Vichy and the Eternal Feminine: A Contribution to a Political Sociology of Gender*, translated by Kathleen A. Johnson (Durham: Duke University Press, 2001), pp. 110-24.

[7] The start of French rationing in 1940 is summarized in Kenneth Mouré, "Food Rationing and the Black Market in France," *French History* 24.2 (2010) 266-68. For ration levels in Occupied Europe, see Hein Klemann with Sergei Kudryashov, *Occupied Economies: An Economic History of Nazi-occupied Europe, 1939-1945* (London: Berg, 2012), Table 17.1, 380, and their discussion of food supply and rations, 375-99. Britain, with significant dependence on imported food, was far better off during the war, with a rationing system claiming to provide "Fair Shares for All." British rations were sufficient, but offered little variety. Bread and potatoes were not rationed during the war. See Ina Zweiniger-Bargielowska, *Austerity in Britain: Rationing, Controls, and Consumption, 1939-1955* (Oxford: Oxford University Press, 2000), pp. 31-45.

The rationing regime rendered shopping for household needs vastly more complicated, frustrating, and time-consuming. Housewives, mothers, in particular, bore the brunt of the changes in consumer freedom. Individual ration cards were distributed from municipal offices (Paris had twenty *arrondissements*, each with its *mairie*), as were the coupons for monthly and weekly rationed goods, and the tickets for daily rations. Consumers queued for their ration documents, which enabled them to then purchase specified quantities of ration goods after queueing again at the relevant shops, if the goods they wanted were still available. The coupons valid for exchange, which varied in timing and quantity according to the season and local supplies, were announced in the press. Consumers had to keep their cards and tickets in order, exchange coupons for tickets when the goods were available, use the correct tickets, and queue at the shops where they had registered, hoping their ration entitlement would be available when they reached the counter.[8] For most rationed food, shops were allocated quantities according to the clients registered to buy from them or the tickets and coupons they turned in to replenish stocks. The system was enormously time-consuming, and highly vulnerable to fraudulent practices on the part of customers, sellers, and wholesale distributors (a matter to which I return below).

The system divided consumers into ration categories according to their age and employment: infants (E) under three years old; initially two and then three categories for children and teenagers (J1 from three to six, J2 from six to twelve, and the J3 category added in 1941 for ages thirteen to twenty-one); adults (A); adults doing heavy labor (T); cultivators (C), and the elderly over seventy (V). Concern for the family and raising healthy children was evident in the extra calories allocated for infants and younger children, especially milk, which was also given to nursing mothers, and the priority cards introduced in 1941 for mothers who were pregnant, nursing, or had several children at home.[9] Apart from its complexity and the opportunities for fraud, the major challenge for consumers was that the rations allowed were below, sometimes far below, daily needs for all categories except E and J1. Consumers needed to obtain unrationed food to survive.

While some extra calories were available at first in foods that were not rationed, these options diminished as consumers bought up available goods, rationing was extended, and unrationed goods declined in quantity and

---

[8] Eric Alary, Bénédicte Vergez-Chaignon and Gilles Gauvin, *Les Français au quotidien, 1939-1949* (Paris: Perrin, 2006), pp. 210-11.

[9] The cards for multiple children were for mothers having at least four children under sixteen years old or three children under fourteen or two children under four. On the abuse of priority cards, Mouré, *Marché Noir*, 137-39.

quality. Fixed prices and illicit demand diverted a growing share of production to the black market. Pétain claimed that rationing was a "cruel necessity," but one that would provide equality of sacrifice and avoid a competitive system in which the wealthy would be unaffected and the poor pay the price: "Everyone must share in the common privations, without wealth saving some and increasing the misery of the others."[10] But the insufficient rations required that consumers find more food. As Dominique Veillon notes of Parisians' adaptations to the challenges of shortages, rationing, and German domination, "They used all sorts of defensive measures that combined inventiveness, solidarity, and illegality."[11]

Feeding Families

In contrast to the Vichy rhetoric and policies that promoted hierarchy, patriarchy, and the family, actual family life after the French defeat emphasized the importance of women as providers, managers, and caregivers. The many men absent because called up for military service, killed in battle, interned in camps as prisoners of war, and later called to do labor service in Germany, shifted the gender balance in households. Wives and mothers had greater responsibilities, duties, and visibility. France mobilized 4.2 million soldiers in 1939-1940; roughly 92,000 died in the battle for France and 1,850,000 were taken prisoner, more than half of whom would remain prisoners in Germany until 1945. French volunteers to work in Germany numbered in the tens of thousands, and the workers requisitioned for labor from late 1942 to 1945 brought about 650,000 French workers (mostly men, some women) to Germany.[12]

Soldiers' families received support in the form of military allowances, and these continued for the wives and children of soldiers taken prisoner in 1940. The allowances were minimal and declined in value as prices rose in Occupied France. Family and Health Secretary Jacques Chevalier advocated for an increase in these allowances in 1941, stating that at their current level, prisoners' wives and children were "condemned to the most severe deprivation," with many wives being forced into prostitution to support their families. Benefits were raised incrementally, in 1941 and 1942, but lagged seriously behind the rising cost of living. Wives sending food packages to their husbands in POW camps gave up food from their own rations and struggled to

---

[10] Philippe Pétain, *Discours aux Français 17 juin 1940 – 20 août 1944*, edited by Jean-Claude Barbas (Paris: Albin Michel, 1989), p. 84; speech from October 10, 1940.
[11] Dominique Veillon, *Paris allemand: Entre refus et soumission* (Paris: Tallandier, 2021), p. 80.
[12] Yves le Maner and Henry Rousso, "La domination allemande," in A. Beltran, R. Frank and H. Rousso, eds., *La vie des entreprises sous l'Occupation* (Paris: Belin, 1994), pp. 26-29.

find income for extras. In May 1941, the state allowed them a paltry two francs per day to help pay for the food in POW parcels.[13]

Under these circumstances, women bore most of the stress in dealing with food shortages. Célia Bertin writes that "Finding food quickly became an obsession. For women especially, who were the first touched by food supply demands. They managed the cards and tickets for their family and soon learned that these tickets they counted on, given the shortages, were not always honored, or honored only in part."[14] The queues became an ordeal, especially in bad weather, as hundreds of customers could line up before stores opened, hoping to obtain their share of limited supplies. Berthe Auroy, who kept a journal to describe experience under occupation to an American friend, described the suffering of waiting in queues in the snow, sometimes for several hours, "to obtain ... oh! not much and sometimes nothing at all, if the food on sale ran out." Auroy had "special equipment" as her "costume de queue," with layers of wool clothing, knitted socks so thick they stood on their own "like the boots of a sewerman," an "artilleryman's" coat, and she wrapped herself in a large grey shawl, with a fur muff underneath for her hands.[15] The shops and market stalls frequently ran out of food; butchers and dairy shops in particular were prone to run out and close early. The Paris police worried about the potential this created for unrest and brought in rules to reduce the time and the length of queues as an obstruction to traffic and a potential for unrest. Reporting on the crowds in the Buci market in central Paris, police recorded that the queues began at 5 a.m. and could number in the hundreds (2000 outside one butcher shop); shops closed with their stock exhausted by 9 a.m.[16] Dominique Veillon notes the case of one housewife who queued for more than four hours one morning in October 1942, at six different shops, at the end of which she had only a list of times when they might have food later that day.[17]

All were not equal in terms of sacrifice and access to food. Geography mattered. Rural families had easier access to food and could have their own gardens, whereas those in cities depended on the food available in markets, and this varied depending on the kinds of agriculture in the surrounding regions. Class and income also mattered. Workers' wages were frozen and the

---

[13] Fishman, *We Will Wait*, 45-54.
[14] Célia Bertin, *Femmes sous l'Occupation* (Paris: Stock, 1993), p. 40.
[15] Berthe Auroy, *Jours de guerre: Ma vie sous l'Occupation* (Paris: Bayard, 2008), pp. 136-37, in a section titled "La grande pénitence. Queues ..."
[16] Archives de la Préfecture de Police, Paris [APP] BA 1808, Commissaire de Police in the 6th arrondissement to the Director of Municipal Police, December 22, 1940.
[17] Dominique Veillon, "La vie quotidienne des femmes," *Le régime de Vichy et les Français*, eds. Jean-Pierre Azéma and François Bédarida (Paris: Fayard, 1992), pp. 631-32.

standard of living fell for the middle and working classes as prices rose. Rationed goods were sold at controlled prices, but the additional food needed to survive had to be purchased at rising black market prices. The Paris police observed in 1941: "The middle and working classes state that circumstances tend to divide consumers into two very distinct clans: those on one side, the owning classes, who can provision themselves almost normally by means of the 'black market,' and on the other side the working classes, who lack essentials. The words of the head of state claiming the equality of all in dealing with restrictions are bitterly underlined."[18] Célia Bertin wrote later, "Never were inequalities due to money more evident. The profits of the black market showed up quickly, and women were the first to notice them.... Apart from the groups who profited from it, the restrictions and black market created an environment unfavorable to the regime. Women, sensitized to injustice because so often its victims, felt they were treated worse than ever."[19]

Family connections made a difference as the food shortages prompted closer relations and exchanges between urban and rural family to provide relatives with food. Beginning in the summer of 1940, farming families sent food packages (*colis familiaux*) to their relatives and friends in the cities. The French railroad system (SNCF) had to set up a special sorting station in Le Mans to handle the food parcels coming from Normandy and Brittany to Paris in the autumn of 1940, and a depot in Paris for the arriving packages at the Gare Saint-Lazare.[20] Despite the opposition of German authorities, the Vichy government allowed such packages officially in October 1941, regulating their contents and setting a maximum parcel weight of 50 kg.[21] These became a major conduit of food to cities; in addition to millions of the parcels that could weigh up to 50 kg, smaller "packets" (*paquets*) of up to 3 kg were commonly used, especially for perishable foods. Their number rose steadily to 34 million in 1941, and 70 million in 1944.[22]

The term "family" was employed to distinguish the parcels sent to meet the needs of families from the traffic in food supplies for profit at black market prices. But many families arranged for a regular shipment of such parcels for payment. This way, farmers could be sure their food went to French

---

[18] APP 220W 4, "Situation à Paris," June 16, 1941.
[19] Bertin, *Femmes sous l'Occupation*, 41-42.
[20] AN F/90/21609; PTT, "Augmentation du trafic à Montparnasse," January 21, 1941; the dépôt in Saint-Lazare opened in January 1941.
[21] Dominique Veillon, *Vivre et survivre en France 1939-1947* (Paris: Payot, 1995), pp. 173-76; German opposition was discussed in AN F/60/1546, reports on meetings in June, September, and October 1941.
[22] AN F/90/21627, "Historique des mesures ayant intéressé l'acheminement des correspondances pendant la période de guerre."

consumers rather than the Germans, and better-off city families could supplement their rations. Most of the parcels sent to Paris went to wealthy districts. Alfred Sauvy thought they should be called "food parcels," and saw them as "a great manifestation of bourgeois hypocrisy," a means for wealthy families in the richest neighborhoods of Paris to undermine the egalitarian impulse behind rationing.[23] The police and the SNCF likewise reported that most parcels went to the wealthy neighborhoods.[24]

The parcels, especially if they arrived regularly, were of course shared amongst family, and also with friends. Diarists in Paris wrote of the parcels in the winter of 1940-1941 as providing vital supplements. Jean Guéhenno observed on January 3, "Life in Paris is growing very difficult. We have ration tickets, but we can't buy anything with them anymore. The shops are empty. At home, we've lived exclusively on parcels sent by friends and cousins in Brittany for the past two weeks."[25] Auroy wrote that distant friends aided "unfortunate Parisians" by sending food parcels; an elderly peasant woman in the Auvergne had sent a parcel that arrived in time for Christmas with eggs, butter, and a pork roast, "a crate of good things unfindable in Paris." In late January, three parcels arrived with lard, butter, eggs, vegetables, and a chicken, from which she made presents to friends and her concierge.[26] The Groult family received their first parcel from relatives in Brittany in February 1941; it included a dozen eggs and a chicken that had started to go bad. They depended on family parcels to supplement their rations.[27]

The volume of parcel traffic increased steadily as an essential means of supply. The preparation and distribution of the food for consumption was mainly done by women, but so was the packaging and sending of the parcels not just from countryside to city, but also from cities to prisoners of war in Germany. Célia Bertin, a literature student at the Sorbonne during the occupation, from a well-off family living on the Île Saint-Louis, did not go hungry or worry about food. She quotes comments from a correspondent she names "Sidonie," in rural France, whose mother sent parcels to two families in Paris, charging them only for the transport costs. While both men and women

---

[23] Alfred Sauvy, *La vie économique des Français de 1939 à 1945* (Paris: Flammarion, 1978), pp. 133-35.
[24] AN F/90/21609; "Augmentation du trafic," January 21, 1941; APP, BA 1806, note of November 19, 1943, and 220W 12, "Situation à Paris," July 26, 1943.
[25] Jean Guéhenno, *Diary of the Dark Years, 1940-1944: Collaboration, Resistance, and Daily Life in Occupied Paris*, translated by David Ball (Oxford: Oxford University Press, 2014), p. 51.
[26] Auroy, *Jours de guerre*, 141-42.
[27] Benoîte and Flora Groult, *Journal à quatre mains* (Paris: Éditions Denoel, 1962; reprint 2002), p. 188.

sought food from farms, "I have only seen women package parcels for the Parisians or other deprived citizens." Sidonie also commented, with regard to women managing food for their families, "I don't know any woman who has not sacrificed some of 'her part' for others when were no other options."[28]

Although Vichy wanted women confined to the private sphere, raising children and supporting their husbands, the quest for sufficient food and women's increased role in household management gave them greater visibility in the proliferation of queues to buy food. These could serve as a center for a new sociability, discussing available food, rumors of food scandals and black markets, and recipes for the unpalatable root vegetables that became a staple for official produce markets.[29] They could also become a site for mobilization to demand more food when the markets were barren. Already visible in queues as public testimony to Vichy's food supply failures, women's demonstrations made their discontent even more evident, taking over public spaces to demand that the state provide food for their families, especially their starving children. Vichy administrators considered the shopping and queues as women's roles; the same view held for the food demonstrations.[30] If the family was the essential cell for social order and the state praised women for their importance as mothers, it was women's right and duty to demand sufficient food, which was clearly available to feed Germans and black-market restaurant customers.

Demands for more food were the most frequent reason for public demonstrations in the first two years of the Occupation. Communist organizers mobilized women shoppers as mothers, encouraging them to demonstrate accompanied by their children. Women protested coal shortages in the winter of 1940-1941 by taking their children on Thursdays (a day out of school) to sit in the heated waiting rooms in municipal offices. They brought sewing and let their children play hide-and-seek, refusing to leave until the

---

[28] Bertin, *Femmes sous l'Occupation*, 49.
[29] See Paula Schwartz, "The Politics of Food and Gender in Occupied Paris," *Modern & Contemporary France* 7.1 (1999) 36-39; Veillon, *Paris allemand*, 113-25, and *Vivre et survivre*, 127-32.
[30] Schwartz, "The politics of food and gender," 35, 39-41; Diamond, *Women in the Second World War*, 49-70. The potential for food unrest to erode support for the government was clear to the Germans in their determination to avoid a repeat of the public unrest at the end of World War I. See Gesine Gerhard, *Nazi Hunger Politics: A History of Food in the Third Reich* (Lanham: Rowman & Littlefield, 2015), and on the popular protest in Berlin, especially by working-class women, and food shortages in Germany in World War I, Belinda J. Davis, *Home Fires Burning: Food, Politics, and Everyday Life in World War I Berlin* (Chapel Hill: University of North Carolina Press, 2000).

mayor met with them and promised more coal for heating.[31] Food protests were sporadic until early 1942, when the lack of vegetables in markets prompted a wave of protests that gained visibility and some concessions in supplementary food distributions. In the largest, in Sète on 20 January, more than a thousand women exasperated by the shortages gathered outside the town hall and demanded "Bread for our kids." When they received no response, they threw rocks and chanted "Down with Pétain, down with Pétain." Municipal authorities responded by distributing rations of dried vegetables.

The Communist party argued that success in Sète should encourage more such demonstrations: direct action would bring success for women's legitimate claims.[32] A wave of smaller demonstrations in southern France gained distribution of supplements of dried vegetables, pasta, and potatoes, and the Gendarmerie added a new category to its monthly summary of activities, titled "Manifestations des ménagères" (housewives' demonstrations).[33] The Vichy administration was clearly anxious about this movement that could spread widely, given the extent of shortages and the importance they accorded to women in their role as mothers. Mayors were ordered to resist housewives' demands and reward peaceable communities. The communist party played an increasing role in 1942, encouraging and organizing protests by housewives and mothers. In April, they proclaimed in a pamphlet, "Action is our strength. In 1789, the women of Paris marched to Versailles to demand bread. In 1942, they must go to the *mairie* and demand it for their little ones."[34]

Later in 1942, two women's protests ended in violence. A demonstration organized for Mother's Day, May 31, called on mothers to take action, "To unite and battle to assure the life of her children." Women gathered outside the ECO grocery store on the rue de Buci in Paris and several, led by Madeleine Marzin, pushed into the store and passed canned goods and sugar to customers outside. Although ECO staff tried to stop them, male comrades were on hand to free the women and assist their getaway. But the security detail shot five policemen, two

---

[31] Lise London, *La mégère de la rue Daguerre: Souvenirs de Résistance* (Paris: Seuil, 1995), pp. 102-03, and Veillon, *Paris allemand*, 68-69.

[32] *L'Humanité*, February 26, 1942, reported that the six women sent to talk to the mayor as representatives of the crowd had been arrested, triggering a larger demonstration in which workers joined their wives in protest, the crowd numbering 2500. AN AJ/41/24, Gendarmerie summary for January 1942, and the account of the demonstration given later, "La révolte des ménagères à Sète," *France*, August 19, 1942. For this wave of protest, see Jean-Marie Guillon, "Le retour des 'émotions populaires': manifestations de ménagères en 1942," in *Mélanges Michel Vovelle, volume aixois* (Aix: Publications de l'Université de Provence, 1997), pp. 267-76.

[33] AN AJ/41/24, Gendarmerie summary for March 1942.

[34] APP, 220W 8, "Situation à Paris," April 13, 1942.

fatally.³⁵ Several weeks later, outside the Felix Potin grocery store on the rue Daguerre, Lise Ricol urged housewives waiting in the queue to protest the waiting in lines and the shortages. Ricol was protected by armed militants, who shot two policemen and one German soldier when police tried to arrest her.³⁶ The organizers and militants were caught and several from the May 31 demonstration were sentenced to death. Three were shot in July and five students from the security squad were executed in February 1943. Marzin escaped. Her death sentence was commuted to hard labor for life, and friends organized her escape in the Gare Montparnasse when she was transferred from Paris to Rennes in August 1942.³⁷

The persuasive power of women's demonstrations for food lay in the sympathy and support they could elicit for a cause in keeping with Vichy's ideology, challenging the state for its failure to provide for families and children. Violent confrontation brought harsh repression; the two events in 1942 took place at an intersection of public protest and the development of armed Resistance. Increasing anti-Vichy politicization, especially by the Communist party, meant there were fewer spontaneous demonstrations demanding food, and more frequent mobilization for political objectives.³⁸ Official supplies declined, and the use of family parcels and the black market increased. Housewives continued to manage family supplies with less expected from the state, from official markets, and from public protest. In the first months of 1944, Paris markets did not have sufficient supplies to honor rations for meat, butter, and potatoes for weeks at a time. Until June, when the Allied invasion disrupted both clandestine and official transport, family food supply depended on cooperative efforts and organization for food supply that mothers played the key role in leading.

Children

Vichy's purported objective of healthy families required attention to the impact of food shortages on children, for whom insufficient nutrition could

---

[35] The rue de Buci demonstration and its organization, aftermath, and legacy, are well-explained in Paula Schwartz, *Today Sardines are Not for Sale: A Street Protest in Occupied Paris* (New York: Oxford University Press, 2020).
[36] London, *La mégère de la rue Daguerre*, 158-62; Roger Linet, *1933-1943: La traversée de la tourmente* (Paris: Éditions Messidor, 1990), pp. 285-91.
[37] Schwartz, *Today Sardines are Not for Sale*, 37, 124-130.
[38] These points are summarized from extensive archival research by Danielle Tartakowsky, "Manifester pour le pain, novembre 1940-octobre 1947," in *Cahiers de l'IHTP* 32-33 [special issue "Le temps des restrictions en France (1939-1949)," edited by Dominique Veillon and Jean-Marie Flonneau] (1996) 465-71.

impair growth and lifelong health. Rations provided sufficient calories for children up to six years old (categories E and J1) but fell significantly short of needs for the J2 children (ages six to twelve) and especially J3 teenagers (twelve to twenty-one).[39] Many studies measured the weight and height of students in school during the war, showing variation that depended on their city and year, but consistently recorded below normal growth, most dramatically in the years 1943 and 1944.[40] The studies also showed vitamin deficiencies and increased susceptibility to disease, most notably tuberculosis, as well as to afflictions like chilblains and impetigo.[41] Efforts to improve nutrition in schools included various services that provided meals for children in school canteens; the *Secours National* [National Aid] provided 405 million meals from January 1941 to Liberation; and a range of food supplements including milk, casein cakes (milk protein), protein cookies, vitamin tablets, and vitaminized cookies and chocolate ("reeking of fish").[42]

Feeding children was primarily organized in their families, with mothers bearing the main responsibility and the greatest sacrifice. Children shared the chore of queuing for food; they could take turns in line, or queue with several family members waiting in more than one line.[43] Families with rural relatives could send their children to stay in the countryside with better food when not in school, and for older children, send them to *colonies de vacances* where they were better fed. Raymond Ruffin went as a *colo* to a farm at la Puisaye (Yonne) in July 1943, planning to stay one month. He returned to Paris finally in mid-October and noted, "We reconnect with the realities of existence under

---

[39] League of Nations, *Food Rationing and Supply 1943/44* (Geneva: League of Nations, 1944), p. 29.

[40] Michel Cépède provides evidence from several studies in *Agriculture et alimentation en France Durant la IIe Guerre mondiale* (Paris: Éditions M.-Th. Génin, 1961), pp. 408-15.

[41] Dominique Veillon, "Aux origines de la sous-alimentation: pénuries et rationnement alimentaire," "*Morts d'inanition*": *Famine et exclusions en France sous l'Occupation*, ed. Isabelle von Bueltzingsloewen (Rennes: Presses universitaires de Rennes, 2005), pp. 31-43; W.D. Halls, *The Youth of Vichy France* (Oxford: Clarendon Press, 1981), p. 208.

[42] Halls, *The Youth of Vichy France*, 205, provides a sampling of the varied and localized measures. For *Secours National* meals in schools, see Jean-Pierre Le Crom, "Helping the Most Needy: The Role of the Secours National," *Vichy France and Everyday Life: Confronting the Challenges of Wartime, 1939-1945*, eds. Lindsey Dodd and David Lees (London: Bloomsbury, 2018), p. 95.

[43] Raymond Ruffin records having queued for two hours in February 1942 to get 2 kg carrots, 2 kg turnips, and one cauliflower, while his mother waited in another queue with three of their five ration cards. In January 1943, he waited nearly four hours for 3 kg of Jerusalem artichokes. Ruffin, *Journal d'un J3* (Paris: Presses de la Cité, 1979) 87-89, 165-66.

the Occupation."⁴⁴ Micheline Bood often visited relatives in Brittany to enjoy a normal diet and bring back food for her family. Watching her mother's and sister's excitement over the 30 kg of food she brought back to Paris in December 1942, she wrote, "It's strange, but when one eats well, one no longer pays much attention to the food."⁴⁵ If they could afford to, families organized their vacations in regions with rich agriculture offering opportunities for a better diet while on vacation and the negotiation of food parcels for the coming winter. Officials began referring to this in the summer of 1942 as *tourisme alimentaire* (food tourism).⁴⁶ But many working-class families could not afford this luxury.

The changes in family food consumption to adapt to the shortages could not help but affect children—not just in the impact on physical health, but also in their understanding of the adult world they were growing up in. The overriding concerns for sufficient food and the search for ways to work around the rules were pervasive. The improvisations needed to obtain scarce goods became known as "le système D," the ability to "make do" (from the verb *se débrouiller*).⁴⁷ A report on the impact of the Occupation on children in *écoles maternelles* (ages four to six), based on observations by teachers in the Marseille region in 1943, provides detailed evidence for the influences of the food shortages on even the youngest students. Children bartered to exchange goods much more than before the war, stole food which they usually consumed on the spot, and reported to the teachers they trusted on their family's successes in finding extra food, including on the black market.⁴⁸

In their games, as well, children imitated the adult behavior they observed around them. While boys played war games, girls played at being mothers providing for their families by queuing for food, having stores include an "arrière-boutique" for black market sales, and complaining of the difficulty in getting food. One conversation between two girls was reported as: "I was in

---

⁴⁴ Ruffin, *Journal d'un J3*, 195.
⁴⁵ Micheline Bood, *Les années doubles: Journal d'une lycéenne sous l'Occupation* (Paris: Robert Laffont, 1974), p. 179. Bood was in high school during the Occupation; her diary has many observations about food, including queuing for one and a half hours on Christmas Day 1940 to get two eggs, and trying to persuade herself that rutabagas and margarine were delicious; ibid, 61, 69.
⁴⁶ For example, AN AJ/41/392, prefect monthly report for September and October 1942, November 3, 1942. Prefects reported the growth of *tourisme alimentaire* in the departments in Normandy and Brittany.
⁴⁷ Veillon, *Vivre et survivre*, 186-95. The term came from the French army in North Africa and became widely known for soldiers' survival tactics in World War I.
⁴⁸ AN F/17/13364, A. Radureau, "Conférences pédagogiques des écoles maternelles," December 17, 1943.

queues until now, but I didn't get anything." "Me neither, but I've got to go tend to my little ones. Ah! This life is miserable!" They found the black market "perfectly lawful" and it provided the best part of their food. "Yesterday we dined really well; we ate a cock, a pie, and a Savoy cake. Mother said it's from the black market and that we shouldn't tell." The report concluded that "Life today is a school of dissimulation, even for the little ones." The children lived "in a climate where there's no longer a distinction between good and bad, where hiding and stealing are allowed: the important thing is to not get caught."[49]

Negotiating the world of rationed goods was replicated in games made for children. In "Tickets S.V.P." (Tickets Please), players roll a die to advance around a board on which they pay with or receive ration tickets, trying to reach the "Pays du rêve 'sans tickets'" (Dreamland "with no tickets") [Figure 10.1]. In "Comme Maman" (Like Mother), a game released on Christmas 1941, children buy goods from shops using the game's ration tickets [Figure 10.2]. The game "Jeu de rutabaga" (Rutabaga Game) replicated the many frustrations and delays in shopping for food. Players roll two dice and go to the square on the board with that dice combination, where they try to buy food to fill all the items on their individual shopping card. Nearly half the stores are closed. At shops with customers waiting, players can purchase with their card but must pay a one-token fine into the bank for each customer ahead of them in line. If they land on "Madame Pie-Borgne" (Madame Magpie, one-eyed, a gossip), they lose two turns. Landing on "Marché noir" incurs a ten-token fine. But landing on "Carte de priorité" gives an extra turn, with no penalty for making a purchase if there is a queue waiting. Landing on "Permis de circulation" gives another turn and five tokens from the bank [Figure 10.3].[50] There was also an Occupation version of the well-known game "Sept familles" (Seven families), with the family names revised to pertain mainly to food. Five families have food-related names and professions: the Bonneterre (good earth) family are farmers, the Lescalope (chop) family are butchers, the Duharengs (herring) are fishermen, the Vermicelle (vermicelli) family are grocers, and the Dupersils (parsley) are gardeners [Figure 10.4]. The altered food regime became part of the new consumer culture to deal with shortages, pervasive in everyday life for children as well as adults.

---

[49] Radureau, "Conférences pédagogiques." For an elaboration of the report's findings see Mouré, *Marché Noir*, 181-83.
[50] My account is based on photographs by Pierre Verrier of games in the Bernard Le Marec Collection, access and permission to use the photos courtesy of the *Centre d'Histoire et de la Résistance et de la Déportation* in Lyon.

Figure 10.1: "Tickets S.V.P.," Collection B. Le Marec, photo © Pierre Verrier.

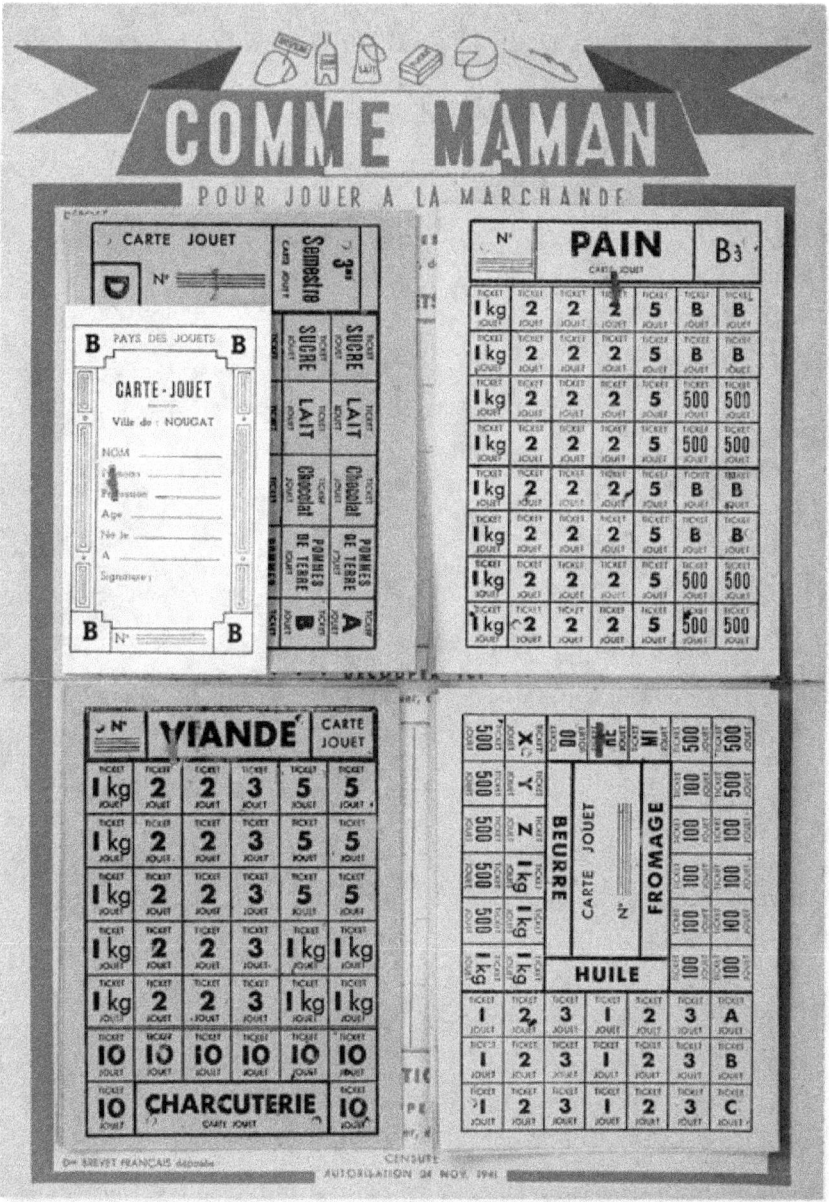

Figure 10.2: "Comme Maman - Pour jouer à la marchande," Collection B. Le Marec, photo © Pierre Verrier.

Figure 10.3: "Jeu de rutabaga," Collection B. Le Marec, photo © Pierre Verrier.

Figure 10.4: "Jeu des 7 familles," Collection B. Le Marec, photo © Pierre Verrier.

This need for adaptation to shortages and respect for improvised solutions (*le système D*) raised concerns about how these changes would influence the honesty and morality of the younger generation. Officials frequently stated their concern when honest work was not enough for survival and there was easier money to be made in trafficking in illicit goods. The prefect in the Vienne reported in 1941, "We must note among the young, particularly those in urban centers, a disastrous morality that is disturbing and for which it is urgent to find efficacious remedies."[51] Marc Chevalier, prefect of Seine-et-Oise, saw rampant moral crisis in 1943. The state was powerless against this because the problem was so widespread, threatening French youth in particular. "The spirit of greed, the indiscipline, the disobedience, are the significant traits of youth that see only bad examples around them."[52]

Family solidarity

Vichy's agenda for families foundered for many reasons, not just the subjection to Nazi orders and interests through collaboration, and the material deprivation it entailed. The internal divisions and the incoherence in Vichy ideas and policies for the family, and their conflict with French republican and democratic political values (the heritage of the French Revolution), fostered skepticism and resistance. The regime's inability to provide sufficient food for its citizens proved to be a major liability, which damaged faith in the regime much earlier than Vichy's politics of collaboration and conflict with Free France. As Fabrice Grenard has shown, the regime's failures to provide adequate food supply were the most important and most precocious factors working to delegitimize the regime, from the first months of the Occupation.[53] The failures in food supply were pervasive, affecting almost everyone, everywhere, every day. For most women struggling to feed their families, the injustices and hypocrisy in Vichy policies were obvious from the start.

Family separations caused by the war—the mobilization, deaths, and imprisonment of soldiers, family dispersal in the exodus, labor requisitions, children sent to rural areas for better food or safety from bombing, and the hidden life of resistance and labor draft evasion—all placed burdens on those left behind, most often women and children. The basic challenge of getting enough to eat, with rations set at a level for "slow starvation," required a greater dedication of time and income for working families, especially those with an absent father. Vichy's emphasis on the family as the foundational cell

---

[51] AN AJ/41/393, "Rapport mensuel," December 3, 1941.
[52] AN AJ/41/391, "Rapport mensuel," July 31, 1943.
[53] Fabrice Grenard, "Les implications politiques du ravitaillement en France sous l'Occupation," *Vingtième siècle* 94 (2007) 199-215.

for society and the nation had tried to place women in positions of subservience, at home, raising children. The economy of penury and inequities in access to essential food made household management far more difficult. It required a public presence to queue for ration documents and food, and it fostered political mobilization to survive. This manifested in public protest against Vichy food policies, and within families who had to work around the rules.

Responses to food scarcity often organized family in solidarity against Vichy controls. Queuing for food and dealing with the regime of cards, coupons, and tickets became a family affair for those who did not have the wealth or the power to have others do this work. Sharing food within families helped make up for the deficiencies of children in the J2 and J3 categories. Family connections were reforged to arrange for food parcels from the countryside, a major supplement for many urban residents, and to provide more food for their children in holiday periods. Vichy's program to rebuild France with strong families, keeping women at home to raise children, and a new commitment to hard work and morality, was strong on rhetoric and propaganda, but did little to help women and children. As Hélène Eck has observed, the relationships between couples and within families under Vichy were in many cases strengthened by the need to overcome adversity.[54] That was especially significant in working together to find ways around or in opposition to the food regime established by the Vichy regime.

---

[54] Hélène Eck, "Les Françaises sous Vichy: Femmes du désastre, citoyennes par le désastre?" in *Histoire des femmes en Occident, Volume V: Le XXe siècle*, ed. Françoise Thébaud (Paris: Plon, 1992), pp. 185-211, 197-98.

Chapter 11

Patriotism and Austerity: Finnish Children and Youth in World War Two

Marianne Junila and Tiina Kinnunen
University of Oulu

Abstract: In histories of consumption, World War II has been described as the first armed conflict between consumer societies. In the interwar period, Finland was still a modest consumer society, but consumer opportunities had diversified towards the late 1930s. The war period – Finland fought two wars against the Soviet Union and one war against Germany in 1939–1945 – marked a radical shift in consumption through severe shortages and rationing. The chapter examines the wartime experiences of Finnish children and youth and the ways the conflict has been remembered decades later in everyday consumer habits and in meanings given to consumer goods. In our recollection material from the early 1990s, scarcity and sacrifices are the all-embracing experiences, whereas the contemporary material from a magazine for children and youth opens up perspectives into the lives of young people from middle-class families who still had some resources for consumption available. Their dreams of sweets and other delicacies show that they were saved from the most extreme scarcity. The experiences of children sent to Sweden – analyzed in fictional and recollection material – show the difference in living standards and consumption between war-waging Finland, where the resources were pushed to the limit, and neutral Sweden, with the abundance of food and other consumer goods available.

Keywords: Finland, Sweden, evacuation, consumption, rationing, shortages, children's magazines

***

"For once, I would like to eat my fill of really, really wonderful food."

(Kultasiipi, 1942)[1]

At the beginning of 1942, the readers of *Sirkka*, a magazine for children and youth, were asked what they would do if rationing ended in Finland and the "good old times" returned. "Kultasiipi's"[2] desire for "really wonderful food" was like the wishes of other readers. The war had begun in the summer of 1941 and was expected to be short and victorious. By the beginning of 1942, after over six months of war, Finns had to get used to the new "normal" characterized by a decline in pre-war living standards and state control of consumption. Both affected the lives of children and young people and influenced how, decades later, they remembered the years 1939–1945.

In histories of consumption, World War II has been described as the first armed conflict between consumer societies.[3] In the late 1930s, Finland was still a modest consumer society, but living standards had risen and consumer opportunities diversified. However, despite the progress made, social and regional differences in living standards remained. For example, studies on the diets of elementary school students showed that affluent families could afford sufficient and varied food, while the poor had to settle for very meager, simple fare.[4] The war marked a shift in consumption as the state regulated the distribution and purchase of goods and services. Those with resources—the families of the *Sirkka* readers among them—could no longer use them as they wished. The volume of private consumption decreased significantly in Finland during the war years through shortages and rationing. In principle then, the reduction of consumer opportunities was perceived as quite democratic: scarcity was distributed to all homes.[5] This chapter examines the wartime experiences of Finnish children and youth and the ways the conflict

---

[1] Kultasiipi [pseud.], "Kysymyksiä ja vastauksia," *Sirkka* 2, 1942. All quotations from the Q and A column are translated by Michelle Mamane.

[2] The readers used pseudonyms in the Q and A column. In this chapter, these pseudonyms are used in the original, Finnish-language form.

[3] For example, Klara Arnberg, Nikolas Glover and Fia Sundevall, "På hemmafronten intet nytt: Kommersiell kvinnlighet under svensk beredskap, 1939–1945," *Historisk tidskrift*, forthcoming 2022.

[4] Less than five percent of pupils were able to enjoy abundant and varied food. *Komiteanmietintö 1940:5. Tutkimuksia kansanravitsemustilan parantamiseksi* (Helsinki, 1940).

[5] Timo Toivonen, *Ainainen puute ja kurjuus? Kulutus ja yhteiskuntakerrostumat Suomessa 1928–1950* (Helsinki: Valtion painatuskeskus, 1986), 9–13; Pauli Arola, "Puutteen sukupolvet. Minun koulumuistoni -keruun köyhyyskertomukset," in "Koulu ja menneisyys," *Suomen kasvatuksen ja koulutuksen historian vuosikirja* 53 (2015) 76.

has been remembered decades later in everyday consumer habits and in meanings given to consumer goods.[6] As young Finns represented over one-third of the total population of approximately 3.7 million during the war years, their attitudes and responses to wartime conditions are significant.

This chapter straddles the history of childhood and youth, consumption studies and material objects, and histories of the experience of war, and its focus is situated in some of the current discussions in these fields. The key premise of the history of childhood and youth is the active agency of minors in relation to the guidance given to them. Studies of consumption and the material have deepened our understanding of the relationship between people and physical objects as well as the agency of 'things.'[7] The relationship between memory and emotions has recently been highlighted in studies about wartime experiences. In this chapter, we explore the emotions of memories of consumption and those surrounding material objects that transcend the war years.[8]

The sources for this chapter include the "Questions and Answers" (*Kysymyksiä ja vastauksia*) column in the *Sirkka* magazine from 1939–1944. The magazine's editor-in-chief was Anni Swan, a well-known Finnish author of books for children and youth. *Sirkka* published stories, serials, and comics, written by adults. The content of the magazine was very cultural, and the war was rarely discussed. The Questions and Answers column was an effort to stimulate a response from young readers. The questions were related to everyday life and were written by both the editor and the readers themselves. *Sirkka* targeted a broad age group, from children to teenagers and those on the threshold of adulthood. The cover photos also included pictures of small children, suggesting that the dividing line between the age groups was not as pronounced as it became in the post-war decades, when teenagers emerged as a special group with an associated identity.[9]

---

[6] In our analysis, we will pay attention to both essential consumption (nutrition, clothing) and to recreational consumption, which allowed for different hobbies. See the categorization by Toivonen, *Ainainen puute*.
[7] See, for example, Leila Koivunen and Taina Syrjämaa, "Esineet ja materiaalisuus historiassa," *Historiallinen Aikakauskirja* 117.2 (2016): 123–24.
[8] The notion of "emotional objects" has been developed by Heini Hakosalo, for example in "Tubipommi ja rautlasi. Emotionaalisia esineitä 1900-luvun alkupuolen suomalaisissa tuberkuloosiparantoloissa," *Historiallinen Aikakauskirja* 117.2 (2016): 165–76.
[9] Sinikka Aapola, "Murrosiän lyhyt historia Suomessa," in *Nuoruuden vuosisata. Suomalaisen nuorison historia*, eds. Sinikka Aapola and Mervi Kaarninen (Helsinki: Suomalaisen Kirjallisuuden Seura, 2003), 94–100.

The chapter also examines children's literature to explore references to food and consumer goods. *Inkeri palasi Ruotsista (Kirsti Comes Home: The Story of a Finnish Girl)*,[10] published in Finnish in 1947 and written by the popular children's author Aili Konttinen, describes a phenomenon central to the wartime experience of Finnish children: between 70,000 and 80,000 Finnish children were sent to Sweden for safety. Konttinen's novel depicts the main character's, Inkeri's (Kirsti's), gradual adjustment to her native Finland after spending many years in Sweden. One of the most important aspects of readjustment was getting used to the significant difference in living standards and consumption between Finland and Sweden.

Other sources include the three-part autobiography written by Eeva Kilpi (née Salo). *Talvisodan aika. Lapsuusmuistelma* (the Winter War period: a childhood recollection), *Välirauha, ikävöinnin aika* (the Interim Peace, a time of longing), and *Jatkosodan aika* (the Continuation War period) were published between 1989 and 1993. Kilpi's (born in 1928) autobiography reflects the shifts in writing about the war that occurred with the collapse of the Soviet Union in the early 1990s. Before the 1990s, memories of Finland's wartime experiences were approached with caution. The war had been lost and the political climate in Finland was dominated by forced sympathy towards the Soviet Union. The patriotic turn that followed the collapse of the Soviet Union allowed people to give more positive—even idealizing—meanings to the war.[11]

Kilpi and her family were evacuated from Finnish Karelia. The war forced them to leave their homes and resettle more than once. Kilpi and her family were middle-class, and she had the opportunity to attend secondary school. Before the war, most Finnish children only went to primary school. Kilpi's work is a memoir of the past but is also a reflection on those memories. She contemplates the nature of memory, its different layers, and how it changes under different circumstances. "How does memory choose what to keep and what to erase?" Kilpi insightfully asks, as do recent scholars of memory.[12] She also discusses the core question about memory: how much of her memory

---

[10] The English translation, by Oliver Coburn and Ursula Lehrburger, was published in 1961 by Coward-McCann. In this chapter, the original Finnish-language book is used as a source material and the quotations into English are made by Michelle Mamane.

[11] Tiina Kinnunen and Markku Jokisipilä, "Shifting Images of 'Our Wars': Finnish Memory Culture of World War II," in *Finland in World War II. History, Memory, Interpretations*, eds. Tiina Kinnunen and Ville Kivimäki (Leiden and Boston: Brill, 2012), 435–82.

[12] Eeva Kilpi, *Talvisodan aika. Lapsuusmuistelma* (Helsinki: WSOY, 2012), 167. (First edition 1989.) All of Kilpi's translations are by Michele Mamane.

concerning the war has been built on the knowledge and experience accumulated since the war?[13]

The chapter also utilizes written reminiscences. In 1999, sixty years after the outbreak of the war, *Kotiliesi* magazine organized a writing competition related to the Winter War, the material of which is stored in the National Archives of Finland. This initiative was carried out at a time when memories of the war years were sought and when the war was widely discussed in various forms in public. Participants of the writing competition included a significant number of the children and youth of the war period.

Together, these sources give insight into wartime experiences as lived, remembered and as contemporary fiction. While not all sources revolve around consumption, they do illustrate some of the shortages of consumer goods and the meanings given them during and after the conflict.

Finland and War

Finland experienced three wars in the period from 1939 to 1945. The Winter War that began in November 1939 was a defensive war waged against a Soviet attack. Finland came close to collapse and was forced to yield to harsh peace terms in March 1940. Wishing to avenge the loss, Finland accepted Germany's offer for support. In June 1941, Finland began combat action termed the Continuation War alongside Operation Barbarossa, Germany's invasion of the Soviet Union. Finland took back territory lost in the Winter War and then occupied the previously non-Finnish areas of Eastern Karelia. Between 1942–1943, the conflict developed into trench warfare. In the summer of 1944, the Soviet Union launched an offensive (against Finland) to push Finland out of the war. Once again, Finland remained independent but was forced to make substantial concessions. The Moscow Armistice, signed in September 1944, forced Finland to expel German troops who were stationed in northern Finland. The resulting Lapland War (1944–1945) saw the retreating German troops destroy the buildings and infrastructure of northern Finland. The population of the region had already evacuated to Sweden or elsewhere in Finland before the outbreak of the war. When they returned, their homes were destroyed. Additionally, Finland was forced to resettle 400,000 Karelian refugees from the territories ceded to the Soviet Union.[14]

---

[13] Kilpi, *Talvisodan aika*, 29; Eeva Kilpi, *Välirauha, ikävöinnin aika* (Helsinki: WSOY, 2012), 194. (First edition 1990.)

[14] Pasi Tuunainen, "The Finnish Army at War: Operations and Soldiers," in *Finland in World War II*, 139–88.

The role played by Finland in World War II has been a popular topic for Finnish historians. From the 1970s and 1980s, research has broadened from histories of battles and military tactics to include the rest of society, activities on the home front, and the experiences of different groups and individuals.[15] With the paradigm shift, scholars have become interested in the experiences and perspectives of children and young people, supported by the establishment of the history of childhood and youth as a research area of its own.[16]

Previous research illustrates how Finland systematically harnessed the home front to aid military efforts in what became total war. The war required the population to work long and exhausting hours, and all Finns aged 15–64 years were subjected to the Work Responsibility Act. Only mothers of young children were exempt. Women's contributions were needed in agriculture, industry, and in various forms of volunteering.[17] Children and adolescents were also encouraged to join activities within various youth organizations. In addition, young people participated in the "struggle for production" by cultivating their own plots of land during the summer. With both parents at work, the war years arguably strengthened a parental style that aimed at early independence.[18] However, in a culture that promoted early independence and self-reliance, efforts were also made to monitor and control children and adolescents. Special attention was paid to the moral resilience of girls and women, and determined efforts were made to curb relations with German soldiers stationed in Finland. This proved difficult because German troops had an abundance of consumer goods that Finland severely lacked. This led to a lively and illicit black market between the Finnish civilian population and German soldiers. Such contact was viewed as a major risk to the morals of young women.[19]

Historians of consumption have pointed out that agriculture-dominated Finland lagged behind the Western countries that had industrialized and urbanized much faster. In the rural areas, consumer goods had only begun to

---

[15] Tiina Kinnunen and Ville Kivimäki, "Uusi sotahistoria Suomessa," *Historiallinen Aikakauskirja* 119.4 (2018): 373–83.

[16] See, for example, Sari Näre, Jenni Kirves, Juha Siltala, Joni Strandberg, eds., *Haavoitettu lapsuus. Sodassa koettua* (Helsinki. WSOY, 2007) and *Uhrattu nuoruus. Sodassa koettua* (Helsinki: WSOY, 2008). The experiences of Karelian evacuee children and war children sent to Sweden have been examined at depth.

[17] Marianne Junila, "Wars on the Home Front: Mobilization, Economy and Everyday Experiences," in *Finland in World War II*, 191–232.

[18] Sari Näre and Jenni Kirves, "Lapsuus sodan keskellä," in *Haavoitettu lapsuus*, 12.

[19] Marianne Junila, *Kotirintaman aseveljeyttä. Suomalaisen siviiliväestön ja saksalaisen sotaväen rinnakkainelo Pohjois-Suomessa 1941–1944* (Helsinki: Suomalaisen Kirjallisuuden Seura, 2000), 146–54.

become more common in the twentieth century. However, even in the 1950s, consumption was still marked by caution. It was not until 1954 that wartime rationing ended, and cultural factors affected attitudes to consumption even in the postwar years.[20] Peasant virtues of frugality, diligence, and decency had been effectively promoted by the consumer education provided by household organizations since the early twentieth century.[21]

While Finns did not suffer the devastating arial bombing of other countries, wartime life was governed by extreme scarcity. The economy was marked by a widespread shortage of raw materials and regulation of all consumption. Resources had to be directed to the war effort and the maintenance of an army that was large in proportion to the population. Finnish rations were one of the lowest in Europe and were comparable to those in occupied countries such as Poland. Rationing put a particular burden on women, who, as housewives, were responsible for procuring groceries and other consumer goods. The scarcity and lack of variety of food had a negative impact on the lives of all age groups, but especially on growing children and adolescents. Likewise, they were particularly affected by the shortage of clothing and footwear.[22] However, there were differences between the various social classes—and thus, between the children and adolescents within them—because consumer goods could be bought through the black market if there was money to spare. Tensions rose between rural and urban areas when more and better food was available in the countryside. [23] In other respects, the living standard in the countryside was inferior to life in the city. For urban children who were sent to the safety of the countryside, it often felt like a foreign country "with no electric lights, no radio, no telephone, no central heating, no plumbing."[24] Differences in consumption opportunities between

---

[20] Juhani Koponen and Sakari Saaritsa, eds., *Nälkämaasta hyvinvointivaltioksi: Suomi kehityksen kiinniottajana* (Helsinki: Gaudeamus, 2019).

[21] Visa Heinonen, *Talonpoikainen etiikka ja kulutuksen henki: kotitalousneuvonnasta kuluttajapolitiikkaan 1900-luvun Suomessa* (Helsinki: Suomen Historiallinen Seura, 1998); Kati Mikkola, "Uutuuksien pyhyys ja pahuus," in "Kansanetiikkaa. Käsityksiä hyvästä ja pahasta," *Kalevalaseuran vuosikirja* 84 (2005), 11–41.

[22] Silvo Hietanen, "Perunan ja rukiin maa. Ravinto ja asuminen sotavuosien Suomessa," in *Kansankunta Sodassa 2: Vyö kireällä*, eds. Silvo Hietanen and Olli Vehviläinen (Helsinki: Valtion painatuskeskus, 1990), 302–6; Aura Korppi-Tommola, "Hungry, but Not Starving: The Experiences of Finnish Children in Town and Country during the Second World War," in *The Landscape of Food: The Food Relationship of Town and Country in Modern Times*, eds. Marjatta Hietala and Tanja Vahtikari (Helsinki: Finnish Literature Society, 2003), 145–53.

[23] Arola, "Puutteen sukupolvet," 75–77.

[24] Kirsti Antturi in the *Kotiliesi* writing competition. National Archives.

children and adolescents were also affected by whether a family had to survive with a single parent. About 90,000 men were killed in the war.

Dreams and Memories of Sweets and Other Delicacies

Sirkka was published monthly. Almost without exception, there was a "Questions and Answers" column. The most common questions dealt with the daily lives, wishes, and dreams of the readers, but consumer habits and spending money were also regularly discussed. The war was rarely discussed. One rare example came in the autumn of 1944, after the armistice. "Kääpiökuningas" described his thoughts while in bed in the evenings: "That peace would come and Finland would have its own borders and every Karelian could go live in their home."[25]

Young readers appreciated the column. For example, according to "Joo-Joo," it was the best part of the magazine because it "allowed all of Finland's youth to converse."[26] Of course, it did not represent all youth, as most readers came from middle-class families. This group was united by a patriotic ethos, and the magazine was indeed felt to unite the "rising generation of a Greater Finland."[27] The school system played a key role in establishing and strengthening patriotism in an independent Finland. The idea of a Greater Finland attracted different social groups at the beginning of the Continuation War, but its strongest support came from the Finnish-speaking middle class, whose offspring had the opportunity to attend secondary school.

Sirkka readers in the war years were born in the late 1920s and in the 1930s. Many had experienced the recession of the 1930s, but also the improvement in material well-being at the end of the decade. It was justifiable to ask these children of at least moderately well-off families about the use of pocket money. Families with the lowest income could not afford to give their children money on a regular basis. A reader by the pseudonym "Voku" asked about the use of pocket money in the October 1939 issue.[28] The answers were received until early November, so they portray the schoolchildren's use of money and consumer habits before the outbreak of the Winter War. Wholescale rationing was not yet underway and only sugar and coffee were rationed. Almost all fifty readers who answered received pocket money and spent it on entertainment and amusements, such as movies and sweets. Other spending included hobbies or hobby equipment, such as books, correspondence supplies, and

---

[25] "Kysymyksiä ja vastauksia," *Sirkka*, no. 10, 1942.
[26] "Kysymyksiä ja vastauksia," *Sirkka*, no. 13, 1942.
[27] Pseud. "An-Lis". "Kysymyksiä ja vastauksia," *Sirkka*, no. 13, 1942.
[28] "Kysymyksiä ja vastauksia," *Sirkka*, no. 10, 1939.

crafting and drawing tools. Not everyone was able to break down their consumption precisely and merely stated that their pocket money dwindled without them noticing, or that it was spent on "trivialities." Very few put their money into savings. The war had not yet affected the consumption of school children. Pocket money was available for hobbies and entertainment, and even sweets hadn't yet disappeared from the shops. Not many thought that saving was necessary, and the answers reveal an unapologetic carelessness: "What a tricky question. My pocket money always runs out so quickly that I don't have the time to notice what I've used it on."[29]

The question about the use of pocket money was presented again in the early autumn of 1944. Interestingly, money was spent in a similar way to almost five years earlier, on different hobbies and school supplies. A few respondents said they were putting their pocket money into savings, but some of the answers displayed the same carelessness as in 1939. For example, the pocket money of "Toroteian" "vanished as if into thin air" when they went to the movies and bought "this and that."[30] However, what was different from 1939 was that pocket money was no longer spent on sweets or other delicacies—as they were hardly available anymore.

In December 1940, *Sirkka*'s readers were asked to consider the question, "How do you currently save?" [31] This discussion took place in the interim peace between the Winter War and the Continuation War. Although Finland was not technically at war, living conditions were on a wartime footing and all essential food products, among other things, were regulated. Saving had become a conversation topic but did not arouse much interest among readers. Saving was understood in two different ways. Firstly, saving was setting aside money for some future consumption or just saving for the sake of saving. Secondly, saving was a way to cut costs. While a year earlier, pocket money was spent on sweets, readers now said they had cut back on them: "I try to go to the movies as little as possible, and I don't buy sweets." [32] Although surely pocket money was saved then, too, it was not a priority: what was more important to most readers was to give something up. Giving up something was one way that the youth felt involved in national efforts to retain independence. Only one reader justified giving up sweets because of their high prices.

The responses about giving up sweets is a little surprising, as recollections from later decades typically emphasized how all sweets had disappeared from the shelves of the shops and how this resulted in a severe longing that was

---

[29] "Kysymyksiä ja vastauksia," *Sirkka*, no.13, 1939.
[30] "Kysymyksiä ja vastauksia," *Sirkka*, no. 8, 1944.
[31] "Kysymyksiä ja vastauksia," *Sirkka*, no. 13, 1940.
[32] "Kysymyksiä ja vastauksia," *Sirkka*, no. 2, 1941.

carefully alleviated with the use of precious sugar. Sweets were, however, available for a surprisingly long time, even though their rations were meager and the price high.[33] They were not accessible to all, but some of *Sirkka*'s readers could still consider giving them up. For example, the sweets factory Hellas still sold "chocolate, sweets, pastilles, drops, toffee, jelly sweets, marzipan, and licorice" in February 1941. A bag of sweets (50 g) of secondary quality cost 2.75 Finnish marks (FIM) and a licorice bag cost 4.20 FIM (30 g)— you could buy half a kilo of crispbread for the price of the bag of sweets.[34] A glass of milk in a restaurant or a cup of coffee substitute cost up to 1.50 FIM.[35]

At the end of 1941, the Continuation War had been waged for half a year, and it had become apparent that the conflict would last much longer than had been expected. Rationing had been going on for so long that the readers of *Sirkka* started to dream. "Nykyajan Eva" asked what the readers would do if the "good old times" were to return and rationing end.[36] There were less than a dozen replies—at least that were published—and most of them were remembering something edible. Many readers imagined that they would stuff themselves with an abundance of delicacies, such as nuts, raisins, pastries, lollies, and chocolate, but just as many would have been satisfied with being able to eat a full meal.[37] The question of the return of the "good old times" and the end of rationing was re-introduced in the February 1942 issue. As at the end of 1941, besides delicacies, the wish list included ordinary food.

The Finnish diet was at its most meager in the spring of 1942,[38] but living on an ever more dwindling and simple diet was reflected in the dreams of children and adolescents as early as December 1941. Although the readers were asked what they would *do*, most answered what they would *eat*. The decline in the variety of diets was more apparent in the youth's writing in 1942. In March, readers were asked a question about the best-tasting root.[39] In April 1942, readers were asked, "what is your favorite food currently?" Young readers responded according to the circumstances and the current availability.

---

[33] "Makeisia valmistetaan ainakin toistaiseksi," *Helsingin Sanomat (HS)*, February 18, 1943; "Karamellitehtaiden sokerin saanti loppunee," *HS*, August 18, 1943.
[34] *Huhtamäki-yhtymän hinnasto*, February 1, 1941. Kansalliskirjaston pienpainatteet.
[35] *Kansanhuoltoministeriön päätös ravinnon ja virvokkeiden sekä niiden hintojen säännöstelystä 30.1.1942*. Kansalliskirjaston pienpainatteet.
[36] "Kysymyksiä ja vastauksia," *Sirkka*, no. 13, 1941.
[37] "Kysymyksiä ja vastauksia," *Sirkka*, no. 2, 1942.
[38] Hietanen, "Perunan ja rukiin maa," 315–16.
[39] "Kysymyksiä ja vastauksia," *Sirkka*, no. 3, 1942.

One reader wrote, "All kinds of vegetables, of course, since currently there's not much else to get."[40]

The question of the "good old times" was also raised in February 1943. The wording of the question is interesting: Readers were asked what "came to mind" when they thought about the time before the war. The respondents remembered "chocolate bars, coffee, good pastries, sweets, honey, ice cream, Tuscan cakes, and pancakes topped with lots of sugar." In addition to the delicacies, they also remembered "a home that no longer exists," "beautiful Karelia," and peace.[41]

However, the young readers of *Sirkka* magazine dreamed about more than just food and delicacies. Valuable items and equipment related to hobbies came up, such as (figure) skates, cameras, and bicycles. Reading remained a hobby through the war for many, as did collecting different types of books or other objects. Libraries provided books at no cost. Collecting required some money, especially when the objects were pictures of film stars, stamps, glossy pictures, and pictures of war collected from magazines.[42]

In the summer of 1944, "Joo-Joo" asked readers what goods they would purchase if there was a month of peace. The large number of responses indicates the experience of shortage was widely shared. "Maratoosa" wanted to hoard food so that "it would last for many years." The author probably did not experience outright hunger; rather, the answer reveals more about the experience of change—food could no longer be taken for granted. There was also a great desire to get fruit again. "Hurjimus" said they remembered "big juicy pears that were [prior to war] in every store," and "Vappu" wrote that they would be grateful if they could "get even a slice of banana." "Riti-Ralla" wanted several kilos of grapes, but "more than anything, I'd like to eat impossible amounts of gingerbread dough." The longing for sweets was strong, and the wish list included both chocolate-topped ice cream and cocoa powder, "Minti mummo" wrote that they wanted "chocolate, chocolate! So much chocolate that I could swim in it!" The memory of sweets was experienced very physically: "My mouth waters when I just think about it." Of course, the wish list also included shoes—real leather shoes—as well as clothes and "dozens" of socks.[43]

---

[40] "Kysymyksiä ja vastauksia," *Sirkka*, no. 4, 1942.
[41] "Kysymyksiä ja vastauksia," *Sirkka*, no. 2, 1943.
[42] "Kysymyksiä ja vastauksia," *Sirkka*, no. 6–7, 1943.
[43] "Kysymyksiä ja vastauksia," *Sirkka*, no. 6–7, 1944.

A Different Consumer Experience for War Children

The term "war children" conveys a different meaning in Finland than in Norway, for example, or any other country occupied by Germany. In Finland, the term refers to the 70,000–80,000 Finnish children sent mainly to Sweden, because living conditions were difficult in Finland and parents felt unable to care for them adequately. This was the largest of all of World War II children's transports. Many children came from large and impoverished families and many of them were Karelian evacuees. The time spent in Sweden affected the children's war experience in many ways, not least because of the pronounced difference in living standards between Finland and Sweden. The wealth of goods in Sweden and the abundance of food with its delicacies was starkly different from the life to which the children were accustomed. The difference was also underlined by the fact that the Swedish families who housed the war children often belonged to the middle or upper classes.[44] Thus, children who were used to the least consumption, even outright deprivation, ended up in extraordinary circumstances.

Sirkka magazine also described the lives of Finnish war children. Anni Swan visited Sweden to see the children's conditions, and the idealized description was published in the spring of 1943. The children in the Salvation Army's children's shelter were described as red-cheeked, spirited, and healthy. "In the kitchen, we marveled at the multitude of delicious sandwiches. There was even more than enough!" The author also admired the number of toys and clothes: "We remembered the wooden and paper shoes of Finnish children and were delighted that at least some of our children had received good and warm clothes."[45]

For many children, leaving Finland was traumatic, but returning and adapting to Finland could be at least as difficult. "I had come from a land of honey and butter and had been thrown into the back streets," a former war child said of her experience about coming back to Finland.[46] During the war, it was important to communicate to Finland, as Anni Swan did above, that sending children to Sweden served the interests of both the children and society. After the war, the discussion shifted. Aili Konttinen's *Inkeri palasi Ruotsista* (1947) can be read as a response to this shift. The novel describes mutual feelings of unfamiliarity, but above all, Inkeri's gradual adaptation to a

---

[44] Heikki Salminen, *Lappu kaulassa yli Pohjanlahden. Suomalaisten sotalasten historia* (Turku: Siirtolaisuusinstituutti, 2007), 197–99; Pentti Kaven, *Sotalapset. Toiveet ja todellisuus* (Helsinki: Minerva, 2011), 51–52.
[45] Anni Swan, "Suomalaisia lapsia Ruotsissa," *Sirkka*, no. 5, 1943.
[46] Sue Saffle, *To the Bomb and Back: Finnish War Children Tell Their World War II Stories* (New York, Oxford: Berghahn, 2015), 65.

life that was characterized by parents who worked from morning to night, and where children were also required to participate in work and negotiate the scarce resources with their siblings. The message of the book was clear: in the end, nothing beats your own country and home, no matter how modest.

The experiences of war children varied depending on the situation of the foster family. The Swedish parents of fictional Inkeri were remarkably wealthy; the girl lived in abundance, and the Swedish parents still remembered her after her return to Finland. Her home in Finland—a small, almost self-subsistent farm—was very modest, the only thing available to the evacuee family after the war. The simple diet—mostly potatoes and sauce—was also a shock to Inkeri. Finnish children were used to this, as is evident in *Sirkka* magazine. The living conditions were cramped. Inkeri was used to her own room full of toys, and when she returned home, she brought gifts for her siblings. They were delighted with the new clothes, but one of the sisters would have preferred chocolate. She tells Inkeri, "I have never been allowed to taste chocolate."[47]

The experience of Christmas was also very different in Finland than in Sweden. Compared to the multitudes of gifts Inkeri received from Sweden, the gifts received from her family, such as the gray mittens knit by her mother and the doll cradle made by her father, seemed very modest.[48] The differences were again highlighted in the novel in the description of the upcoming spring as a period when children started going without shoes. The siblings marveled at how strange Inkeri found the idea of walking barefoot throughout the summer.[49]

The differences between Finland and Sweden described in Konttinen's novel are repeated in the oral histories conducted in recent years that address the experiences of war children. They reveal that the abundance encountered by war children in Sweden was not limited to the dinner table. Foster homes were often spacious and beautifully decorated, with enough bedrooms for every child. When Inkeri was sent back to Finland, she was shocked when she was not allowed to take back home more than a few toys. She wondered what could be more important than her own, dear things.[50] In her study, Sue Saffle quotes the nine-year-old daughter of a family evacuated from Karelia and sent to Sweden. She was the seventh child in her family. She was in awe when she arrived in her new home: "[b]eing in a big house with a room of my own. I had never seen so

---

[47] Aili Konttinen, *Inkeri palasi Ruotsista* (Porvoo, Helsinki: WSOY, 1947), 32.
[48] Konttinen, *Inkeri palasi*, 84.
[49] Konttinen, *Inkeri palasi*, 129–30.
[50] Ibid, 9.

many beautiful things." Initially, she even refused to touch them because they were so different from the simple things she was used to at home.[51]

The beautiful environment, delicious food, and lovely clothes made a six-year-old girl, whom Saffle also quotes, feel like a princess, just like the fictional Inkeri in Konttinen's description: "Though I missed my mother, I felt like a princess."[52] "Beautiful" was indeed a word that the war children often used to describe their new circumstances: the home, its interior, the clothes they received, how their foster mother dressed. After returning to Finland, Inkeri recalled her Swedish mother: "How beautiful mamma was when she was dressed up!"[53] In addition to the abundance, the children noticed and appreciated the beauty of the environment and objects. It was clearly not necessary to be satisfied with getting the most essential and cheapest things in Sweden; consumer habits were also driven by taste, style, and fashion.

Remembered Scarcity

As revealed above, the "Questions and Answers" column in *Sirkka* magazine discussed scarcity, but in accordance with the requirements of the time, this experience was tinged with community spirit and survival. Affixing scarcity to the struggle for the homeland—something bigger than oneself—as a shared experience gave it a positive meaning. In the early 1990s, when recollections of the war, including Eeva Kilpi's autobiographical works, increased, Finland was again experiencing scarcities. When the Soviet Union, with which Finland had a lively trade, collapsed, the effects were also felt in Finland. The results were a wave of bankruptcies, increased unemployment, and a significant increase in income disparities. At this point, remembering the war years also had nostalgic dimensions. The years of conflict, especially the Winter War, were discussed as a time when the nation struggled to achieve a common goal.[54]

Many of Eeva Kilpi's memories are related to food, and they are reminiscent of the experiences in *Sirkka* about the changes in diet and the increase in scarcity. Food was simple even before the war, even if a family was middle class, but because of the war, it was even simpler than before. Kilpi remembered, "I take a bite of fermented bread and a sip of tea from a cup. I still remember how they taste. There was no sugar in the tea. There was no

---

[51] Saffle, *To the Bomb and Back*, 183.
[52] Ibid, 151.
[53] Konttinen, *Inkeri palasi*, 36–7.
[54] Ebba Sarasjoki-Holopainen, *Kotiliesi* writing competition, PK 22.22, National Archives.

butter on the bread. For the first time, I realized that until now, we had always had sugar and butter."[55]

As noted above, sweets did not completely disappear from Finland during the war period but were a rare treat and the object of constant fantasy. This is also evident from Kilpi's descriptions. Obtaining traditional sweets was still possible during the interim peace. The desire for sweets and other sugary delicacies was not fully satisfied even after the war, as rationing and shortages continued. Children could even eat the toothpaste received as aid from America to satisfy a sweet tooth.[56]

Kilpi remembers agonizing over endless stinginess and forced inventiveness when she was approaching her teens: "socks patched several times, dyed and reversed clothes, hats sewn from sofa cushions."[57] Almost the only way to get clothes for a growing adolescent was to modify the clothes of the adults in one's immediate circle, "which mom gave up piece by piece."[58] You could also barter for clothes: "The green checkered flannel blouse was the result of mom's relentless hoarding, its price may have been an 'illicit' block of butter to the haberdasher."[59]

Austerity also affected the hobbies of children and adolescents. Kilpi writes that it "inspired" her to do various experiments. The use of potatoes as glue was limited by the fact that it was also eaten. Shoe finish, which was used to extend the life cycle of non-paper shoes, was also suited to painting: "When using the remainders of shoe finish, you didn't even have to ask for money for artistic hobbies. And shoe finish stayed on almost anything it was once applied to. It inspired me to come up with a new technique: scraping."[60]

With her scraping technique, Eeva conjured up flower patterns on her mother's cream jar lid. Her mother admired the cream jar, which meant a lot to her daughter: "It was a significant recognition. After all, parents didn't have the time to stop in the middle of their hurries to look at what their children scribbled who knows where."[61] The description illustrates not only the inventiveness brought on by the shortage that extended to all walks of life and all social classes, but also the author's desire to assign positive meanings to both the shortage and the adaptive behavior of parents. An understanding towards mothers is present in *Kotiliesi*'s writing competition material as well,

---

[55] Kilpi, *Talvisodan aika*, 171.
[56] Arola, Puutteen sukupolvet," 75.
[57] Kilpi, *Välirauha*, 175.
[58] Kilpi, *Välirauha*, 24, 115.
[59] Kilpi, *Jatkosota*, 101.
[60] Kilpi, *Jatkosota*, 218.
[61] Kilpi, *Jatkosota*, 218, 219.

reminding readers of the unreasonable workload they bore when fathers were on the front.[62]

Emotional objects

Although the readers who wrote to *Sirkka* magazine lived in financially stable conditions, their lives were also not characterized by an abundance of goods. Hobby-related items such as ice skates, bicycles, and cameras were valuable and treated accordingly. Oral histories and memoirs, however, provide the most detailed descriptions of the emotional importance of items. For those children and adolescents who had to leave their home regions and homes, memories reflect experiences of lost and saved personal items. It was not easy to replace lost items in austerity-era Finland, and for that reason alone the items salvaged had a special significance. In addition, they, as well as the lost goods, were associated with feelings of grief, longing and nostalgia, which were dealt with much later.[63]

In *Kotiliesi*'s writing competition material, one respondent describes a quick evacuation after the outbreak of the Winter War at the end of November 1939: "I run upstairs to say goodbye to my summer play nook. And there they are. At the top step of the stairs, my most beautiful shoes, black patent leather shoes with their straps and holes. . . I look at my lovely shoes. I sigh. I set my beautiful shoes back on the top step of the stairs and run to the sleigh ready to go."[64] Another respondent had to leave his pedaled rocking horse Urho. He remembered his last night with his dear horse: "As the last day gave way to the evening, I made my Urho chaff fodder in an old white enamel basin, and I gave my horse plenty of hay. How would one know if it took as long as two weeks before we meet again?"[65]

The salvation of objects important to oneself is remembered from decades ago. The dearest treasures of a girl, who in her adulthood wrote for the *Kotiliesi* competition, were paper dolls drawn by herself and their clothes drawn according to the designs in fashion magazines. There was an air alarm and her mother told her to throw away the box of paper dolls so that running would be easier, "but I was definitely more concerned for my paper dolls than for my life."[66]

---

[62] See, for example, Kaarina Huhtinen, *Kotiliesi* writing competition, PK 22.22, National Archives.
[63] Tuomas Tepora, "Sota-ajan leikit ja koulu," in *Haavoitettu lapsuus*, 47–50.
[64] Laila Hirvikangas, *Kotiliesi* writing competition, PK 22.22, National Archives. All the translations of the material by Michele Mamane.
[65] Viljo Hämäläinen, *Kotiliesi* writing competition, PK 22.22, National Archives.
[66] Leea Hakkarainen, *Kotiliesi* writing competition, PK 22.22, National Archives.

When the Winter War ended and the information came out about the loss of territory outlined in the peace terms, Eeva Kilpi's family, along with others involved in military operations, had a few days to return to their home region to retrieve their belongings. In addition to valuable furniture, the mother salvaged items that were important to her two daughters: the dolls Sinikka and Keiju obtained from America with porcelain legs and real dark hair, as well as some books, *Grimm's Fairy Tales*, and *One Thousand and One Nights*. At the time of writing her autobiographies, Kilpi still had all these objects, invested with memories of her childhood in the lost Karelia.[67]

Conclusion

Based on selected contemporary and recollection material, this chapter has analyzed how Finnish children and youth wrote about their consumption during the war years—how the extreme shortage was dealt with and what young people dreamed of—and how experiences of war-related shortage were remembered decades later during a nostalgic surge in war memories. Additionally, the novel about a fictional war child sent to Sweden offers a perspective into the extreme differences in the living standards of neighboring countries.

The reduction of consumer opportunities affected everyday living for the whole population in war-waging Finland. This democratization has been highlighted in previous research and in many recollections—despite the factual differentiation between various groups of people. In our recollection, material scarcity is the all-embracing experience, whereas the contemporary material—*Sirkka* magazine with its mostly middle-class readers—opens a perspective into the lives of young people who still had resources for consumption available. There were reductions that affected their lives, but the dreams of the readers—in many cases associated with sweets and other delicacies—show that they were saved from the most extreme scarcity. For them, giving up the accustomed level of consumption signaled their contribution to the nation that was required from everybody. In the recollection material, the focus is more clearly on the experience of scarcity and, in some cases, of great personal sacrifices, for instance, in terms of lost objects. We want to suggest that this focus reflects the narrative that highlights the high price that the whole nation was ready to pay for its survival, a price that has only accumulated in interpretations of collective memory since the end of the war.

---

[67] Kilpi, *Talvisodan aika*, 194–95.

Contributors

Allison Scardino Belzer is an associate professor of History at Georgia Southern University in Savannah, Georgia, where she teaches Italian and British history. She earned her PhD from Emory University (2002). Her book *Women and the Great War: Femininity under Fire in Italy* (Palgrave, 2010) investigates how the war affected women living at home and near the fighting front. Recent publications include "Identifying Patriots: Women in Uniform in Italy" in *Cutting a New Pattern: Women in Uniform in the Great War* (Smithsonian, 2020) and "Women's Experiences with War" in *Italy in the Era of the Great War* (Brill, 2018); they examine different facets of Italian women's wartime experience, with attention to situating them in an international context.

Gina Benavidez is a PhD student at the University of New Mexico where she studies modern European history with a regional emphasis in Spain and a thematic emphasis on gender. Her dissertation focuses on the Women of the International Brigades in the Spanish Civil War and the conflict as a theater for international actors. The chapter in this volume is based on one of her dissertation chapters.

Nupur Chaudhuri is Professor of History at Texas Southern University and teaches European and British history. She is the author of numerous articles and chapters on British and French history and is co-author, with Mary Elizabeth Perry and Sherry Katz, of the award-winning collection *Finding Women in the Archives: Collection of Essays on Women from India, Iran, Spain, Poland, Mexico, Mozambique and the U.S.* (University of Illinois, 2010) and co-editor with Eileen Boris of *Voices of Women Historians: Personal, Professional and Political* (University of Indiana, 1999); with Ruth Roach Pierson of *Nation, Empire, Colony: Critical Categories of Gender and Race Analysis* (University of Indiana, 1998) and with Margaret Strobel of *Western Women and Imperialism: Complicity and Resistance* (University of Indiana, 1992).

Mark J. Crowley is Associate professor in the Department of Management at the David Eccles School of Business, University of Utah. He is a graduate of the Universities of Wales (Cardiff), Oxford and London. Crowley has published articles on nineteenth-century British trade unionism, Welsh nationalism, devolution in Wales and women's employment in the Second World War.

Crowley co-edited (with Erika Rappaport and Sandra Trudgen Dawson) *Consuming Behaviours: Identity, Politics and Pleasure in twentieth-century Britain* (London, 2015) and (with Sandra Trudgen Dawson) *Home Fronts: Britain and the Empire at War, 1939-45* (Boydell, 2017). He is currently completing his monograph, *Post Office Women at War, 1939-45* (forthcoming, Bloomsbury Academic).

Sandra Trudgen Dawson is Executive Administrator of the Berkshire Conference of Women Historians. She received a PhD in History and Feminist Studies from the University of California, Santa Barbara, in 2007. Her first book, *Holiday Camps in twentieth-century Britain: Packaging Pleasure*, was published by Manchester University Press in 2011 as part of their Popular Culture Series. Dawson co-edited (with Erika Rappaport and Mark J. Crowley) *Consuming Behaviours: Identity, Politics and Pleasure in twentieth-century Britain* (Bloomsbury Academic, 2015) and edited (with Mark J. Crowley) *Home Fronts: Britain and the Empire at War, 1939-45* (Boydell, 2017). Her current project, *Midwives and Mothers: Reproductive Labours in Interwar and Wartime Britain* is forthcoming with Lexington Books.

Patrick José Dawson is Director of the Albin O Kuhn Library & Gallery at the University of Maryland, Baltimore County. He also served as Dean of Libraries at Northern Illinois University and in various positions at the University of California on the Riverside, Irvine, and Santa Barbara Campuses. Besides a degree in Library Science from the University of Arizona, Dawson holds a Bachelor's degree in History and a Master's degree in History from the University of New Mexico. Dawson's Master's focus was the history of colonial Latin America and the Spanish Empire.

Suzanne Dunai is an assistant professor of history at Southwestern Oklahoma State University. She completed he dissertation 'Food Politics in Postwar Spain: Eating and Everyday Life during the Early Franco Dictatorship, 1939-1952' at the University of California San Diego in 2019. Her research analyzes the ideological motivations of food policies during the period of rationing in Spain (1939-1952) and their social consequences. Along with European History, her teaching and research interests include Food Studies, Women, Gender, and Sexuality Studies, and Latin American Studies. She is the recipient of a Fulbright student grant from the U.S. State Department and Hispanex grant from the Foreign Ministry of Spain, which have funded her research for several publications on Spanish daily life during the 1940s.

Marianne Junila is a research fellow at the Department of History, University of Oulu, Finland. Her research interests relate to the social history of the 20th-century wars in general, and to history of children, health and welfare in particular. She is also interested in gender history and history of emotions. Her articles published in English include, among others, "War through the Children's Eyes in The Finnish Civil War 1918: history, memory, legacy" (2014) and "Wars on the home front: mobilization, economy and everyday experiences in Finland" in *Finland in World War II: history, memory, interpretations* (2012). In Swedish she published an article on health care of Finnish children sent to Sweden during WW II (Junila & Karin Zetterqvist Nelson, "Gränsöverskridande socialmedicin: vård av finska sjuka barn i Sverige 1942–1949", *Socialmedicinsk tidskrift* 5/2017, 610–618).

Tiina Kinnunen is professor of History at the University of Oulu, Finland. Her scholarship deals with the history of European feminisms, social and cultural history of war, and history of historiography. Within social and cultural history of war, she has published widely on Finnish women at war, and memory cultures of Finnish Civil War and Finland's WW II. Her publications include a co-edited volume (with Ville Kivimäki) *Finland in World War II: history, memory, interpretations* (2012), which has become standard work in the field. In 2018, she co-edited a special issue of *Historiallinen Aikakauskirja* (Historical Journal) on social and cultural history of WW II in Finland. Kinnunen is the chair of a scientific committee of the Centre for War and Peace, to be opened in Mikkeli, Finland in 2021.

Mary Laurents is a lecturer in the History Dept. at the University of Maryland Baltimore County and in the Public History Department at Stevenson University. She has a PhD in Language, Literacy, and Culture. Laurents' area of focus is the effects of war on sociological factors like collective identity and the transformation of collectivities under traumatic conditions. Her monograph, *British Identities in WWI: The Lost Boys*, was published in 2020 by Lexington Books.

Kenneth Mouré is Professor of History at the University of Alberta. Mouré published, *The Gold Standard Illusion: France, the Bank of France, and the International Gold Standard, 1914-1939*, with Oxford University Press, 2002, and *Managing the Franc Poincaré: Economic Understanding and Political Constraint in French Monetary Policy, 1928–1936*, Cambridge University Press, 1991. His research on black-market activity in France during World War II has been published in journal articles; his monograph *Marché Noir: The Economy* *of Survival in Second World War France* was published by Cambridge University Press in 2023.

Andrew Orr is Associate Professor of History and Security Studies at Kansas State University. He holds a Ph.D. in European History from the University of Notre Dame and specializes in military and women's history. Orr is the author of *Women and the French Army during the World Wars, 1914 – 1940* from Indiana University Press (2017) and has published articles on French military and women's history in *French Historical Studies, French History*, and the *Journal of Military History*. In 2020 he was a Visiting Fellow at the University of St. Andrew's Centre for French History and Culture.

Laurie S. Stoff is Teaching Professor and Honors Faculty Fellow at Barrett, The Honors College, at Arizona State University, and affiliated faculty in the Melikian Center for Russian, Eurasian, and East European Studies at ASU. She holds an M.A. and PhD in History from the University of Kansas and specializes in Russian, East European, women's and gender history, and the history of war and society. Her research focuses on the intersections of gender and war, specifically, Russian women and the Great War, and the ways that wartime experience transcended conventional conceptions of military activity. She has written a number of works on this subject, including two monographs: *They Fought for the Motherland: Russia's Women Soldiers in World War I and the Revolution* (University Press of Kansas, 2006), and *Russia's Sisters of Mercy and the Great War: More than Binding Men's Wounds* (University Press of Kansas, 2015) – winner of the Southern Conference for Slavic Studies Best Book Prize and the Southern Historical Association's Smith Award for Best Book in European History. Additionally, as part of the international editorial team for the multi-volume project Russia's Great War and Revolution, she served as lead editor, with Anthony J. Heywood, Boris I. Kolonitskii, and John W. Steinberg, for the recently published volume *Military Affairs in Russia's Great War and Revolution, 1914–22, Book 1: Military Experiences* (Bloomington: Slavica Publishers, 2019).

Michelle Tusan is Professor of History at the University of Nevada Las Vegas where she teaches and writes about gender, liberalism, and empire. Her publications include *Woman Making News: Gender and Journalism in Modern Britain* (2006), *Smyrna's Ashes: Humanitarianism, Genocide and the Birth of the Middle East* (2012) and *The British Empire and the Armenian Genocide: Humanitarianism and Imperial Politics from Gladstone to Churchill* (2017).

Bibliography

Abella, Irving and Harold Troper. *None Is Too Many: Canada and the Jews of Europe, 1933–1948*. Toronto: University of Toronto Press, 2012.

Acier, Marcel. *From Spanish Trenches; Recent Letters from Spain*. New York: Modern Age Books, 1937.

Adams, Christine. *Poverty, Charity, and Motherhood: Maternal Societies in Nineteenth-Century France*. Urbana: University of Illinois Press, 2010.

Alpert, Michael. *A New International History of the Spanish Civil War*. London: Palgrave, 1998.

___. Alpert, Michael. "Humanitarianism and Politics in the British Response to the Spanish Civil War, 1936-9." *European History Quarterly* 14 (1984) 423-40.

Anderson, Lara. *Food and Francoism: Food Discourse, Control and Resistance in Franco Spain*. Toronto: University of Toronto Press, 2020.

Anderson, Peter. "The Struggle over the Evacuation to the United Kingdom and Repatriation of Basque Refugee Children in the Spanish Civil War: Symbols and Souls." *Journal of Contemporary History* 52: 2 (2017) 297-398.

Ash, Susan. *Funding Philanthropy: Dr. Barnardo, Metaphor, Narrative and Spectacle*. Liverpool: Liverpool University Press, 2016.

Audoin-Rouzeau, Stephane. Children and Adolescents. *Brill's Encyclopedia of the First World War.* Leiden: Brill, 2012, 103-107.

Austin, Linda M. "Childhood: Nostalgia and the Romantic Legacy," *Studies in Romanticism* 42.1 (2003) 75-98.

Ball, Alan M. *And Now My Soul Is Hardened: Abandoned Children in Soviet Russia, 1918-1930*. Berkeley: University of California Press, 1994.

Baron, Nick, ed. *Displaced Children in Russia and Eastern Europe, 1915-1953: Ideologies, Identities, Experiences*. Boston: Brill, 2016.

Barranquero Texeira, Encarnación and Lucía Prieto Borrego. *Así Sobrevivimos al Hambre: estrategias de supervivencia de las mujeres en la postguerra española*. Málaga: Servicio de Publicaciones, Centro de Ediciones de la Diputación de Málaga, 2003.

Baughan, Emily. "The Imperial War Relief Fund and the All-British Appeal: Commonwealth, Conflict and Conservatism within the British Humanitarian Movement, 1920-25," *Journal of Imperial and Commonwealth History* 40.5 (2012) 845–61.

Bennet, Judith and Angela Wanhalla, eds. *Mothers' Darlings of the South Pacific: The Children of Indigenous Women and U.S. Servicemen, World War II*. Honolulu: University of Hawai'i Press, 2016.

Bland, Lucy. *Britain's "Brown Babies": The Stories of Children Born to Black GIs and British Women in the Second World War*. Manchester: Manchester University Press, 2019.

Blas, Verónica Sierra "A Lost Generation? Children and the Spanish Civil War." James Matthews, ed. *Spain at War: Society, Culture and Mobilization, 1936–44*. London: Bloomsbury Academic, 2019. 158–76.

Bell, Adrian. *Only for Three Months: The Basque Refugee Children in Exile.* Earls Barton: Wrightsons, 2007.

Benjamin, Natalia, ed. *Recuerdos: Basque Children Refugees in Britain.* Oxford: Mousehold Press, 2007.

Bhatti, Anil and Johannes H. Voigt, eds. *Jewish Exile in India, 1933–1945.* New Delhi: Manohar, 1999.

Blakeney, Michael. *Australia and the Jewish Refugees, 1933–1948.* Sydney: Croom Helm, 1985.

Bock, Gisela. "Racism and Sexism in Nazi Germany," *When Biology Became Destiny: Women in Weimar and Nazi Germany,* ed. Bridenthal et al. New York: Monthly Review Press, 1984. 271-296.

___. "Antinatalism in National Socialist Racism," *Nazism and German Society, 1933- 1945,* ed. David Crew et al. New York: Routledge, 1994. 110-140.

Bosworth, R. J. B. *Mussolini's Italy: Life Under the Fascist Dictatorship, 1915-1945.* New York: Penguin, 2007.

Breakwell, Suan Sheridan. "'Knowing how to be a Mother': Parenting, Emotion and Evacuation Propaganda during the Spanish Civil war, 1936-1939." In *Parenting and the State in Britain and Europe, c. 1870-1950: Raising the Nation.* Hester Barron and Claudia Siebrecht, eds. Palgrave Macmillan, 2017. 207-230.

Brittain, Vera. Bishop, Alan, ed. *Chronicle of Youth: The War Diary 1913-1917.* New York: William Morrow and Company, Inc. 1982.

Brittain, Vera. *Testament of Youth.* New York: Penguin Books, 1994.

Broad, Graham. *A Small Price to Pay: Consumer Culture on the Canadian Home Front, 1939-45.* Vancouver: University of British Columbia Press, 2013.

Buchanan, Tom. East Wind, China and the British Left, 1925-1976. Oxford University Press: Oxford Scholarship Online, 2012.

___. "'Shanghai-Madrid Axis? Comparing British Responses to the Conflicts in Spain and China, 1936 - 39," *Contemporary European History* 21.4 (2012): 533-552.

___. "The role of the British Labour Movement in the Origin and the Work of the Basque Children's Committee, 1937-9." *European History Quarterly* 18 (1988) 155-174.

___. *Britain and the Spanish Civil War.* Cambridge: Cambridge University Press, 1997.

Cabalerro Jurado, Carlos. *The Condor Legion: German Troops in the Spanish Civil War.* Oxford: Osprey Press, 2013.

Cabanes, Bruno. *The Great War and the Origins of Humanitarianism, 1918–1924.* Cambridge: Cambridge University Press, 2014.

Cañete Quesada, Carmen. "Salaria Kea and the Spanish Civil War: Memoirs of a Negro Nurse in Republican Spain." *In Black USA and Spain: Shared Memories in the 20th Century,* edited by Rosalía Cornejo-Parriego, New York: Routledge, 2020. 113-33.

Cardoza, Thomas. *Intrepid Women: Cantinières and Vivandières of the French Army.* Bloomington: Indiana University Press, 2010.

Caron, Vicki. *Uneasy Asylum: France and the Jewish Refugee Crisis, 1933–1942*. Redwood City: Stanford University Press, 1999.

Carroll, Peter N. *The Odyssey of the Abraham Lincoln Brigade: Americans in the Spanish Civil War*. Stanford, California: Stanford University Press, 1994.

Castells, Manuel. *The Power of Identity*. Oxford: Wiley-Blackwell, 2010.

Cazorla Sánchez, Antonio. *Fear and Progress: Ordinary Lives in Franco Spain, 1939-1975*. Malden: Wiley-Blackwell, 2010.

Cenarro, Ángela. *La sonrisa de Falange: Auxilio Social en la guerra civil y en la posguerra*. Barcelona: Critica, 2006.

___. *Los Niños del Auxilio Social*. Madrid: Espasa Calpe, 2009.

Chang, Iris. *The Rape of Nanking: The Forgotten Holocaust of WWII*. New York: Basic Books, 1997.

Clegg, Arthur. "Aid China, 1937-1949: A Memoir of a Forgotten Campaign." *Science and Society* 56.1 (1992). 164-165.

Clements, Barbara, Barbara Engel and Christine Worobec, ed. *Russia's Women: Accommodation, Resistance, Transformation*. Berkely, California: University of California Press, 1991.

Collingwood, Lizzie. *The Taste of War: World War Two and the Battle for Food*. New York: Penguin, 2013.

Connelly, John. *From Peoples into Nations: A History of Eastern Europe*. Princeton: Princeton University Press, 2020.

Crane, Cynthia. *Divided Lives: The Untold Stories of Jewish-Christian Women in Nazi Germany*. New York: St. Martin's Press, 2000.

Curtis, Norah and Cyril Gilbey. *Malnutrition: Quaker Work in Austria 1919–24 and Spain 1936–39*. London: Oxford University Press, 1944.

Damousi, Joy. *The Humanitarians Child Refugees and Australian Humanitarians in a Transnational World, 1919-1975*. Cambridge: Cambridge University Press, 2022.

Darrow, Margaret. *French Women and the First World War: War Stories of the Home Front*. New York: Berg, 2002.

Davies, Hywel. *Fleeing Franco: How Wales Gave Shelter to Refugee Children from the Basque Country during the Spanish Civil War*. Cardiff: University of Wales Press, 2011.

Dawson, Sandra Trudgen. *Holiday Camps in Twentieth-Century Britain: Packaging Pleasure*. Manchester: Manchester University Press, 2011.

___. "Refugee Children and the Emotional Cost of International Humanitarianism in Interwar Britain," *Journal of British Studies* 60 (2021) 115-139.

___. "Working-Class Consumers and the Campaign for Holidays with Pay," *Twentieth Century British History* 18.3 (2007). 277-305.

Deacon, Valerie. "Fitting into the French Resistance: Georges Loustaunau-Lacau and Marie-Madeleine Fourcade at the intersection of Politics and Gender." *Journal of Contemporary History* 50 (April 2105). 259-273.

D'Eath, Jessica. "'A noi': The Emergence of the Gallant Fascist in Italian Children's Literature of the Inter-war Period." In *Politics and Ideology in Children's Literature*. Edited by Marian Keyes and Aine McGillicuddy. Dublin: Fourcourts Press, 2014, 115-126.

De Grand, Alexander. "Women under Italian Fascism," *The Historical Journal* 19.4 (1976) 947-968.

DeGroot, Gerard J. and C. Peniston-Bird. *A Soldier and a Woman: Sexual Integration in the Military.* London: Longman, 2000.

Deslandes, Paul. "Selling, Consuming, and Becoming the Beautiful Man in Britain: The 1930s and 1940s," *Consuming Behaviours: Identity, Politics, and Pleasure in Twentieth-Century Britain,* eds. Erika D. Rappaport, Sandra Trudgen Dawson, and Mark J. Crowley London: Bloomsbury, 2015. 53-70.

Diamond, Hanna. *Women and the Second World War in France, 1939-1948: Choices and Constraints.* London: Longman, 1999.

De Pauw, Linda Grant. *Battle Cries and Lullabies: Women in War from Prehistory to the Present.* Norman: Oklahoma, 1998.

Displaced Children in Russia and Eastern Europe, 1915-1953. Nick Baron, ed. Leiden: Brill, 2017.

Dodd, Lindsey and David Lees, eds. *Vichy France and Everyday Life: Confronting the Challenges of Wartime, 1939-1945.* London: Bloomsbury, 2018.

Dominé, Jean-François. *Les Femmes au Combat: L'arme feminine de la France pendant la Seconde Guerre mondiale.* Paris: Service historique de la Défense, 2008.

Downs, Laura Lee. *Childhood in the Promised Land: Working-Class Movements and the Colonies de Vacances in France, 1880-1960.* Durham: Duke University Press, 2002.

Duff Cooper, Alfred. *Old Men Forget.* London: Faber and Faber, 2011.

Durbach, Nadja. "British Restaurants and the Gender Politics of the Wartime Midday Meal," *Home Fronts: Britain and the Empire at War, 1039-45,* eds. Mark J Crowley and Sandra Trudgen Dawson. London: Boydell and Brewer, 2017. 19-36.

Eby, Cecil. *Between the Bullet and the Lie; American Volunteers in the Spanish Civil War.* New York: Holt, Rinehart and Winston, 1969.

Edgar, Adrienne. "Bolshevism, Patriarchy, and the Nation: The Soviet 'Emancipation' of Muslim Women in Pan-Islamic Perspective," *Slavic Review* 65.2 (2006) 252-272.

Ekmekcioglu. Lerna. *Recovering Armenia: The Limits of Belonging in Post-Genocide Turkey.* Stanford: Stanford UP, 2016.

Elshtain, Jean Bethke. *Women and War.* New York: Basic Books, 1987.

Emanuel, Muriel and Vera Gissing. *Nicholas Winton and the Rescued Generation: Save One Life, Save the World.* London: Vallentine Mitchell, 2002.

Enloe, Cynthia. *Does Khaki Become You? The Militarisation of Women's Lives.* London: Pluto, 1983.

___. *Maneuvers: The International Politics of Militarizing Women's Lives.* Berkeley: University of California Press, 2000.

Falcoff, Mark, and Fredrick B. Pike. *The Spanish Civil War, 1936-39: American Hemispheric Perspectives.* Lincoln: University of Nebraska Press, 1982.

Fast, Vera K. *Children's Exodus: A History of the Kindertransport.* London: I. B. Taurus, 2011.

Fava, Sabrina. *Percorsi critci di letteratura per l'infanzia tra le due guerre.* Milano: Vita e pensiero, 2004.

Fawaz, Leila. *A Land of Aching Hearts.* Cambridge: Harvard UP, 2014.

Ferrall, Charles and Anna Jackson. *Juvenile Literature and British Society, 1850-1950: The Age of Adolescence.* New York: Routledge, 2010.

Fishman, Sarah. *We Will Wait; Wives of French Prisoners of War, 1940-1945.* New Haven: Yale University Press, 1991.

Fitzpatrick, Sheila. *Everyday Stalinism: Ordinary Life in Extraordinary Times: Soviet Russia in the 1930s.* Oxford: Oxford University Press, 2000.

Fochesato, Walter. *Raccontare la guerra: Libri per bambini e ragazzi.* Novara: Interlinea, 2011.

Fort, Adrian. *Nancy: The Story of Lady Astor.* London: St. Martin's Griffin, 2014.

Francis, Hywel. *Miners Against Fascism: Wales and the Spanish Civil War.* London: Lawrence & Wishart, 2012.

Friedländer, Saul. *Nazi Germany and the Jews, Volume 1: The Years of Persecution, 1933–1939.* New York: HarperCollins, 1997.

___. *The Years of Extermination: Nazi Germany and the Jews, 1939–1945.* New York: HarperCollins, 2007.

Fuchs, Rachel G. *Abandoned Children: Foundlings and Child Welfare in Nineteenth-Century France.* Albany: SUNY Press, 1984.

Fuhr, Lini. *Up from the Cellar.* Minneapolis, MN: Vanilla Press, 1979.

Fussell, Paul. *The Great War and Modern Memory.* New York: Oxford University Press, 1989.

Fyrth, J. *The Signal Was Spain: The Aid Spain Movement in Britain, 1936-1939.* Palgrave: London, 1986.

Gallego Méndez, María Teresa. *Mujer, Falange y Franquismo.* Madrid: Taurus, 1983.

Gaterell, Peter. *Russia's First World War: A Social and Economic History.* London: Pearson, 2005.

Gerassi, John. *The Premature Antifascists: North American Volunteers in the Spanish Civil War, 1936-39: An Oral History.* New York: Praeger, 1986.

Gildea, Robert. *Fighters in the Shadows a New History of the French Resistance.* Cambridge, MA: Harvard University Press, 2015.

Giráldez Lomba, Antonio. *Sobrevivir en los Años del hambre en Vigo.* Vigo: Instituto de Estudios Vigueses, 2002.

Giorgi, Marisa. *(Re)Forming Italians: Children's Literature in Italy, 1929-1939.* PhD Dissertation, City University of New York, 2012.

Goldman, Nancy. *Female Soldiers—Combatants or Non-Combatants?: Historical and Contemporary Perspectives.* Westport: Greenwood Press, 1982.

Goldman, Wendy. *Women at the Gates Gender and Industry in Stalin's Russia.* Cambridge: Cambridge University Press, 2002.

___. *Women, The State and Revolution: Soviet Family Policy and Social Life, 1917-1936.* Cambridge: Cambridge University Press, 1993.

Goldstein, Joshua. *War and Gender: How Gender Shapes the War System and Vice Versa.* Cambridge: Cambridge University Press, 2003.

Gottlieb, Julie. *Feminist Fascism: Women in Britain's Fascist Movement, 1923-1945.* London: I.B. Tauris, 2003.

Goodenough, Elizabeth and Andrea Immel, eds. *Under Fire: Childhood in the Shadow of War.* Detroit: Wayne State University Press, 2008.

Graebner, Norman A. and Edward M. Bennett. *The Versailles Treaty and Its Legacy: The Failure of the Wilsonian Vision.* Cambridge: Cambridge University Press, 2014.

Grayzel, Susan and Tammy Proctor, eds. *Gender and the Great War.* Oxford: Oxford University Press, 2017.

Grossmann, Atina. "Feminist Debates about Women and National Socialism," *Gender and History* 3.3 (1991) 350-58.

___. "A Question of Silence: The Rape of German Women by Occupation Soldiers," *October* 72 (1995) 43–63.

Guido, Alani and Cormac O Grada, eds. *Famine in European History.* Cambridge: Cambridge University Press, 2017.

Hallett, Christine. *Veiled Warriors: Allied Nurses of the First World War.* Oxford: Oxford University Press, 2014.

Harris, Mark Jonathan and Deborah Oppenheimer. *Into the Arms of Strangers: Stories of the Kindertransport.* New York: Bloomsbury, 2017.

Hawkes, Louise Restieaux. *Before and After Pinocchio: A Study of Italian Children's Books.* Paris: The Puppet Press, 1933.

Heineman, Elizabeth D. *What Difference Does a Husband Make? Women and Marital Status in Nazi and Postwar Germany.* Berkeley: University of California Press, 1999.

Henshaw, Jonathan, Craig A. Smith, and Norman Smith, eds. *Translating the Occupation: The Japanese Invasion of China.* Vancouver: University of British Columbia Press, 2021.

Herbert, Melissa. *Camouflage Isn't Only for Combat: Gender, Sexuality and Women in the Military.* New York, 1998.

Higonnet, Margaret, ed. *Nurses at the Front: Writing the Wounds of the Great War.* Boston: Northeastern University Press, 2001.

Higonnet, Margaret, Jene Jackson, Sonya Muchel, and Margaret Weitz, eds. *Behind the Line: Gender and the Two World Wars.* New Haven: Yale UP, 1987.

Hochschild, Adam. *Spain in Our Hearts: Americans in the Spanish Civil War, 1936-1939.* Boston, MA: Houghton Mifflin Harcourt, 2016.

Holm, Jeanne. *Women in the Military: An Unfinished Revolution.* Novato: Presidio Press, 1992.

Honeck, Mischa and James Marten, eds. *War and Childhood in the Era of the Two World Wars.* Cambridge: Cambridge University Press, 2019.

Hughes, Karen. "Transnational Struggles for Racial Justice: Australian Indigenous Women's Marriages to American Servicemen During the Second World War." *Engendering Transnational Transgressions: From the Intimate to the Global,* eds. Eileen Boris, Sandra Trudgen Dawson and Barbara Molony. New York: Routledge, 2020. 115-132.

Irujo, Xabier. *Expelled from the Motherland: The Government of President Jose Antonio Agirre in Exile, 1937–1960.* Cameron J. Watson and Jennifer Ottman trans. Reno: University of Nevada Press, 2012.

Ivanova, Iu. N. *Khrabreishchie iz prekrasnykh: Zhenschiny Rossii v voinakh.* Moscow: "Rossiiskaia politicheskaia entsiklopediia," 2002.

Jackson, Angela. *British Women in the Spanish Civil War.* London: Routledge, 2002.

Jinks, Rebecca. "'Marks Hard to Erase': The Troubled Reclamation of 'Absorbed' Armenian Women, 1919–1927." *American Historical Review* 123.1 (2018) 86-123.

Joshi, Vandana. *Gender and Power in the Third Reich: Female Denouncers and the Gestapo, 1933-1945.* New York: Palgrave MacMillan, 2003.

Katchadourian, Stina. *The Lapp King's Daughter: A Family's Journey Through Finland's Wars.* Fithian Press, 2010.

Kater, Michael H. *Hitler Youth.* Cambridge: Harvard University Press, 2006.

Keegan, John. *The First World War.* Vintage, 2000.

Khan, Yasmin. "Sex in an Imperial War Zone: Transnational Encounters in Second World War India," *History Workshop Journal* 73.1 (2012) 240–58.

Kinealy, Christine. *Charity and the Great Hunger in Ireland: The Kindness of Strangers.* London: Bloomsbury, 2013.

Kinnunen, Tiina and Ville Kivimäki (eds). *Finland in World War II. History, Memory, Interpretations.* Leiden, Boston: Brill, 2012.

Koonz, Claudia. *Mothers in the Fatherland: Women, the Family and Nazi Politics.* New York: St. Martin's Press, 1987.

Kowalsky, Daniel. "The Soviet Cinematic Offensive in the Spanish Civil War." *Film History* 19. 2007.

___. *Stalin and the Spanish Civil War.* New York: Columbia University Press, 2004.

Korppi-Tommola, Aura. "War and Children in Finland during the Second World War." *Paedagogica Historica* 44.4 (2008): 445–55.

Kuusisto-Arponen, Anna-Kaisa and Ulla Savolainen. "The Interplay of Memory and Matter: Narratives of Former Finnish Karelian Child Evacuees", *Oral History* 44.2 (2016): 59–68.

Lacour-Astol, Catherine. *Le genre de la Résistance. La Résistance féminine dans le Nord de la France.* Paris: Les Presses de Sciences Po, 2015.

Lagarreta, Dorothy. *The Guernica Generation: Basque Refugee Children of the Spanish Civil War.* Reno: University of Nevada Press, 1984.

Lambert, Angela. *Unquiet Souls: A Social History of the Illustrious, Irreverent, Intimate Group of British Aristocrats Known as "The Souls."* New York: Harper & Row, 1984.

Laurents, Mary. *British Identity in World War I: The Lost Boys.* Lexington, 2020.

Laycock, Jo and Francesca Piana. *Aid to Armenia: Humanitarianism and Intervention from the 1890s to the Present.* Manchester: Manchester University Press, 2020.

Lear, Walter J. "American Medical Support for Spanish Democracy, 1936-1938." *Comrades in Health: U.S. Health Internationalists, Abroad and at Home,* edited by Theodore M. Brown and Anne-Emanuelle Birn, New Brunswick, NJ: Rutgers University Press, 2013. 65-81.

Leckie, Jacqueline, Angela McCarthy, and Angela Wanhalla. *Migrant Cross-Cultural Encounters in Asia and the Pacific.* New York: Routledge, 2016.

Lehtola, Veli-Pekka. "Second World War as a Trigger for Transcultural Changes among Sámi People in Finland." Acta Borealia 32.2 (2015): 125-147.

Leverton, Bertha and Shmuel Lowensohn. *I Came Alone: The Stories of the Kindertransports.* Lewes: Book Guild, 1990.

Levi D'Ancona, Luisa. "Modern Italy." *Jewish Women: A Comprehensive Historical Encyclopedia* (27 February 2009), Jewish Women's Archive, https://jwa.org/encyclopedia/article/italy-modern.

Limonero, Colomina. *Dos patrias, tres mil destinos Vida y exilio de los niños de la guerra de España refugiados en la Unión Sovietica.* Madrid: Ediciones Cinca, 2010.

London, Louise. *Whitehall and the Jews, 1933–1948: British Immigration Policy, Jewish Refugees and the Holocaust.* Cambridge: Cambridge University Press, 2001.

Lopatkina, Nataliya L. *Kul'turupologicheskie aspekty v razvitii sestrinskogo delo.* Kemerovo: 2009.

Marten, James, ed. *The Lessons of War: The Civil War in Children's Magazines.* Wilmington, DE: SR Books, 1999.

Mahood, Linda. *Feminism and Voluntary Action: Eglantyne Jebb and Save the Children, 1876-1928.* London: Palgrave Macmillan, 2009.

Mahood, Linda and Vic Satzewich. "The Save the Children Fund and the Russian Famine of 1921–23: Claims and Counter-Claims about Feeding 'Bolshevik' Children," *Journal of Historical Sociology* 22.1 (2009) 57–83.

Marcus, Leonard. *Minders of Make-Believe: Idealists, Entrepreneurs, and the Shaping of American Children's Literature.* Boston: Houghton Mifflin, 2008.

Marshall, Dominique. "Humanitarian Sympathy for Children in Times of War and the History of Children's Rights, 1919–1959." James Marten, ed. *Children and War: A Historical Anthology.* New York: New York University Press, 2002. 184-199.

Marwick, Arthur. *The Deluge: British Society and the First World War.* London: MacMillan, 1965.

Mason, Tim. "Women in Nazi Germany," *History Workshop Journal* 1 (1976) 74-113.

McDermid, Jane and Anna Hillyar. *Women and Work in Russia, 1880-1930: A Study in Continuity Through Change.* London: Taylor & Francis, 2014.

McLean, Eden K. *Mussolini's Children: Race and Elementary Education in Fascist Italy.* Lincoln: University of Nebraska Press, 2018.

Melman, Billie, ed. *Borderlines: Gender and Identity in War and Peace: 1870-1930.* New York: Routledge, 1990.

Melosh, Barbara, *"The Physician's Hand:" Work Culture and Conflict in American Nursing.* Philadelphia: Temple University Press, 1982.

Melucci, Alberto. *Nomads of the Present: Social Movements and Individual Needs in Contemporary Society.* Philadelphia: Temple University Press, 1989.

Miller, Montserrat. *Feeding Barcelona, 1714-1975: Public Market Halls, Social Networks, and Consumer Culture.* Baton Rouge: Louisiana State University Press, 2015.

Moore, Bob. *Refugees from Nazi Germany in the Netherlands, 1933–1940.* Dordrecht: M. Nijhoff, 1986.

Morcillo, Aurora G. *True Catholic Womanhood: Gender Ideology in Franco's Spain.* DeKalb, Ill: Northern Illinois University Press, 2000.

Mosby, Ian. *Food Will Win the War: The Politics, Culture, and Science of Food on Canada's Home Front.* Seattle: University of Washington Press, 2015.

Mouré Kenneth. "'Economic Tyranny' and Public Anger in France, 1945-1947." *Journal of Contemporary European History.* August 2022. 1-14.

___. *Marché Noir: The Economy of Survival in Second World War France.* Cambridge: Cambridge University Press, 2023.

Muel-Dreyfus, Francine. *Vichy and the Eternal Feminine: A Contribution to a Political Sociology of Gender*, translated by Kathleen A. Johnson. Durham: Duke University Press, 2001.

Myers, K. P. F. "Englishness, identity and refugee children in Britain, 1937-1945." Unpublished Thesis. Coventry University (2000).

Nelson, Cary, and Jefferson Hendricks, eds. *Madrid, 1937: Letters of the Abraham Lincoln Brigade from the Spanish Civil War.* New York: Routledge, 1996.

Nevala-Nurmi, Seija-Leena. "Girls and Boys in the Finnish Voluntary Defense Movement." *Ennen ja Nyt* 6.3-4 (2006). https://journal.fi/ennenjanyt/article/view/108351/63368.

Ofer, Inbal. *Señoritas in Blue: The Making of a Female Political Elite in Franco's Spain.* Brighton: Sussex Academic Press, 2010.

Ojala, Jari, Jari Eloranta and Jukka Jalava. *Road to Prosperity: Economic History of Finland.* Helsinki: Suomalaisen kirjallisuuden seura, 2006.

Orr, Andrew. *Women and the French Army during the World Wars*, 1914-1940. Bloomington, IN: Indiana University Press, 2017.

Pakula, Hannah. *The Last Empress: Madame Chiang Kai-shek and the Birth of Modern China.* New York: Simon & Schuster, 2009.

Pole, Adrian. "'Soldiers of Culture' and their 'Little Comrades': The International Brigades and the Children of Civil War Spain, 1936-1939." *Journal of Contemporary European History.* 2022. 1-15.

Parker, Peter. *The Old Lie: The Great War and the Public School Ethos.* London: Constable and Company Limited, 1987.

Paris, Michael. *Over the Top: The Great War and Juvenile Literature in Britain.* Westport, CT: Praeger, 2004.

Passmore, Kevin. *Women, Gender and Fascism in Europe, 1919-1945.* New Brunswick, NJ: Rutgers University Press, 2003.

Patai, Frances. "Heroines of the Good Fight: Testimonies of U.S. Volunteer Nurses in the Spanish Civil War, 1936-1939." *Nursing History Review* 3 (1995): 79-104.

Paul, Lissa, Rosemary R. Johnston, and Emma Short, eds. *Children's Literature and Culture of the First World War.* New York: Routledge, 2016.

Paxton, Robert O. *Vichy France: Old Guard and New Order 1940-1944.* New York: Columbia University Press, 1972.

Posternak, A. V. *Ocherki po istorii obshchin sestry miloserdiia.* Moscow: Izdateltsvo Sviato-Dimitreevskii uchilishche sester miloserdiia, 2001.

Pedersen, Susan. *The Guardians: The League of Nations and the Crisis of Empire.* New York: Oxford University Press, 2016.

Pretus, Gabriel. *Humanitarian Relief in the Spanish Civil War (1936–1939).* Lewiston: Edward Mellen, 2013.

Qualls, Karl D. *Stalin's Niños: Educating Spanish Civil War Refugee Children in the Soviet Union, 1937-1951.* Toronto: University of Toronto Press, 2020.

___. "Defining the Ideal Soviet Childhood: Reportage about Child Evacuees from Spain as Didactic Literature." *War and Childhood in the Era of the Two World Wars.* Mischa Honeck and James Marten, eds. Cambridge: Cambridge University Press, 2019. 71-86.

___. "From Hooligans to Disciplined Students: Displacement, Resettlement, and Role Modeling of Spanish Civil War Children in the Soviet Union, 1937-1951," in Nick Baron, ed. *Displaced Children in Russia and Eastern Europe, 1915-1953: Ideologies, Identities, Experiences.* Leiden, 2017. 131-54.

___. "From Niños to Soviets?: Raising Spanish Refugee Children in House No. 1, 1937-51." *Canadian-American Slavic Studies* 48 (2014) 288-307.

Qiu, Peipei. *Chinese Comfort Women: Testimonies from Imperial Japan's Sex Slaves.* Vancouver: University of British Columbia Press, 2013.

Rappaport, Erika. *Shopping for Pleasure: Women and the Making of London's West End.* Princeton: Princeton University Press, 2000.

Read, Christopher, Peter Waldon, and Adele Lindenmeyr, eds. *Russia's Home Front in War and Revolution, 1914-22. Book 4: Reintegration—The Struggle for the State.* Bloomington, IN: Slavica Publishers, 2018.

Recuerdos: Basque Children Refugees in Britain. Natalia Benjamin, ed. Oxford: Mousehold Press, 2007.

Reese, Dagmar. *Growing Up Female in Nazi Germany*, trans. William Templer. Ann Arbor: University of Michigan Press, 2006.

Reid, Alastair J. *United We Stand: A History of Britain's Trade Unions.* London: Allen Lane, 2004.

Rempel, Gerhard. *Hitler's Children: The Hitler Youth and the SS.* Chapel Hill: University of North Carolina Press, 1990.

Report of the Committee on Alleged German Outrages, Appointed by His Britannic Majesty's Government and Presided Over by the Right Hon. Viscount Bryce, O.M. December 1914.

Reyah, Mario Ojeda. *Mexico and the Spanish Civil War: Domestic Politics and the Republican Cause.* Eastbourne: Sussex Academic Press, 2015.

Richmond, Kathleen. *Women and Spanish Fascism: The Women Section of the Falange, 1934-1959.* London: Routledge, 2003.

Roberts, Joan and Thetis Group. *Feminism and Nursing: An Historical Perspective on Power, Status, and Political Activism in the Nursing Profession.* Westport, CT: Praeger Publishing, 1995.

Rodríguez Barreira, Oscar, ed. *El Franquismo desde los márgenes: Campesinos, mujeres, deatores, menores...* Lleida: Editorial Universidad de Almería, 2013.

Román Ruiz, Gloria. *Delinquir o morir. El pequeño estraperlo en la Granada de posguerra.* Granada: Editorial Comares, 2015.

Sabin-Fernandez, Susana. "The Basque Refugee Children of the Spanish Civil War in the UK: Memory and Memorialisation." Ph.D. diss. University of Southampton (2010).

Sanborn, Joshua. *Drafting the Russian Nation: Military Conscription, Total War, and Mass Politics, 1905-1925.* DeKalb: Northern Illinois University Press, 2003.

___. *Imperial Apocalypse: The Great War and the Destruction of the Russian Empire.* Oxford: Oxford University Press, 2014.

Sarfatti, Michele. *The Jews in Mussolini's Italy: From Equality to Persecution.* Translated by John and Anne C. Tedeschi. Madison, WI: The University of Wisconsin Press, 2006.

Sasson, Tehila. "From Empire to Humanity: The Russian Famine and the Imperial Origins of International Humanitarianism," *Journal of British Studies* 55.3 (2016) 519-37.

Schwarzkopf, Jutta. "Combatant or Non-Combatant? The Ambiguous Status of Women in British Anti-Aircraft Batteries during the Second World War", *War & Society* 28.2 (2009) 105-31.

Seikaly, Sherene. "A Nutritional Economy: The Calorie, Development and War in Mandate Palestine," *Home Fronts: Britain and the Empire at War, 1039-45,* eds. Mark J Crowley and Sandra Trudgen Dawson. London: Boydell and Brewer, 2017. 37-58.

Senin, A. S. "Zhenskie batal'ony i voennye komandy v 1917 godu," *Voprosy istorii,* 10 (1987): 176-82.

Shapiro, Martin F. "Medical Aid to the Spanish Republic During the Civil War (1936-1939)." *Annals of Internal Medicine* 97 (July 1982): 119-124.

Shaw, Caroline. *Britannia's Embrace: Modern Humanitarianism and the Imperial Origins of Refugee Relief.* Oxford: Oxford University Press, 2015.

Silver, Hillary. "Social Exclusion and Social Solidarity: Three Paradigms." *International Institute for Labour Studies.* 133 (1994). 531-578.

Smith, Harold L. *War and Social Change: British Society in the Second World War.* Manchester: Manchester University Press, 1986.

Solomon, Susan Gross and John F. Hutchinson, eds. *Health and Society in Revolutionary Russia.* Bloomington: Indiana University Press, 1990.

Stephenson, Jill. *Hitler's Home Front: Württemberg under the Nazis.* New York: Continuum, 2006.

Steer, G. I. *The Tree of Gernika: A Field Study of Modern War.* London: Hodder and Stoughton, 1938.

Stille, Alexander. *Benevolence and Betrayal: Five Italian Jewish Families under Fascism.* New York: Picador, 2003.

Stites, Richard. *The Women's Liberation Movement in Russia: Feminism, Nihilism, and Bolshevism, 1860-1930.* Princeton: Princeton University Press, 1991.

Stoff, Laurie. *Russia's Sisters of Mercy and the Great War: More than Binding Men's Wounds.* Lawrence: University Press of Kansas, 2015.

___. *They Fought for the Motherland: Russia's Women Soldiers in World War I and the Revolution.* Lawrence: University Press of Kansas, 2006.

Stoff, Laurie, Heywood, Anthony, Kolonitskii, Boris, and John W. Steinberg, eds. *Military Affairs in Russia's Great War and Revolution, 1914-22, Book 1: Military Experiences.* Bloomington: Slavica Publishers (Indiana University), 2019.

Stone, Tessa. "Creating a (Gendered?) Military Identity: The Women's Auxiliary Air Force in Great Britain in the Second World War", *Women's History Review* 8.4 (1999) 605–624.

Summerfield, Penny. *Women Workers in the Second World War: Production and Patriarchy in Conflict.* Manchester: Manchester University Press, 1984.

Suny, Ronald. *They Can Live in the Desert but Nowhere Else: A History of the Armenian Genocide.* Princeton: Princeton University Press, 2015.

Takseva, Tatjana and Arlene Sgoutas, eds. *Mothers Under Fire: Mothering in Conflict Areas.* Ontario: Demeter Press, 2015.

Threat, Charissa J. *Nursing Civil Rights: Gender and Race in the Army Nurse Corps.* Urbana: University of Illinois Press, 2015.

Travers, Susan and Susan Holden. *Tomorrow to Be Brave: A Memoir of the Only Woman Ever to Serve in the French Foreign Legion.* New York: Touchstone, 2007.

Tremlett, Giles. *International Brigades: Fascism, Freedom and the Spanish Civil War.* London, UK: Bloomsbury Publishing, 2020.

Tuchman, Barbara; *The Proud Tower: A Portrait of the World Before the War: 1890-1914.* New York: Bantam Books; 1967.

Tusan, Michelle. "The Business of Relief Work: A Victorian Quaker in Constantinople and Her Circle." *Victorian Studies* 51.4 (Summer 2009) 633-662.

Vehviläinen, Olli. *Finland in the Second World War.* New York: Palgrave Macmillan, 2002.

Vernon, James. *Hunger: A Modern History.* Cambridge: Harvard University Press, 2007.

Vinyes, Ricard, Montse Armengou, and Ricard Belis. *Los niños perdidos del franquisimo.* Barcelona, 2003.

Von Saldern, Adelheid. "Victims or Perpetrators? Controversies about the Role of Women in the Nazi State," *Nazism and German Society, 1933-1945*, ed. David F. Crew. Ann Arbor: University of Michigan Press, 2002.

Wanhalla, Angela. *Matters of the Heart: A History of Interracial Marriage in New Zealand.* Auckland: Auckland University Press, 2014.

Watenpaugh, Keith. "Between Communal Survival and National Aspiration: Armenian Genocide Refugees, The League of Nations, and the Practices of Interwar Humanitarianism." *Humanity Journal* 5:2 (2014).

Whitehead, Winifred. *Old Lies Revisited: Young Readers and the Literature of War and Violence.* Concord, MA: Pluto Press, 1991.

Waugh, Alec. *The Loom of Youth.* London: Cassell & Company Ltd. 1917.

Weindling, Paul. "Medical Refugees in Britain and the Wider World, 1930–1960: Introduction," *Social History of Medicine* 22.3 (2009) 451–59.

Weiss-Wendt, Anton, ed. *The Nazi Genocide of the Roma: Reassessment and Commemoration.* New York: Berghahn, 2015.

Weitz, Margaret Collins. *Sisters in the Resistance: How Women Fought to Free France, 1940–1945.* New York: Wiley, 1995.

Welshman, John. *Churchill's Children: The Evacuee Experience in Wartime Britain.* Oxford: Oxford University Press, 2010.

Wheelwright, Julie. *Amazons and Military Maids: Women Who Cross-Dressed in the Pursuit of Life, Liberty and Happiness.* London: Pandora, 1994.

Wildman, Allen. *The End of the Russian Imperial Army, Vol. 1: The Old Army and the Soldiers' Revolt (March-April, 1917).* Princeton: Princeton University Press, 1980.

___. *The End of Russian Imperial Army, Vol. 2: The Road to Soviet Power and Peace* Princeton: Princeton University Press, 1987.

Willson, Perry. *Women in Twentieth-Century Italy.* New York: Palgrave Macmillan, 2010.

Willson, Perry. *The Clockwork Factory: Women and Work in Fascist Italy.* Oxford: Oxford University Press, 1993.

___. *Peasant Women and Politics in Fascist Italy: The Massaie Rurali.* London: Routledge, 2002.

Yoshiaki, Yoshimi. *Comfort Women: Sexual Slavery in the Japanese Military During World War II.* New York: Columbia University Press, 1995.

Zafra, Enrique, Rosalía Crego y Carmen Heredia. *Los Niños Españoles Evacuados A La URSS (1937).* Madrid: Ediciones De La Torre, 1989.

Zahra, Tara. *Kidnapped Souls: National Indifference and the Battle for Children in the Bohemian Lands, 1900–1948.* Ithaca: Cornell University Press, 2008.

Index

A

American Medical Bureau 117, 118, 122, 123, 124, 132, 133, 134
American Women xxii, 117, 118, 119, 121, 134
Anti-Communist 152
Anti-Fascist 57, 71, 111, 130, 134
Armenia 88, 91, 92, 93, 96
Armenians 82, 83, 84, 85, 86, 87, 88, 91, 92, 93, 94, 95, 97
Armenian Genocide xi, xviii, xxi, 79, 81
Armenian Red Cross 91
Astor, Lady 135, 136
Authoritarian Dictatorship 119, 156

B

Basque 100, 101, 103, 107, 108, 119, 125
Basque Child Refugees 99, 103, 110
Basque Children Committees 103, 107
Basque Children Repatriation Committee (BCRC) 108
Black market xviii, xxii, 158, 169, 173, 178, 180, 182, 184, 186, 187, 200, 201
Boycott xxii, 135, 137, 139, 140, 141, 142, 144, 151
Brittain, Vera xxi, 3, 4, 6, 7, 8, 9, 10, 11, 12, 13, 14, 15, 16, 17, 18, 19, 55, 84, 135, 148, 151
British Women xx, xxii, 7
Burgess, Ann Mary 79, 80, 81, 83, 84, 85, 86, 87, 88, 96, 97

C

Chen, W. C. 146
Cheng, C.S. 148
Chiang Kai-Shek, Madame 146
Children's Fiction xxi, 57
China 136, 137, 138, 139, 140, 141, 142, 143, 144, 145, 146, 147, 148, 149, 150, 151
"China Day" 145
China Mission 146, 147
"China Sunday" 146
China Campaign Committee 136, 137, 138, 139, 140, 141, 142, 143, 144, 145, 146, 147, 148, 149, 150, 151
Chinese Women 135, 143, 146, 148
Citrine, Walter 135, 137
Collective Identity 3, 4, 5, 6, 8, 9, 11, 15, 18
Colonias 99, 102, 107
Combatant xiii, xv, xxi, 22, 32, 35, 39, 41, 42, 43, 46, 48, 50, 53, 55, 56
Communism 101
Communist xvii, 99, 108, 110, 113, 115, 117, 118, 120, 182
Communist Party 51, 111, 122, 123, 124, 183, 184
Consumption xvi, xx, xxii, 135, 155, 158, 165, 169, 171, 181, 186, 195, 196, 197, 198, 199, 200, 201, 203, 206, 211

D

Democratic xi, 132, 192, 196
Democratically elected 118
Democracy 117, 119, 122, 131, 145, 175
De Vries, Lini 117
Disillusion xxi, 3, 4, 6, 16

E

Eastern Front xxi, 21, 22, 23
English Women 83, 84
Evacuation 102, 103, 112, 195, 210

F

Family xxii, 6, 8, 10, 11, 25, 28, 37, 38, 63, 68, 71, 72, 74, 90, 91, 108, 109, 112, 113, 115, 122, 124, 131, 139, 143, 145, 155, 156, 157, 159, 160, 161, 162, 163, 165, 173, 174, 175, 176, 177, 178, 179, 180, 181, 182, 184, 185, 186, 187, 192, 193, 198, 202, 207, 208, 211
Famine xvi, xvii, xviii, xix, xxii, 79, 82, 110, 149, 171
Fascist xxi, 57, 59, 59, 62, 65, 68, 72, 73, 74, 119, 132, 134, 135, 136, 137, 146, 156
Fascist Japan 137
Fascist Party 63, 66, 73
Fascist Regime 58
Fascist Spain 103, 120
Fascism xxii, 57, 58, 63, 64, 72, 73, 75, 100, 101, 111, 113, 115, 117, 118, 119, 120, 123, 124, 130, 133, 134, 136, 137, 138, 143, 146, 147
Falange (Party) 156, 162
Feminism 3, 89, 91

FET-JONS 156, 157, 158, 159, 160, 162, 163, 164, 165, 166, 168, 170, 171
Finland xix, xxii, 47, 195, 196, 198, 199, 200, 202, 203, 206, 207, 208, 209, 210, 211
Firebombing 99, 100, 101, 102
"Flag Day" 147
French Women xxi, 39, 40, 42, 44, 51, 55
Food Charity 155, 156, 160, 161, 168, 171
Food Controls 173
Food Policies xvii, xxii, 171, 173, 193
Franco, Francisco xxii, 101, 103, 106, 108, 110, 114, 115, 117, 119, 120, 125, 156, 157, 158, 159, 160, 163, 164, 165, 166, 169, 171
Francoist Ideology 155, 156
Free French Army 39, 42, 49
French Resistance 41, 47, 50
French Women xxi, 39, 40, 42, 44, 51, 55
Fuhr, Lini 118, 130, 133

G

German Occupation (of France) 173, 174
Great War xi, xii, xvi, xvii, xix, xxi, 3, 4, 21, 22, 23, 24, 31, 32, 37, 57, 58, 60, 63, 64, 66, 69, 70, 72, 73, 75
Guernica 99. 100, 101, 102, 103, 110, 115

H

Hitler, Adolph (Adolf) 59, 119, 136
Humanitarian xiii, xxi, xxii, 79, 80, 82, 83, 84, 89, 91, 95, 96, 99, 102,

103, 107, 110, 115, 122, 136, 157, 158
Humanitarianism xiii, xv, xvii, xviii, xxii, 79, 82, 96, 99, 111, 115

I

International Brigades xxii, 117, 118, 120, 121, 122, 126, 129, 136, 138
International Press 99, 100, 101
Italy xi, xxi, 49, 57, 58, 59, 60, 61, 63, 64, 67, 68, 69, 70, 72, 73, 74, 99, 103, 117, 119, 146
Italian xii, xxi, 17, 47, 48, 58, 59, 60, 61, 62, 68, 71, 73, 74, 101, 102
Italian Children's Literature (juvenile, books) 58, 68, 74, 75
Italian Front 58
Italian History 65
Italian Jews 69
Italian National Anthem 66
Italian Publishers 60
Italian War Literature 67
Italian Women 57, 58, 72

J

Japan 136, 137, 138, 140, 141, 142, 144, 145, 151
Japanese Fascism xxii, 137
Japanese Goods xxii, 137, 139, 140, 142, 144
Japanese Imperial Army xix, 145
Japanese Occupation (of Manchuria) 136, 143
Japanese Products 139, 140, 141, 142, 143
Jarama, battle of 117, 127, 128, 129

K

Key, Salaria 131, 133, 134
Koneye, Prince 143

L

League of Nations xii, xvii, 19, 83, 88, 95, 143, 146, 176
Lost Generation xxi, 3, 4

M

Magazine(s) xxii, 52, 195, 196, 197, 199, 202, 205, 206, 207, 208, 210, 211
Martin, Fredericka 117, 122, 123, 129, 131
Masculinity 3, 42, 74
Meric, Marie-Madeleine 39, 42, 52, 53, 54, 55
Middle East 47, 79, 82
Military Camp 45, 157
Military Equipment 26, 120
Military Hospital(s) 13, 16, 18
Military Service 10, 12, 13, 40, 41, 44, 46, 49, 163, 178

N

Nanjing 135, 136, 137, 144
National Socialist(s) 119
Nazi 68, 192
Nazism 123
Nazi Germany xii, xviii, 47, 55, 103, 114, 157, 166, 174
Nazi troops 47
Ninos xx, 99, 110, 113
Non-combatant xxi, 22, 39, 40, 41, 42, 43, 44, 46, 47, 48, 49, 50, 52, 55, 56, 103
Non-fiction 57, 60, 63, 66, 69

Nurses xvii, xxi, 22, 24, 25, 30, 31, 32, 33, 36, 37, 62, 71, 112, 117, 118, 119, 122, 123, 124, 128, 129, 130, 131, 132, 133, 134

O

Occupation xxi, 30, 34, 50, 68, 74, 94, 135, 143, 179, 181, 186, 187, 192
Occupation zones 176
Occupied France 39, 42, 173, 174, 178
Ottoman Christians 79, 81, 82, 83

P

Pacifism 3, 29, 87
Patriarchal 26, 34, 37, 42, 83, 91
Patriarchy xvii, 96, 173, 178
Patriotism xvii, 17, 57, 58, 63, 64, 66, 202

Q

Quaker xviii, 79, 81, 83, 84, 88, 103

R

Rations 14, 71, 161, 169, 174, 176, 177, 178, 181, 182, 183, 184, 185, 192, 201, 204
Rationing xviii, xxii, 115, 161, 176, 177, 178, 181, 195, 196, 201, 202, 204, 209
Refugees xv, xviii, xx, 62, 87, 88, 92, 99, 101, 102, 103, 104, 106, 107, 108, 109, 111, 112, 113, 115, 125, 126, 137, 138, 142, 143, 146, 160, 199
Republican 99, 100, 101, 102, 103, 106, 114, 118, 120, 121, 122, 125, 126, 133, 136, 137, 160, 192

Russia xi, 21, 22, 23, 24, 25, 27, 28, 29, 30, 33, 34, 35, 36, 123
Russian xx, xxi, 23, 24, 25, 26, 27, 28, 31, 33, 34, 37, 49, 87, 92, 113, 122
Russian Armenia 93
Russian Feminists 29
Russian Orthodox Church 31
Russian Revolution xvii, 21
Russian Women 24, 26, 28, 30, 35

S

Second World War (see also World War II) xii, xiv, xvi, xviii, xx, 39, 44, 55, 65, 68, 135, 138, 150, 151
Seymour, Horace 146
Shih-Chieh, Wang 146
Shortages xviii, xix, xxii, 28, 40, 105, 115, 167, 168, 171, 174, 176, 178, 179, 180, 182, 183, 184, 186, 187, 192, 195, 196, 199, 209
Sisters of Mercy 22, 31, 32, 33
Social Aid Program 155, 156, 157, 158, 160, 162, 167, 170, 171
Southampton 99, 104, 105, 108, 149
Soviet xix, xx, 31, 37, 96, 111, 112, 113, 114, 115
Soviet Central Committee 110
Soviet Communist International (Comitern) 118
Soviet Ideology 113
Soviet Regime 21, 22
Soviet Union xvii, xx, xxii, 47, 99, 102, 103, 104, 110, 111, 112, 113, 115, 120, 195, 198, 199, 208
Spanish Civil War xvii, xx, xxii, 115, 117, 120, 134, 155, 156, 159, 162
Spanish Medical Aid 104
Spanish Women 129

Stalin, Joseph xx, 96, 111, 114, 115
Starvation xvi, xviii, 104, 173, 175, 176, 192
Sweden xx, 47, 125, 195, 198, 199, 206, 207, 208, 211

T

Typhoid 106
Trades Union Congress 136, 137
Travers, Susan 39, 42, 46, 47, 48, 49, 50, 55

U

United States (of America) 60, 120, 128, 133, 144

V

Vichy (France) xviii, xxii, 45, 46, 52, 53, 54, 55, 173, 174, 175, 176, 178, 180, 182, 183, 184, 192, 193

Villa Paz 131, 133

W

Western Front xxi, 14, 21, 22
Women authors 57, 64, 69
World War I (See also Great War, First World War) xxi, xxii, 4, 5, 6, 18, 21, 39
World War II (see also Second World War) xxi, xxii, 39, 40, 79, 80, 81, 195, 196, 200, 206
Wounded xvii, 15, 21, 31, 33, 35, 62, 69, 71, 73, 90, 100, 117, 118, 126, 128, 131, 135, 137, 140, 143, 144, 149, 150

Y

Yessayan, Zabel 79, 81, 83, 89, 90, 91, 92, 93, 94, 95, 96, 97

www.ingramcontent.com/pod-product-compliance
Lightning Source LLC
Chambersburg PA
CBHW071350290426
44108CB00014B/1495